SWORDS INTO PLOWSHARES

Swords Into Plowshares

A Collection of Plays
About Peace and Social Justice

Ingrid Rogers

The Brethren Press, Elgin, Illinois

SWORDS INTO PLOWSHARES

Cover Design by Kathy Kline

Illustrations by Lisa Miller

Library of Congress Cataloging in Publication Data
Main entry under title:

Swords into plowshares.

1. Religious drama, American. 2. Peace—Drama.
3. American drama—20th century. 4. Drama in religious education.   I. Rogers, Ingrid.
PS627.R4S9   1983   812'.008'0382   82-24492
ISBN 0-87178-827-6

Published by The Brethren Press, Elgin, Illinois 60120

Printed in the United States of America

Acknowledgements and Information About Performance Rights

The plays and skits in this book may be photocopied for performances unless copies should be ordered as indicated below. Reprint permission needs to be requested from the holder of the copyright.

Dougherty, Peter. "Elfie." Published with the author's permission.

Drescher, James. "A Letter From Freddy," © 1982 by James Drescher; reprinted with permission. "Oh Yes — I Guess," © 1969 by James Drescher; reprinted with permission. Copies of each play should be ordered from MIJIM Enterprises, 675 Hartman Station Road, Lancaster, PA 17601.

Ferguson, John. "Carie," © 1977 by John Ferguson; first published by the Fellowship of Reconciliation in *Reconciliation Quarterly*, New Series 7.4 (December 1977) pp. 26-32; reprinted with the author's permission. "The Trial," © 1957 by the Epworth Press; used with permission. There is no fee for performances, but reprint permission should be secured from the author at Selly Oak Colleges, Birmingham B29 6LQ, Great Britain.

Fisherfolk, "Sam and Ivan," © 1976 by Celebration Services (Int'l) Ltd; The Cathedral, Millport, Isle of Cumbrae, Scotland. All rights reserved. Used by permission. Non-commercial performances of the skit do not require special permission. For rights to reprint or perform commercially please contact Celebration Services, Box FF, Woodland Park, CO 80863.

Frantz, Evelyn M. "Winds of Change," © 1977 by Evelyn M. Frantz; for permission to reprint or perform, contact Evelyn M. Frantz, 5144 Ridgeview Dr., Harrisburg, PA 17112.

Friesen, Dorothy. "Naboth's Vineyard," published with permission. The author asks no royalties but would like to know where the play is produced. Write to SYNAPSES, 1821 W. Cullerton, Chicago, IL 60608.

Gurian, Jay. "A Man in a Loin Cloth," © 1969 by Jay P. Gurian; reprinted with permission. A full-length play by the same title is also available and may be obtained from Jay Gurian, American Studies Department, University of Hawaii, Honolulu, Hawaii 96822.

Houser, Gordon. "A Candle in the Dark," published with the author's permission.

Lehman, Celia. "The Middle Man," published with permission. For reprint or performance rights contact the author at 13170 Arnold Road, Dalton, Ohio 44618.

Lindley, Jonathan. "Don't Cry, Chiisai, Don't Cry," published with the author's permission.

Maloy, Kate. "Hagwine and Geneva, or War and Peace." Rights to reprint and perform are granted without fee, but the author would like to know when and where performances are given and, if a profit is made, would appreciate donations to the Woolman Alliance, c/o Kate Maloy, 5507 Hays Street, Pittsburgh, PA., 15206.

Moyer, Jean. "And Marybai is Hungry." Published with the author's permission.

Numrich, Charles. "State of Siege." Published with the author's permission.

Reba Place Fellowship Drama Group. "Good Friday," © 1982 by Reba Place Fellowship, 727 Reba Place, Evanston, IL 60202; reprinted with permission.

Rogers, Ingrid. "Genesis." "King Midas III." "The Stone Wall," © 1982 by United Church Press. "To Feed the Hungry." "Visions of the Messiah." The author asks no performance fees but would like to know where the skits are produced. Reprint permission needs to be requested from the author at 707 North Sycamore Street, North Manchester, IN 46962.

Shenk, Lois Landis. "A House For David," © 1982 by Lois Landis Shenk; reprinted with permission. For rights to reprint or perform, contact the author c/o Blossom Hill Mennonite Church, 330 Delp Road, Lancaster, PA 17601.

Somerville, John. "The Last Inquest: A Preventable Nightmare in One Act," © 1981 by the Canadian Peace Research Institute. First published in *Peace Research*, 1981, Vol. 13, No.2. Reprinted with permission. For copies of this play write to the author at 1426 Merritt Drive, El Cajon, CA 92020.

This book is dedicated
to you as a peacemaker
for handing on the blessing you received.

CONTENTS

INTRODUCTION   11

PART ONE: HISTORICAL PEACEMAKERS

1. Jesus as Prince of Peace   17

A House for David, *by Lois Landis Shenk*   19
Visions of the Messiah, *by Ingrid Rogers*   27
Good Friday, *by the Reba Place Fellowship Drama Group*   30

2. Other Workers for Peace   45

Winds of Change, *by Evelyn Frantz*   47
William's Pruning Hooks, *by Luise Van Keuren*   74
Carie, *by John Ferguson*   88
A Man in a Loin Cloth, *by Jay Gurian*   93

PART TWO: PROBLEMS FACING PEACEMAKERS TODAY

3. Idolatry   107

The Middle Man, *by Celia Lehman*   109
King Midas III, *by Ingrid Rogers*   125
Hagwine and Geneva, *by Kate Maloy*   129

4. The Threat of Nuclear War   146

Sam and Ivan, *by the Fisherfolk*   148
Elfie, *by Peter Dougherty*   152
Civil Defense Satire, *by the State of the Union Players*   154
The Last Inquest, *by John Somerville*   159

5. Prejudice   174

The Stone Wall, *by Ingrid Rogers*   177
Don't Cry, Chiisay, Don't Cry, *by Jonathan Lindley*   181
The Trial, *by John Ferguson*   201

6. Militarism, the Draft, and War Taxes 217

State of Siege, *by Charles Numrich* 218
Oh Yes — I Guess, *by James Drescher* 221
His Own Household, *by Arleta Unzicker* 228
A Letter From Freddy, *by James Drescher* 236

7. World Hunger and Human Rights Violations 241

To Feed the Hungry, *by Ingrid Rogers* 244
And Marybai is Hungry, *by Jean Moyer* 248
Naboth's Vineyard, *by Dorothy Friesen* 255

8. Fear, Apathy, and Hopelessness 260

Alligator, *by Don Yost* 262
A Candle in the Dark, *by Gordon Houser* 273
Genesis, *by Ingrid Rogers* 280

POSTSCRIPT 283

INTRODUCTION

Drama as a Teaching Tool for Congregations

Drama in the churches? Of course! Why leave the acting to the actors and the plays to the theaters! There is no other medium that can present Christ's gospel of love and justice more vividly. In a theatrical performance, verbal and visual stimuli blend in exciting new ways, making a message come alive and causing it to linger in our hearts and minds. A play that we have seen or performed becomes part of us. Therefore drama, with its power to captivate and change people, is an excellent tool to transmit the Biblical message. It deserves to be included in our church services.

In a sense, acting has always been a vital part of worship. Ritual is reenactment, and as we partake in it, the meaning unfolds. The communion meal repeats the Last Supper, itself a reenactment of the Passover meal in Exodus. Baptism and the feetwashing ceremony, with their symbolism of cleansing, rebirth, and new beginnings, dramatize New Testament events as well as the crossing of the Jordan and the Red Sea. Ritual in the church owes much of its strong appeal to its inherent dramatic qualities.

Drama is part of our worship service in yet another way. To illustrate abstract ideas, a good preacher will enliven sermons by weaving in suspenseful anecdotes, stories, and bits of dialogue. Jesus himself frequently used this method. When he wanted to explain to the common people what God's Kingdom would be like, he chose to do so by means of dramatic tales. He talked about a businessman robbed and beaten on the road, about a son who squandered his father's wealth, about people hired to work in the fields. Concreteness lies at the heart of Jesus' parables. Rather than preach abstract notions, he told stories to which people could relate, stories filled with characters with whom people could identify. The concept of asking and showing forgiveness took shape in the story of the Prodigal Son; love of neighbor was illustrated in the Good Samaritan; the command to bear fruit in witness was embodied in the parables of the sower and of the talents. Through these many cherished stories the gospel has become tangible, concrete, intelligible to the lay person.

In the Middle Ages, when biblical knowledge had become a perogative of the clergy because the common people did not know Latin, the Church decided to bring the gospel to the people in a way that everyone could understand. To hand on the biblical message,

11

the clergy introduced miracle and mystery plays. Christ's birth, his temptation, his baptism, and his healings were portrayed in the church. These dramas enjoyed great popularity. The gospel gained relevance as its connection to the life of the people became obvious.

Today again we must allow people to see. We suffer from abstractions as foreign to most of us as Latin was to the medieval peasants who gathered in their village chapels. Who can understand $500 billion spent on armaments each year? Who can fathom millions of people starving, millions without shelter, millions imprisoned and persecuted? Again we need to translate. The Word of God is as valid as ever. Christ's message of love, peace, and justice can still confront the evils of the world. But as in Christ's parables or the medieval miracle and morality plays, truth must be made visible in the context of our daily lives.

There are many reasons for dramatizing Christ's gospel of peace and justice. One, of course, is the visibility and immediacy of a theatrical performance. Rather than be told about the theory of nonviolence, we observe a conflict in which this theory is tested; along with the characters, our minds grapple for a solution. Instead of hearing about racism or world hunger, we see a person exposed to abuse and suffering right in front of our eyes — it is real and tangible. Though we may never directly confront some of the problems revealed in the plays, their performance makes that confrontation possible. We still need our tales of human agony and desire for healing, and we still need to see our faith illustrated through a setting and characters we recognize as our own.

In addition to the visual impact and the immediacy, drama has a strong emotional appeal. Plays transfer a message more wholistically than sermons because the audience experiences feelings beyond the spoken words. Observers of a play become co-creators as they let themselves identify with the characters or situations and relate these to their own lives.

Another important reason for using drama as an educational tool is the value of participation. Many congregations seek new ways to involve members in worship. Drama here has several advantages. First, it is a group process, an exercise in interaction. Second, it appeals to children and teenagers, the age groups that all too often do not feel part of traditional worship services. Third, the performing group can be intergenerational and thus allow the development of relationships which are not possible in many Sunday School classes. And finally drama may draw out hidden talents of people who find that this is the way they most want to participate.

Role-playing in itself has other values. Often a person's aggressive behavior is linked to inability to see a situation from another's perspective. In a play, we may well assume the role of an adversary. Or we may try out and practice a new stance. Even if we completely identify with a character we portray, we are not speaking our own words but someone else's. This is a valuable exercise. Both the audience and the players learn to deal with a conflict objectively by looking at it from the outside or from another's point of view. For conflict resolution, this process is crucial.

Probably the most important argument for dramatizing the gospel of peace and justice is that as Christians we are compelled to pass on Christ's message. Healing, feeding the hungry, taking care of the poor, freeing the oppressed, suffering violence without seeking to retaliate — this is the example given by Chirst and this is the example we must follow if we claim the Prince of Peace as Lord. It is our duty to decry injustices and to seek alternatives consistent with our faith in a loving God.

The History of This Anthology

Two years ago I wrote an Easter play for our congregation entitled "Visions of the Messiah." It portrayed wrong conceptions people once held of the Christ: the violent revolutionary of the Zealots, the king who would end domination by the Romans. The play showed how difficult it was to accept Jesus appearing as the suffering servant or as the one who had come to free the oppressed, heal the sick, and proclaim the kingdom of love and justice.

Several things became obvious during the course of that performance and the months thereafter. First, the message stuck. Why? Mainly because it presented a life-like situation. Theater is the oldest form of audio-visual performance in front of a large audience. The dialog sounds familiar; the characters are easy to identify with; conflict and suspense keep us involved mentally. In a church community, there is the added pleasure of seeing friends or relatives perform, which creates a sense of unity. And the memory lingers on. Months after the performance of another skit at our church, a youth commented during a conversation about the arms race: "That's just like that play we saw upstairs . . . "

With every new skit we staged, it became more and more obvious that the activity was valuable not only for the audience, but even more so for the performers. The plays proved to be excellent teaching tools. Rather than just listening to explanations of Christian ideals, people acted them out on stage, formulated them, reiterated them, presented them on their own, and finally taught them to others. It filled the participants' need for fun with peers, for independent creativity, and for faith development through search and participation.

From the beginning, our plays involved peace issues. The first skit set the stage, presenting Christ's nonviolent alternative to the evils of his society. It was a logical step from there to start exploring Christian alternatives in our own age. How do we deal with "defense" needs? Why are we so little disturbed by world hunger, the most cruel and widespread form of violence? How do we live responsibly in a world in which all people, regardless of nationality or race, are our brothers and sisters in Christ?

The next play I wrote dealt with our idolatrous willingness to sacrifice human lives for the sake of a high standard of living. Without my knowledge, my pastor submitted this play for publication, and it was accepted. The enthusiastic response not only from our church community but also from others overwhelmed me. Along with this came various requests for plays on specific topics.

Soon the idea was born to put together a collection of plays related to peace and social justice. I sensed there were people all over the nation writing chancel drama and wanting to promote the cause of the Prince of Peace through acting. So why not share our work? An advertisement appeared in several peace publications calling for contributions. And they came! It was exciting to get in touch with this grassroots network of artists willing to share their talents, their insights, and their faith. Maybe this collection of dramas and skits will inspire others to write and contribute to future volumes of peace plays.

Criteria for the Selection of Plays

The plays had to be selected to fit the needs not of a specific denomination, but rather of any group of people who desired to be introduced to, confronted with, or reinforced in Christ's message of peace. These then were the criteria which determined the choice:

1. Each drama had to be useful as a teaching tool. Artistic beauty was important, but secondary to the educational purpose.
2. Since the plays would be performed in churches, on the street, or at peace gatherings, we needed plays with fairly unsophisticated stage technology, simple dialogue, and clearly discernible message.
3. Last but not least, the plays had to be faith-centered. I mean by that not necessarily religious terminology or phrases within the play, but rather a set of ideas rooted in the Bible and Christ's teachings: love your neighbor as yourself; do good to those who persecute you; turn the other cheek; love your enemies; what you have done to the least of my brothers, that you have done to me.

14

Suggestions How to Use the Plays

Keep your audience in mind as you select plays for performance. Although the plays included in this collection have similar goals, they vary in tone and may appeal to groups at different levels of awareness. Some plays are perhaps more appropriate for people who have already struggled with the problem expressed; others serve better as an introduction to the issue. The idea is to move one step further toward peace, not to alienate or reinforce hostility.

Peace education can happen at any time, in any place. One way to use the plays, therefore, is simply to read and ponder them.

Another possibility is to employ them in Sunday School. The plays could either just be read aloud with divided roles or be performed, script in hand. The more engaged people become in the dialogue, the more certain the impact will be. The plays read in Sunday School can serve as a prelude to discussions about social justice issues of our time. To facilitate the ensuing conversation, questions for discussion are provided at the end of each play. Of course, these are only suggestions. Sunday School teachers and members will want to add or substitute their own.

Third, the plays can be used as part of the Sunday service. Several skits take no longer than five to ten minutes to perform and could therefore easily be incorporated in worship. Longer dramas such as "Good Friday" could be presented in place of a sermon or as a complete special service by itself.

Finally, the plays may be performed at special gatherings for the specific purpose of peace education. Any of the plays would be appropriate, depending on the needs of the audience and on the thematic emphasis desired. After the performance, it is a good idea to allow a few minutes of silence for people to reflect how the play relates to their own faith. If the audience is large, it may be advisable to form groups of six to eight for dicussion.

The church is not the only place to spread Christ's gospel of peace and justice. Peace education needs to happen in the schools as well as on the streets, on college campuses as well as in the factories, in homes as well as on the market place. Many of the plays have a sense of urgency, and rightfully so. Peace is no longer an idealistic end; it is the only realistic means to ensure survival. To act for peace, on stage and otherwise, is to affirm God's creation. Almost two thousand years after it was stated, Christ's message of nonviolence and sacrificial love speaks to us more urgently than ever.

HISTORICAL PEACEMAKERS

Peacemaking is not a new idea. It is as old as the human race which, from the beginning, had to choose between living in an Eden of unity with God and each other, or turning away from God to hate and kill like Cain. Repeatedly, human beings have chosen the second option. Our history books overflow with stories of war. Every weapon designed, from bayonets to nuclear bombs, we have subsequently used to take other people's lives. The bloody tales of human cruelty include not only the stories of those killed in war but also of those whose humanity we threaten out of personal hatred or of those whom we let starve by insisting on our own affluence. Every time we cease to see the brother or sister in the other person, every time we deny our responsibility as "keepers" and egocentrically pursue only our self-interest, we repeat Cain's crime.

Fortunately, there is also another side. Repeatedly in human history people have sought alternatives to evil. They have chosen to suffer rather than exercise violence. They have courageously risked their lives by refusing to kill. For them, love of God necessarily included love of neighbor.

Christians have a mixed tradition of war and peacemaking. With Constantine, it became acceptable for Christians to serve in the army. Augustine gave further sanction to warfare with his "just war" theory. Millions of people have since been murdered in the name of Christianity. From participating in the crusades, to carrying coins which say "In God We Trust" but which in fact pay for the nuclear bombs we trust even more — Christians have been caught in the contradiction of proclaiming love while promoting death.

But here again the alternative witness cannot be denied. Christianity during the first centuries was a completely pacifistic movement. After all, its followers modeled themselves on Jesus who preferred having himself killed over destroying his enemies. This pacifist strand survived throughout the centuries. Among the groups of believers who came to America to seek religious freedom were the Anabaptists who deduced from Jesus' teachings that they could not participate in wars. Quakers, Mennonites, and Brethren were the three historic peace denominations whose members, after many years of persecution and acts of civil disobedience, gained the legal right to conscientious objection. Individual members of other congregations also witnessed effectively for peace. These stories need to be told and remembered. It is important for us to feel we belong to a rich heritage. Today in our global community we also must recognize and rejoice in the fact that other religious traditions have emphasized the need for peace and are seeking to promote it. Let us celebrate Mother Theresa and Mahatma Gandhi, Martin Luther King and Archbishop Romero, Dom Helder Camara and Dorothy Day, and the many other people who can serve as models for us.

This first section of the book presents plays about historical peacemakers: Jesus as he clarifies his role as messiah; a minister of an early Brethren congregation who lives out his convictions about love of enemies; a Quaker merchant who refuses to hand over weapons; a missionary's wife who, when her life is threatened, responds out of faith with a love that disarms her enemies;and Gandhi trying to lead India peacefully out of colonial oppression. These are but a few of the thousands of people who worked to turn our planet into a peaceable garden. I hope this book will stimulate readers to write more plays about other peace heroes, so that more volumes can soon be published to celebrate the contribution of these great men and women.

Jesus as Prince of Peace

Jesus is the perfect example of a peacemaker. He healed people who experienced inner conflict and were physically or mentally sick. He ignored social barriers by eating with the tax collector, by talking to the Samaritan woman at the well, and by forgiving the prostitute. He encouraged others to seek reconciliation when he blessed all peacemakers during his Sermon on the Mount. He ignored the law when it stood in the way of doing good to others. He broke through cultural and national biases by holding up the Good Samaritan to illustrate what it means to love one's neighbor. He refused to accept Peter's violent action when Peter drew his sword in Gethsemane, even though it was for Jesus' own protection. Finally, at Golgatha, he suffered abuse and crucifixion to show that love would not be conquered by death.

The following three plays raise the question of what kind of messiah Jesus was. All three affirm him not in the role of the mighty ruler who promises to bring freedom by militaristic means but rather in the role of suffering servant obedient to God. "The House of David" dramatizes the temptation in the desert. All three temptations deal directly with the messiahship of Christ; all would have been plausible, "tempting," and certain of public acclaim. But they were not the option of the Prince of Peace.

"Good Friday" shows the logical outcome of Jesus' messiahship. Death on the cross awaits someone who his whole life proclaimed a kingdom of love and justice. He dies betrayed by Judas, abandoned by the disciples, denied by Peter, ridiculed and abused by the masses, forgotten by us today as we prepare to kill those for whom he died. Yet the miracle of the cross is that it has come to stand as a symbol not of death, but of ultimate victory over death. We are a resurrection people. The promise of the kingdom is still there, tangible, if we are willing to act — and maybe die — out of Christlike love for one another.

A HOUSE FOR DAVID

by Lois Landis Shenk

CHARACTERS

JESUS, *age 30*
SATAN, *a traveler*
NATHAN, *a prophet*
ISAIAH, *a prophet*
ZECHARIAH, *a prophet*
TWO ANGELS, *dressed in white*

The wilderness of Judean hills. Optional backdrop contains painted desolate hills and yellow-white sky containing a few buzzards. In the middle of the stage is a pile of boulders, one large, one medium with flatish top, and smaller rocks around the base. Sounds of a dry wind, and a few eerie bird cries. Lighting is bright and hot-looking. The scene waits for a few minutes, to establish mood.

Man enters, left. He is intense, an obviously gaunt, weary, dusty man, age 30. He wears a beard, and his long hair is combed in spite of being dirty. Atop his head is a headband (optional) upon which is fastened a white dove, wings in flight position.

The man stumbles up to boulder and flings himself upon it. Gethsemane-style. He groans, sweets, throws hands heavenward. It is important that these motions do not appear melodramatic. His demeanor should suggest that he is Jesus.

JESUS. Abba! Abba! I took the baptism, and you said I'm your beloved son! Abba! Show me the way!
   [*His voice echoes into the deep silence, which hangs long and heavy, broken only by a few faint bird-calls. JESUS lies face down upon the large boulder, motionless. SATAN enters, from right. He is dressed as a desert traveler. It is not apparent that he is the Devil. He carries a walking stick, a flask of water and a traveler's bundle. He approaches the prostrate form cautiously, then pokes him in the rib to see if he is alive.*]
JESUS. [*Sitting up suddenly*] Who are you! [*Jesus is sensitized from long fasting, wary, but yearning also for companionship.*]
SATAN. Oh, me? I'm going thata way. [*He motions with his stick pointing in a vague direction.*] Just happened to see you and

19

thought maybe the bandits got you. I see you're lively enough, though you look like you could use a meal and something to drink. Here, I've got some water. [*SATAN uncorks the flask and hands it to JESUS, who takes a few parched sips and then returns it.*]

JESUS. Thank you.

SATAN. [*He shrugs and smiles.*] It'd be a heartless devil that couldn't spare a drink for a fellow traveler in this God-forsaken desert. [*JESUS gives a start at the idea that God might have forsaken him.*]

JESUS. Well, [*he speaks with irony*] I came out here to find God.

SATAN. *Some* claim to find him here. Take David, the shepherd singer, who hid from Saul in these Godless hills. Went on to be king — God rewarded him for being good, I guess. [*A quickly suppressed gleam enters SATAN's eye.*] A man after God's own heart, they say.

[*SATAN shifts his position.*]

SATAN. But here I go babbling about nothing and you looking like Elijah when his brook dried up! Here — [*SATAN offers the flask.*] Have another.

JESUS. Thanks. [*He opens it and drinks long and deep, his appetite returning in the friendly atmosphere.*]

SATAN. [*digging in knapsack*] I think I have some barley cake, somewhere . . . best barley cake in Palestine . . . [*SATAN rummages, building suspense and muttering to himself comments such as "Mmmm. May be down here," "Well, then it's gotta be over here . . ."*] Melts in your mouth, it does. I had some just a bit ago.

[*SATAN frowns, shows frustration. JESUS has been showing discreet signs of returning hunger, licking lips, changing position, etc.*]

SATAN. What a pity! I must've eaten the last crumb. What a pity! [*pause*] The moistest barley cake this side of the Dead Sea, and I have to go and eat it all just when I need it for you.

[*SATAN slowly re-ties bundle, gathers up flask and staff, then sits by the boulder or leans against it. He absent-mindedly picks up a loaf-sized stone and fingers it slowly, tracing thoughtful circles around its perimeter. A sly, creative gleam almost impreceptibly steals over his face.*]

SATAN. As I said, what a pity. [*Pause.*] You know, Elijah made oil and meal out of nothing for the widow and himself. [*SATAN kicks a small stone.*] You came out here to find God. Did you find him? They say he gave Moses bread in the desert, too. If you're a "son of God" like those others, tell these stones to turn into bread. There'll be enough for you and me — and we can give the rest to the poor.

[*JESUS picks up a stone and caresses its smoothness. He*

reaches with his hand to his head and settles the headband with
dove. His senses have been sharpened by deprivation.]
JESUS. [aside] Son of God . . . "This is my beloved son . . . "
SATAN.[looking to sky for time of day] It's just about dinner time,
I see. [Pause.] If you could make bread — Think! No more
trouble in the world — Bread for everybody!
   [SATAN places the stone on top of the boulder, balancing it
there.]
SATAN. It's not fair the way the kings and the rich snatch the very
living out of the peasants' mouths. Steal more than the poor
folks have, and then the rich grind into powder the hands that
are already worked to the bone. Sorry and sad mothers and
babies,   fathers   who   work   and   work   and   never   get
anywhere — Does God want that? [Pause]
If you've got a prophet's power, join the others and cry for
justice! What do you think God's power is for, anyhow? Justice,
prophet, justice! The world has suffered long enough! [SATAN
sounds sincere and intense. There is silence during which JESUS
picks up the stone on the boulder and muses to self. SATAN
peers intently at Jesus and sits with his hand holding his chin.]
JESUS. Could this be your will, Abba? This boulder might become
an altar where I serve you . . . [JESUS hesitates, looking heavenward.]
SATAN. [urgently] Are you going to let the people destroy each
other for bread — when you can do something about it? Give
them food, and for the first time since Eden the world will be
peaceful. [SATAN taps the boulder resolutely with his stick.
JESUS is composed, but very intense. His eyes have narrowed in
deep concentration.]
JESUS. Suppose I did make sure everybody in the world had
enough food . . .
SATAN. Thank God for that day!
JESUS. Even after the manna, the children of Jacob complained . . .
SATAN. Fathers would have more time to love their children and
wives; families would be happy; contented families make a
happy world.
JESUS. Is this the way things work?
SATAN. [sarcastically] Don't try it, and we'll never know how
good it might have been, here on earth!
JESUS. [After thoughtful pause, he speaks with clear perception,
but with no hint of making a dictum.] It's written in God's Law
that man does not live by eating only bread, but by every word
that comes from God's mouth.
SATAN. [He shrugs and yawns, stretching arms to set a relaxed
atmosphere. Shrugs again.] Have it your way, prophet. But a lot
of good you'll do, that way. You're like them all — got their
heads in the clouds. [SATAN gathers up his belongings.] Well,
I'd best be going or it will be dark before I arrive.

JESUS. Where are you headed?

SATAN. Jerusalem—to worship. Come along? You've been out here long enough, from the looks of you. We'll go to the temple together, and gather in Solomon's porch . . .

JESUS. [*He chuckles at a pleasant memory.*] When I was twelve I stood in Solomon's porch, right by the front pillar, the day my parents thought I was lost. I didn't mean to frighten them—just couldn't tear myself away. We had the most stimulating discussion! My Uncle Zechariah introduced me to the high priest . . . [*a faraway look is in JESUS' eyes*] . . . So exhilarating! Only twelve, I was. And there I talked with the people closest to God . . . Or so I *thought* they were close, then . . .

SATAN. Yes, I know what you mean. Things aren't always the way they seem.

[*SATAN, leading JESUS gently by the arm, walks with him around the stage once, slowly like pilgrims, bowed heads. SATAN quotes aloud from Psalms, "How lovely is thy dwelling place, O Lord Most High!" SATAN and JESUS stop at center front stage, gazing ahead as they stand side by side.*]

SATAN. You must have had quite a conversation, when you were twelve. Did they agree with your ideas?

JESUS. You know those teachers of the Torah. They would think they were wrong if they thought they knew what they believed!

SATAN. I know what you mean . . . interpretations, interpretations. [*He appears genuinely empathetic, philosophical.*] Yes, it's a shame. Andy they're the leaders, too. [*Pause*] Yet you got to wonder, why does God make it so difficult to find the way? Why doesn't he give them something they can't mistake—a sign so everybody can be sure. [*SATAN, the sly, creative gleam in his eyes, glances sideways at JESUS*]. . . See all those sincere people? [*He motions and peers into the audience.*] If only they could be sure . . . [*SATAN spins around abruptly to face JESUS.*] I got it! Climb onto the roof there—the highest pinnacle by the alter—and show them they ought to listen to you. Cast yourself down—

JESUS. I see what you mean.

SATAN. "He shall give his angels charge over thee, to bear thee up lest thou dash thy foot against a stone."

JESUS. [*aside*] "Thou art my beloved son, in whom I am well pleased." The one who baptised me heard it, too. Yes! How could they help but believe, then! I could teach them how to live, and Eden would come again! [*JESUS exhalts, hands held high in victory expression. Then he catches himself.*] But wait—What is it—Something doesn't feel right—.

SATAN. Senseless people, they are, who can't understand anything they read! [*He speaks with a low growl-like tone.*] How else are they gonna know the truth? Why does it take everybody

22

so long to learn! [*Pause.*] Yes, I can see you're a prophet — an extra-ordinary one. They really should listen to you. You've got so much they should know!

JESUS. [*His manner is intense, composed.*] And yet — What is it — What is it? [*musingly*] If God is my servant, then I am his master, and not his "beloved son." [*excitedly*] Yes! I see it now! A son does not force his father's hand. [*JESUS looks squarely, and assuredly, at SATAN.*] "You shall not tempt the Lord your God," says Scripture.

SATAN. [*He affects a look of condescension.*] Yes, that's what it says, but . . . [*SATAN sweeps hand toward audience*] . . . You really ought to help them. Can they help it if God is so hard to understand? [*Emphatically*] The people will die in their sins, and it will be your fault.

[*JESUS gazes steadily and determinedly into the audience, then turns abruptly, head bowed and resolute, and walks over to the boulder. He seems to forget anyone else is around. SATAN walks quietly to back left stage, where he turns to stare over the Judean hills, his back to audience. He leans pensively and petulantly on his staff. JESUS, in authentic struggle, mops brow, throws himself upon rock, beating on it, face turned toward sky.*]

JESUS. Abba! Abba! You love them! Why can't they see! Why can't they know the truth! Why can't they love you? Why can't they love each other! Abba. Show me the way!

[*JESUS lowers his head into his arms and waits, looking gaunt and exhausted. There is deep silence except for a desert owl's hoot. JESUS still waits. After some time, SATAN gathers his belongings and turns, then stalks deliberately toward JESUS. He jabs JESUS in the rib, more severely than at the first meeting.*]

SATAN. That's no way for a prophet to act! Get up! What did God tell Elijah? Up!

[*In SATANS' eye is an evil gleam as he quotes from Psalm 2, pausing at appropriate places to poke JESUS in scorn, designed to arrouse JESUS to action.*]

SATAN. Why are the nations in turmoil? [*He gives a mocking hiss.*] Why do the peoples hatch their futile plots? [*dramatic pause*] The Kings of the earth and the Rulers conspire against the Lord and his anointed King. [*poke*] "Let us throw off God's chains," they say.

[*SATAN pauses, walks to rear stage, points to sky over the Judean hills and bursts into raucus laughter.*]

SATAN. "The Lord who sits enthroned in heaven laughs them to scorn!" [*SATAN strides quickly to where JESUS lies motionless on the rock. SATAN pokes JESUS urgently.*] "Then He rebukes them in anger, he threatens them in his wrath!"

[*SATAN is aroused and paces left and right, behind the*

boulder, waving and brandishing stick like a sword. Then he rushes to JESUS and goads again.]

SATAN. You are my son! says God. This day have I become your Father! [*SATAN continues in low, intense tones.*] "Ask of me what you will: I will give you nations as your inheritance, the ends of the earth as your possession! You shall break them with a Rod of Iron! [*swipes with stick*] You shall shatter them like a clay pot!"

[*SATAN pauses to see if his words have an effect. He takes a deep breath and stomps to right front stage, spending a piercing look over the audience. He punctuates his words by jabbing the air with his stick as he speaks.*]

SATAN. "Be mindful, then, you Kings! Learn your lesson, rulers of the earth! Worship the Lord with reverence! Tremble — and kiss the son, lest the Lord by angry and you are struck [*swipes like sword*] down in mid course."

[*SATAN swaggers to boulder and stands in warlike posture with one foot on the rock. He taps the rock for emphasis as he speaks.*]

SATAN. "For . . . his . . . anger . . . flares . . . up . . . in . . . a . . . moment!"

[*SATAN bends down and whispers loudly into JESUS' ear.*]

SATAN. Your father King David said that! Save the people from their warrings! Save them from their vain imaginations! Make them treat each other fairly! Make them worship God.

[*SATAN pauses, limp after his outburst. JESUS gives signs that the words are taking effect. He lifts his face, glowers at the rock, a look of intense concentration on his face.*]

SATAN. [*calmly, in conversational tone*] Gather your warriors together like your father David, and beat the heathen into the sea. God will be worshipped and again be pleased. You must show them what is good for them, if you ever want peace and justice to come to the land.

[*JESUS, his gaunt face dark with righteous indignation, reaches for the stick which SATAN holds out to him. JESUS holds the stick, turning it over and considering. Still holding the rod, he slowly kneels by the boulder, raises the stick from SATAN high above his head in both hands, and calls heavenward.*]

JESUS. ABBA! What of the sword of David? Is it mine?

[*JESUS holds the position, waiting expectantly. Suddenly off stage a trumpet blast is heard. JESUS gently lays the stick on the boulder, and still kneeling, prepares to hear. One by one in turn (one on the stage at a time) THREE PROPHETS march across the rear of the stage, from right to left. Each prophet carries a placecard bearing his name, to identify himself as NATHAN, ISAIAH, or ZECHARIAH. The trumpet blast heralds each en-*

trance. Each prophet in his turn pauses center stage and intones his message, careful to break the lines with appropriate pauses and gestures for right emphasis.]

[*Trumpet blast. Nathan enters first.*]

NATHAN. O David, my servant! Are you the man to build me a house to dwell in? *You* shall not build a house in honor of my name, for *you have been a fighting man and you have shed blood.* I will build up *your* royal house!

[*ISAIAH enters.*]

ISAIAH. Who could have *believed* what we have heard, and to whom has the power of the Lord been revealed? . . . He grew up before the Lord like a young plant whose roots are in parched ground! . . . No beauty . . . no majesty . . . no grace . . . disfigured . . . despised . . . tormented and humbled by suffering . . . [*Loudly*] We thought God was against him! . . . Yet *on himself* he bore our sufferings . . . the chastisement he bore is health for us, and by *his* scourging we are healed . . . Without protection, without justice, he was taken away . . . He was assigned a grave with the wicked, a burial-place among the refuse of mankind, though *he had done no violence and spoken no word of treachery.*

[*ZECHARIAH enters.*]

ZECHARIAH. These are the words of the Lord of Hosts: "Administer true justice, show loyalty and compassion to one another." But they refused to accept instruction and all that the Lord of Hosts had taught them by his spirit through the prophets of old, and they suffered under the anger of the Lord of Hosts. These are the words of the Lord of Hosts: "In those days, when ten men from nations of every language pluck up courage, they shall pluck the robe of a Jew and say. 'We will go with you because we have heard the God is with you.'"

[*Trumpet blast, as if to announce the arrival of a king. ZECHARIAH turns expectantly toward entrance, right, and when trumpet ceases he continues to speak.*]

ZECHARIAH. Rejoice! Rejoice! Daughter of Zion! Shout aloud, Daughter of Jerusalem! for see — Your king is coming to you, his cause won, his victory gained, *humble* . . . and mounted on an [*ironically*] *ass*, on the foal of a [*ironically*] *she* ass!

[*ZECHARIAH shakes his head in amazement at the paradox. He lays down his placard and walks reverently to the kneeling JESUS. ZECHARIAH places his hand on JESUS' shoulder and continues speaking, in an instructive tone.*]

ZECHARIAH. He shall banish chariots from Ephraim and warhorses from Jerusalem . . . The warrior's bow shall be banished. He shall speak peaceably to *every* nation, and his rule shall extend from sea to sea, from the river to the ends of the earth.

[*ZECHARIAH holds a prayerful pause, hand on JESUS'*

shoulder, then turns, and moves toward exit.]

[*Silence. Desert birds call. JESUS rubs his eyes as if awakening from a dream. He retrieves the stick from the altar-boulder, and returns it to SATAN.*]

JESUS. This is your weapon, not mine. You are Satan. Get behind me. You do not savor the things of God; and it is written that "thou shalt worship the Lord thy God and *Him only* shalt thou serve."

[*JESUS picks up the water flask and hands it to SATAN. Without a word SATAN accepts it, gathers himself together, and walks off stage, purposefully as if continuing on an endless journey. He appears as he did when he first entered the stage. JESUS watches SATAN disappear.*

Suddenly JESUS, exhausted, crumples in death-like weariness. Two ANGELS in white enter, one from right and one from left. One ANGEL holds a crystal goblet and pitcher of ice water. The other ANGEL carries a basket of bread and a small tablecloth. The two ANGELS kneel beside JESUS, spread the cloth on the smaller boulder and pour the goblet full of water and hold it to JESUS' lips. ANGELS continue ministering until JESUS rises.]

JESUS. All power is given unto me in heaven and in earth; Go ye, therefore, and teach all nations . . .
Teaching them to observe all things
Whatsoever I have commanded you . . .
A new commandment I give unto you, that ye love one another.
He that is greatest among you, let him be as the younger; And he that is chief, as he that doth serve.
In my father's house are *many mansions* . . .
My house shall be called a house of prayer for *all nations* . . .
How blessed are the peacemakers;
God shall call them his children.
God shall call them his children.

Suggestions for Discussion

1. Picture the consequences if Jesus had succumbed to any of Satan's temptations. Jot down a list of results on a chalkboard. Distinguish between immediate and long-term effects. Brainstorm about the mindset and ambitions of his followers in each case.

2. Consider how each of the three prophesies contributes to Jesus' awareness of his messiahship.
   — Why does Nathan proclaim that David is *not* the right one to build God's temple? How, then, can Jesus later say that if the temple is destroyed, he will raise it up in three days?
   — What are the attributes of the Messiah described by Isaiah? By Zechariah?

3. Define in your own words why Jesus' desert experience was crucial for his mission.

VISIONS OF THE MESSIAH

by Ingrid Rogers

CHARACTERS

A ROMAN SOLDIER
A ZEALOT
A PHARISEE
A WOMAN WHOSE DAUGHTER WAS HEALED ON A SABBATH

[*A woman goes through the center aisle, announcing the arrival of the Messiah.*]
WOMAN. Listen to me, people of Israel—the Messiah has come! Wonderful things are happening! The lame are walking, the blind can see! "Jesus of Nazareth" they call him. Yesterday, he healed my sick daughter when we all had given up hope. There is beauty and strength in him, and a marvellous vision of the Kingdom to come! Don't just sit there and look at me in this astounded fashion; go and try to meet him! Seek him, and you shall find the Messiah you longed for!

[*A soldier, having come in from back, grabs her arm.*]

SOLDIER. What is this, messiah-talk again? You better be careful, woman. You know how we Romans feel about these tales. You better stop witnessing about these rebel types in public. Who is this fellow, anyway?

WOMAN. Well, I'm not sure he fits your image of a rebel type, but he has come to free us, and he has such power that no Roman in the world will be able to stop him.

[*Woman quickly sits down on bench and hides.*]

SOLDIER. Hey, wait a minute. Where are you? Aw nuts — she escaped in the crowd! If these people could just keep quiet, pay their taxes and let everybody go about his business! All this Messiah stuff all the time!

[*Soldier off*]

ZEALOT. [*rising from another bench*] My word, that was interesting! I must find this woman. Ah, there she is! Excuse me, I just heard you speak to that Roman soldier. Is it really true, you have seen the Messiah?

WOMAN. Yes, and I want to tell the whole world about it!

ZEALOT. Can it be? The leader for whom we have waited for such as long time has finally arrived? Tell me more about him. What did he say?

WOMAN. He is proclaiming the good news that the time has come when the Lord will save his people. The captives will gain liberty, the blind will see, all the oppressed will be set free.

ZEALOT. Listen, woman, I need to get in touch with him. I have a band of 40 people under me, and we have over a thousand followers who are armed and waiting for a signal to begin the revolution. We are ready to help him overthrow the oppressors. We'll show him how strong we are! But what's the matter? What are you shaking your head for?

WOMAN. I — I am not sure that Jesus would approve such violence. Just yesterday I heard him speak of peace, and of loving your neighbor and well — even loving your enemies! He is healing people. He hasn't come to destroy. He says that we will find our freedom in loving others.

[*Zealot turns away very disappointed.*]

Wait! Can't you see? What good will it do to replace one kind of oppression with another? Violence won't really change anything! Stay, friend! Listen to him, at least . . . .

[*He is gone.*]

WOMAN. [*after a pause, addressing the public — pleading, but happy.*] Friends, look what is happening. There is great wonder in this land. You all know the situation we are in. You all know that we cannot get out of it by ourselves. But there is hope now! The Messiah — he is actually with us!

PHARISEE. [*solemnly walking up*] Now, now, lady . . . let's just be a bit sensible about all those proclamations. Did you say that this Jesus healed your daughter yesterday? Why, that was a Sabbath, wasn't it? Now wouldn't the Messiah — if he were the real one — know enough about the law of Moses not to pick a Sabbath for his healing? So just be cautious and calm, lady. Take a rest. Go on vacation for a while. Follow the law, and let *us* worry about the Messiah.

[*He walks on, nodding to himself.*]

WOMAN. [*to audience*] But the Messiah *is* here! I've seen him! My daughter is well! There is hope for all of us!

Suggestions for Discussion

1. If someone proclaimed the arrival of a messiah today, how would you check whether this person is sent from God or is just a false prophet?

2. Which people today are seeking liberty for the captives and freedom for the oppressed? Talk about the work of Amnesty International, Martin Luther King, and other groups or individuals with similar motivation.

3. What are some promises from people you have heard who claim to be speaking in the name of God but do not make love of neighbor and social justice a high priority?

4. Can you think of a modern equivalent of a Zealot? Of a Pharisee? Of the woman in the skit?

GOOD FRIDAY

by the Reba Place Fellowship Drama Group

CHARACTERS

NARRATOR
JOSHUA, *a chief priest*
CAIAPHAS, *high priest*
JUDAS
JESUS
PETER
JAMES
JOHN
3 SOLDIERS
HIGH PRIEST'S SERVANT
    [*in arrest scene*]

WOMAN
SERVANT TO CAIAPHAS
3 MEN
PILATE
PILATE'S OFFICER
MARY, *mother of Jesus*
MARY MAGDALENE
SALOME
SIMON OF CYRENE
CROWD
    [*about ten more people*]

PROLOGUE

NARRATOR. Jesus, taking the Twelve aside, said to them, "Behold, we are going up to Jerusalem, and everything that is written of the Son of man by the prophets will be accomplished. For he will be delivered to the Gentiles, and will be mocked and shamefully treated and spit upon. They will scourge him and kill him and on the third day he will rise." But they understood none of these things; this saying was hid from them, and they did not grasp what he said.

The chief priests and the Pharisees gathered the council and said, "What are we to do? For this man performs many signs. If we let him go on like this, everyone will believe in him, and the Romans will come and destroy both our holy place and our nation." But Caiaphas, who was high priest that year, said to them, "You know nothing at all; you do not understand that it is expedient for you that one man should die for the people and not that the whole nation should perish." He did not say that of his own accord, but being high priest that year, he prophesied that Jesus should die for the nation, and not for the nation only, but to gather into one the children of God who are scattered abroad. So from that day on they took counsel how to put him to death.

30

SCENE I: In the Home of Caiaphas

Caiaphas and Joshua come on stage, talking vigorously.

JOSHUA. I tell you, my Lord Caiaphas, he watches his words carefully. He says nothing against Rome. Nothing, at least, that could be held against him.

CAIAPHAS. But you must press him. I told you, it's not enough just to spy on him.

JOSHUA. We did. We did, my lord! Just as you suggested!

CAIAPHAS. You asked him about taxation?

JOSHUA. Yes, yes! Is it lawful to give tribute to Caesar or not? I put the question to him myself.

CAIAPHAS. And what did he say? Tell me exactly, word for word.

JOSHUA. He told us to show him a coin, and then he asked, "Whose face and name are on it?" Someone answered, "Caesar's!" Then he said, "Well then, give to Caesar the things that are Caesar's and to God the things that are God's."

CAIAPHAS. What? [*pondering*] . . . Give to Caesar what is Caesar's and God what is God's . . . What do you make of that, Joshua? Does he say to pay the tax, or not?

JOSHUA. The coin belongs to Caesar.

CAIAPHAS. And then what belongs to God?

JOSHUA. He didn't say . . .

CAIAPHAS. Obviously, he's trying to avoid a direct answer. That in itself is mighty suspicious. What's the mood of the people?

JOSHUA. Excitement! You can feel it building, day by day.

CAIAPHAS. Annas says I should arrest him, and worry later about the charges. What would you say to that?

JOSHUA. No, my Lord. I'd very strongly advise against it. If you arrest him now, in the presence of the people, you're going to have a worse problem on your hands . . .

CAIAPHAS. Then there's nothing to do, but hope that things won't explode until *after* Passover . . .

JOSHUA. Either that or . . . [*Hesitates*] . . . but no, I guess not.

CAIAPHAS. Or what, Joshua?

JOSHUA. Well, I was just thinking, perhaps we could arrest him secretly, at night, or some time when he's alone . . . [*Stops, shakes head*] . . . but even that would be risky, and with these crowds it would be hard to find a time, even at night, when that could be done without causing a riot.

CAIAPHAS. [*Decisively*] All right then, we'll wait until after Passover. In the meantime, keep a close watch on him. Let me know at once, day or night, of any new developments . . .

[*Servant enters.*]

SERVANT. My lord Caiaphas, please forgive me for interrupting, but there's a man outside who insists on seeing you at once.

CAIAPHAS. Who is it?

SERVANT. He won't tell me his name, nor what he wants. He insists that you will want to see him.

CAIAPHAS. All right, send him in.

[Servant exits, and immediately returns with Judas.]

SERVANT. This is the man, your holiness. [He exits.]

CAIAPHAS. Now, sir, what is it you wanted?

JUDAS. I understand you want to arrest Jesus the Nazarene.

CAIAPHAS. Arrest him? Well . . . you might say, we're keeping a close watch on him. Do you know him?

JUDAS. [Coming close to Caiaphas] I know him well . . . very well. Until today I've been one of his disciples.

CAIAPHAS. A disciple! Then what brings you here?

JUDAS. [Intensely] I follow him no more. He's a fraud! He promised us the Kingdom of God. I thought he was the Messiah. But he deceived me.

CAIAPHAS. Well, my friend, you're not the first to be led astray by false Messiahs. And unfortunately, I'm afraid, you'll not be the last.

JUDAS. [Almost wild] No . . . you don't understand. He wasn't like any other. There was power in him. But now . . .

CAIAPHAS. [Breaking in] Friend, what's your name?

JUDAS. Judas . . . Judas Ishkariot.

CAIAPHAS. Ishkariot! You're not a Galilean, then? I thought his disciples were Galileans. Judas, what did you come here to tell us?

JUDAS. [Collecting himself slowly] How much money will you pay me, if I help you arrest him?

CAIAPHAS. [Astonished] Help us arrest him? . . . Well, now . . . how could you do that?

JOSHUA. [Breaking in] Caiaphas, perhaps he could tell us where we might find him along, and we could possible take him without the crowds knowing it.

JUDAS. Exactly! I could do it. You'd have no trouble.

JOSHUA. Why, this is most fortunate!

CAIAPHAS. Yes, my good man! Perhaps you could be of help to us. You spoke of money?

JUDAS. Right! I deserve something, don't I, for all the months I've wasted with him?

CAIAPHAS. Well, what would you say . . . thirty pieces of silver? Will that be enough? [Slaps him jovially on the shoulder] With that you could buy yourself a slave and make up for lost time, eh?

JUDAS. Agreed!

CAIAPHAS. What do you suggest then? When would be the best time? Tonight? It's Passover, of course. Where will he eat the Passover?

JUDAS. That's one thing I don't know. He's been very secretive about it.

CAIAPHAS. Well, then, what do you suggest?

JUDAS. [*Thinking, then suddenly*] Oh . . . listen . . . I must get back, or he'll wonder where I've been. [*Begins to exit.*] As soon as I know his plans, I'll return . . .

CAIAPHAS. All right, all right . . . but . . . [*stops him*] here, let me pay you before you leave . . .

[*Caiaphas counts out to him the silver. Judas puts the money in a pouch and exits immediately, without a word. Caiaphas calls after him:*]

Now be sure you follow through on your part. Let us know the first opportunity when we can arrest him.

JOSHUA. [*Also calling*] . . . And be sure it's a time when there are no crowds.

CAIAPHAS. [*Exuberant, slapping Joshua on the back*] Well, Joshua, we're in luck. [*Begins to exit.*] Just wait until Annas hears about this.

SCENE 2: In the Garden of Gethsemane

NARRATOR. When Jesus and his disciples had sung a hymn, they went out to the Mount of Olives. And Jesus went with them to a place called Gethsemane.

[*A musical ensemble, choir, or soloist sings a verse of a song related to Jesus' preparation in Gethsemane. A possible choice would be "Go To Dark Gethsemane" from the Brethren and Mennonite Hymnals.*]

[*Offstage, Jesus is heard talking quietly to his disciples, coming closer as he talks.*]

JESUS. [*Offstage behind risers*] . . . I have told you that one of you would betray me. Now the time is coming when *all* of you will fall away; for it is written, "I'll strike the shepherd and the sheep will be scattered." But don't be discouraged. After I am raised up, I'll go before you to Galilee . . .

PETER. [*Offstage*] Master, what are you saying . . . that we're going to run away from you, if trouble comes. [*Vigorously*] Well, I don't know about the others, but I'll never leave you, even if the rest do.

JESUS. Peter, this very night, before the cock crows twice, you'll deny me three times.

PETER. [*Vehemently*] No, master, even if I must *die* with you, I'll not deny you.

JAMES. [*Offstage*] Nor I, master.

JOHN. [*Offstage*] Nor I.

[*Pause*]

JESUS. [*Offstage*] Brothers, stay here . . . I want to spend some time in prayer. [*Pause.*] Peter, James, John . . . I want you three to come with me . . .

[*Peter, James, John and Jesus come to center stage.*]

JESUS. My soul's so full of sorrow, I can hardly bear it. Would you stay here and watch with me while I go over there to pray?

DISCIPLES. Certainly, Master.

[*Peter, James, and John remain center stage, seating themselves. Jesus moves on a short distance, just offstage.*]

JOHN. [*Stage whisper to James and Peter*] I've never seen him so troubled.

PETER. I don't understand. He seemed happy enough during the Passover meal.

JAMES. Where's Judas?

PETER. Judas?

JAMES. Yeah . . . you saw him leave, didn't you? Right in the midst of the Passover.

PETER. That was strange, wasn't it? I wonder where he is.

JESUS. [*Offstage*] Father . . . Father . . .

JOHN. Listen! He's praying . . . Look at his face!

JESUS. . . . Anything is possible for you, Father . . . Take this cup away from me . . . Yet . . . not what I will, but your will be done . . .

PETER. [*Stage whisper to John*] John . . . the cup? He had us *drink* from *his cup*?

JAMES. And didn't he say he'd not drink with us again until we drink it in the Kingdom of God?

JOHN. . . . The way he struggles there . . . It worries me. He's never been like this before.

PETER. [*Yawning*] I just can't stay awake . . . must be the Passover meal. James, would you keep an eye out? I've gotta get some sleep. [*Peter makes himself comfortable, and is quickly asleep.*]

JAMES. [*Yawning too*] I'm gonna have to get a little sleep myself. If you're awake anyway, John, perhaps you could watch for the rest of us.

[*John remains in a seated position, but he too soon begins to nod. After a pause, Jesus comes on stage and approaches Peter.*]

JESUS. [*Quietly, but a little disturbed*] Simon! Simon! Are you sleeping?

PETER. [*Waking with a start*] Oh . . . What? Oh, Master. I guess I . . . I guess I dozed off a little.

JESUS. I wanted you to stay awake and watch with me. Couldn't you even watch one hour? Watch and pray, Peter, that *you* don't come into temptation. [*Spoken as Jesus exits*] The spirit is willing, but the flesh is weak.

PETER. John! Are you awake?

JOHN. Yes, Peter. I heard everything.

PETER. He wants me to watch . . . I don't know what for. But I'm still so sleepy. I don't know if I can make it . . .

JESUS. [*Offstage*] Father . . . remove this cup . . .

JOHN. [*Whispering to Simon*] It's the same prayer, Peter . . . He's in *such* a struggle . . . But what about?

PETER. [*Yawning*] I wish I knew . . . [*Yawning, stretching, settling down*] . . . But I guess we'll find out soon enough. [*He sleeps again.*]

JOHN. [*To himself, after Peter sleeps.*] . . . What's going to happen to us? [*Pause, then to Peter:*] Peter . . .! Peter . . .! Sound asleep. Brr . . . It's getting chilly. [*He pulls his coat around himself and soon nods.*]

[*After a pause, Jesus returns, sees them sleeping again, shakes his head sorrowfully and slowly returns.*]

JESUS. My Father, if this cannot pass unless I drink it, your will be done.

[*After a pause, Jesus comes decisively on stage. He speaks rather loudly now.*]

Are you still sleeping, brothers? Well, it's enough, now. The hour is come. Get up! See, the Son of Man is now about to be handed over to the power of sinful men. Come, let's go. See! There he comes . . . the man who's going to betray me . . .

[*The three disciples struggle to get awake during this. They get to their feet, very confused. Judas, followed by Joshua, three soldiers, and the high priest's servant, enters from the left risers.*]

JUDAS. [*Quiet and intense*] The one I kiss is the man. Seize him. [*He walks directly to Jesus and embraces him.*] Rabbi! Peace be with you.

JESUS. What, do you betray me with a kiss, Judas?

[*The soldiers immediately close in on Jesus, grab him by the arms and begin tying his hands behind his back. Suddenly Peter, now fully aroused, begins to flail with a sword. He hits the high priest's servant on the side of the head. The servant doubles up in pain, his hand over his ear. A soldier goes after Peter. It looks for a moment as though a fight will break out. Then Jesus speaks, loud and decisive about the melee:*]

Peter! Enough. Put away your sword. They who take the sword will perish with the sword. [*He goes to the high priest's servant, places his hand on the injured ear, and heals it.*]

JAMES. [*To Peter*] Peter, let's get out of here, before they arrest us, too. [*They, together with John, exit hastily.*]

[*Things quiet down momentarily. The soldiers return the Jesus, and continue binding him.*]

JESUS. [*More quietly now, to the soldiers*] Did you have to come with swords and clubs to capture me, as though I were an outlaw? Day after day I was with you teaching in the temple, and you didn't arrest me.

SOLDIER. [*Finishing tying Jesus' hands, he speaks loudly:*] Come on, now . . . No smart talk . . . There, that should do it . . .

JOSHUA. [*Almost whispering*] Soldiers, not so loud. We want to get him out of here without waking the whole countryside.

SOLDIER. Where are we taking him?

JOSHUA. To Caiaphas . . . to be tried at the Sanhedrin.

SOLDIER. Okay, then . . . Get a move on . . . Come on . . .

[*They lead Jesus roughly offstage, Joshua and Judas following.*]

SCENE 3: The Courtyard of the High Priest

NARRATOR. Then they led him away, bringing him into the high priest's house. And Peter followed at a distance.

[*Music group hums one verse of the hymn sung at the beginning of scene 2.*]

[*Woman comes on stage from left. It is night.*]

WOMAN. Brr. What a chilly night! Wonder why Caleb hasn't built a fire. I guess I'll build one myself . . .

[*She begins gathering wood and starting a fire. Servant comes on stage from right.*]

Caleb, why haven't you built a fire?

SERVANT. I was just coming to do that very thing. [*He begins helping her.*] It's been a busy night here. The whole Sandhedrin has gathered.

WOMAN. They called a meeting in the dead of night? And during Passover? That's mighty strange!

SERVANT. I heard them talking. It's something to do with the Nazarene. I think they're going to arrest him.

WOMAN. People have been talking about him all week, ever since last Sunday when he came riding on a donkey, leading that big parade.

SERVANT. I'm surprised they've let him alone as long as they have.

[*Noise heard offstage left of someone hammering at the gate.*]

JOSHUA. [*Offstage*] Hallooo . . . Is anyone here?

[*Caleb starts toward the gate, but just then Caiaphas hurries across stage from right.*]

CAIAPHAS. Never mind, Caleb. I'll get it.

[*Caiaphas goes to the gate and returns in a moment with Joshua and Judas, followed by one of the soldiers pushing Jesus roughly ahead of him. They cross the stage and exit on the right.*]

WOMAN. Poor man. I wonder what they intend to do with him.

SERVANT. From what I hear, they want to put him out of the way.

WOMAN. Put him out of the way? Now what does that mean?

SERVANT. That means, lady . . . kill him!

WOMAN. No! What a pity!

[*A knock is heard at the gate.*]

PETER. [*Offstage*] Hello. May I come in?

WOMAN. I'll go. [*She exits.*] Well . . . and who are you?

PETER. It's cold out here. May I warm myself at your fire?

WOMAN. But who are you? And what are you doing wandering around here at this time of night?

PETER. Listen, woman . . . all I want is to warm myself by your fire.

WOMAN. Well, come on in. It is a mighty chilly night. [*She leads him to the fire, then suddenly looks at him closely.*] Say . . . You're not one of the disciples of the man they just brought in here, are you?

PETER. Well . . . well, of course not. [*There is an awkward silence, and he averts his face so the light doesn't shine directly on it.*]

SERVANT. Shalom, friend!

PETER. [*Barely audible*] Shalom.

SERVANT. And who are you?

PETER. Simon. Simon bar Jonah.

SERVANT. Say. Haven't I seen you somewhere?

PETER. I doubt it. I'm not from Jerusalem.

SERVANT. No, but just in the past several days . . . why, yes! I have seen you . . . at the temple . . . with the Nazarene.

PETER. No, you must be mistaken.

SERVANT. [*Shaking his head*] Really! I'd have sworn that I'd seen you somewhere. [*Pause.*] You've heard of the Nazarene, haven't you? The one that claims to be the Messiah? [*Silence*] They've arrested him, you know. He's inside there right now being questioned by the Sanhedrin.

[*Courtyard scene freezes, and we hear the trial from behind the risers.*]

CAIAPHAS. Does the accused have anything to say for himself? [*Silence*] I repeat. Does the accused have anything to say for himself? [*Silence*] All right, then . . . We shall proceed with the accusations. Gentlemen, what charges are there against this man?

MAN 1. My Lord Caiaphas, I heard the accused speak against Caesar, saying we should refuse to pay our taxes . . .

MAN 2. My Lord, I object. I don't wish to take exception with my honorable colleague, but others of us heard him speak on that subject, and I don't believe it could be said he advocated non-payment of taxes.

CAIAPHAS. What did he say, then?

MAN 2. I believe his words were that what belongs to Caesar should be paid to him.

CAIAPHAS. And did he mean that the tax belongs to him?

MAN 2. I believe so, sir.

MAN 1. I disagree, Lord Caiaphas. He distinctly said . . .

CAIAPHAS. [Interrupting] Gentlemen, let's drop that accusation. There seems to be confusing testimony on the issue. I suggest we hear what other charges there are against him.

MAN 3. My lord, I heard him say that he will tear down God's temple and build it back up again three days later.

CAIAPHAS. You heard him say that?

MAN 1. And I heard him say the same thing, sir.

CAIAPHAS. We have two witnesses, then! What does the accused say to this? Is it true that you spoke of destroying God's temple? [Jesus remains silent.] I repeat. Was it really your plan to destroy God's temple? [Silence] What! Do you refuse to answer me? [Pause] Enough of this! Let me ask you a final question, and I put you under oath to answer. Tell us once and for all: Do you claim to be the Messiah, the Son of God?

JESUS. [Quietly] If I tell you, you'll not believe me anyway . . . But from now on, The Son of Man will be seated at the right side of Almighty God, and coming with the clouds of heaven . . .

JOSHUA. [Breaking in vigorously] Do you claim, then, to be the Son of God?

JESUS. You say that I am.

CAIAPHAS. Honorable members of the Sanhedrin. What further need do we have of witnesses? You have heard the blasphemy out of his own mouth. What shall we do with this man?

MAN 1. Guilty!

MAN 2. He should be put to death.

MAN 3. Take him to Pilate!

MAN 1. To Pilate and to judgment . . .

ALL. He should be crucified . . . Crucify him.

CAIAPHAS. Very well, then. Sanhedrin dismissed. Soldiers, we'll take the prisoner to Pilate at once.

[Cock crows]

[They cross the stage again and exit at left gate. As Jesus reaches center stage the cock crows, and he turns and looks into Peter's eyes, a long, sorrowful gaze. Then the soldiers push Jesus forward again, and Peter turns and hides his face in his hands, sobbing softly. Judas, bringing up the rear, now stops center stage. The enormity of what he has done has just dawned on him. He holds up the money bag and looks at it in horror and disgust. He drops it on the floor and tears his hair in remorse. Suddenly, he picks up the money bag and runs out the gate.]

[Peter now begins to sob aloud. The woman and the servant have been looking back and forth from Peter to Judas, dumb-founded; now they look at each other, shaking their heads in

wonderment. They exit quietly. After a few moments Peter
stumbles off stage left. His sobs change to bitter wailing. His
weeping is all we hear for a few moments.]

[*Music group sings about Jesus' suffering. "Ah, Holy Jesus,"*
Mennonite Hymnal No. 158, stanzas 1 and 2, could be used.]

[*Immediately after Peter's cries have died away, the soldiers*
bring Jesus, blindfold him, punch him around, and then place
him face against the wall and flog him. Then they tie his arms
behind his back, and one of the soldiers brings him to Pilate.]

[*The Narrator continues after the music is ended and Jesus'*
hands are tied.]

SCENE 4: In Pilate's Court

[*Pilate enters as Narrator speaks, preceded by his officer, who*
sets a chair for him a bit forward under the spotlights. The of-
ficer takes his place to Pilate's left, slightly behind his chair. At
the same time the three men come down and take chairs in the
audience near the front. There is a scene-within-a-scene, where
Judas returns money to the chief priests. This will take place
behind the trial, under separate south spotlights.]

NARRATOR. Then they bound him and led him away, and
delivered him to Pilate, the governor.

SOLDIER. [*Presenting Jesus to Pilate*] Your Honor, the prisoner.

PILATE. [*Looking Jesus up and down, his tone faintly sarcastic*]
So. You are the King of the Jews? [*Jesus makes no reply. Pilate*
turns to the audience.] Exactly what accusations are you bringing against this man?

MAN 1. We found him perverting our nation.

MAN 2. That's right. He told us not to pay taxes to Caesar.

MAN 3. And he claims to be the Messiah. A king.

PILATE. [*To Jesus*] Are you King of the Jews?

JESUS. You have said so.

PILATE. [*He wishes they wouldn't bother him with their internal*
religious disputes. To the crowd, annoyed.] What do you want of
me? I don't find any crime in this man.

MAN 1. But he stirs up the people with his teachings — all over
Judea and Galilee, and right here in Jerusalem as well.

PILATE. I don't find anything to condemn him for under Roman
law. Take him yourselves, and judge him by your own laws.

MAN 2. But it's against Roman law for us to put anyone to death.

PILATE. [*Ponders a moment*] I'll tell you what. I have one of two
prisoners whom I could release for you in honor of your
Passover. There's the murderer, Barabbas. You all know how he
led an insurrection. [*Sarcastically*] I know how concerned you

39

are for the welfare of our Roman government. I'm sure you wouldn't want me to release Barabbas. So how about this Jesus?

CROWD. No! No! Not Jesus. We want Barabbas! We want Barabbas! Give us Barabbas! [*etc.*]

PILATE. Then what shall I do with this man whom you call King of the Jews?

CROWD. Have him crucified! Yes! Crucify him! Crucify!

PILATE. [*Exasperated*] Why? What evil has he done?

CROWD. [*Chanting, fists thrust into the air*] Crucify him! Crucify him! Crucify him!

PILATE. [*To officer*] Manilaeus, bring me a basin of water. [*The officer exits to get a basin of water and towel. Trial scene freezes. Spotlights shift to another part of the stage where the following scene takes place. It is in the temple, where Judas has come to confess his guilt to the chief priests. Joshua and Caiaphas enter from the right as the crowd is still chanting, "Crucify him!" Immediately Judas comes hurrying up to them, money pouch held out, his face contorted, his voice agitated.*]

JUDAS. Here. I can't keep this. Take it back. I have sinned. I have betrayed innocent blood.

CAIAPHAS. [*Coldly, waving the money away*] What's that to us? See to it yourself.

JUDAS. [*Fist clenching and unclenching, so devastated he can hardly speak*] Can't you hear me? I said . . . I said . . . [*He throws the money pouch with all his force at their feet, then with a loud wail:*] I have betrayed innocent blood! [*He turns and runs out west exit.*]

[*Spotlights go back to the previous spot where the trial scene continues.*]

OFFICER. [*He returns just as Judas is running out.*] Here you are, my lord.

PILATE. [*To crowd, loudly, distinctly, slowly, with cold, suppressed anger*] I want you to know I am innocent of this man's blood. See to it yourselves.

MAN 3. Right! His blood be on us.

MAN 1. His blood's on us.

MAN 2. Yes. We'll take his blood on us . . .

PILATE. [*Curtly, to soldier*] Take him away. Have him flogged. Then turn him over to the centurion. He'll be crucified this morning with the other two. [*To the crowd, rising*] Now leave! Out of my sight! All of you! Just go!

[*Pilate turns on his heel and stomps out, followed by the officer. Jesus, pushed roughly ahead by the soldier, exits after them, head bowed.*]

NARRATOR. Then Pilate released for them Barabbas, and having scourged Jesus, delivered him to be crucified.

[*Music group sings two verses of "They Led My Lord Away," or another appropriate song.*]

SCENE 5: Mockery by the Roman Soldiers

[*Three soldiers enter from right with mock ceremony. The lead soldier carries the crown of thorns on the purple robe, folded like a pillow. The other two push and manhandle Jesus, now weak from torture. They pantomime the action as the Narrator reads. Exit left.*]

NARRATOR. Then the soldiers of the governor took Jesus into the praetorium, and they gathered the whole battalion before him. And they stripped him and put a scarlet robe on him . . . . Then they put a crown of thorns on his head, and put a reed in his right hand . . . and kneeling before him, they mocked him, saying, "Hail, King of the Jews!" And they spit upon him. And when they had mocked him, they stripped him of the robe, and led him away to crucify him . . . .

SCENE 6: Procession to Golgatha

[*Immediately form up for the procession to Golgatha. Jesus with cross and soldiers first, followed by centurion with spear, John and the mother of Jesus, Mary Magdalene, and Salome. The rest of the crowd follows in natural groupings. Procession follows the same route as the Palm Sunday one. On reaching stage center, Jesus stumbles under the weight of the cross, and the centurion orders Simon of Cyrene to carry it for him. Simon, Jesus, and the soldiers go behind the risers. The centurion directs the "watchers" to the stage and stays with them.*]

NARRATOR. So they took Jesus, and he went out bearing his own cross, to the place called the place of a skull, which is called in Hebrew, Golgatha.

[*Quoir sings during the procession. Refrains should be repeated until the procession to Golgatha is finished and the "watchers" at the cross are in place, stage center.*]

SCENE 7: The Crucifixion

[*"Watchers" face the risers. The centurion and Jesus' mother and friends stand close to the risers. The others arrange themselves in groupings behind them, leaving space just behind and next to the centurion for the soldiers who will return to stand guard. Jesus speaks his lines from the top of a high ladder, hidden from the audience by a screen on top of the risers. All other dialogue is spoken by the Narrator, and pantomimed by the actors. The only other sound is the "weeping" of the women from time to time, as appropriate.*]

NARRATOR. And when they came to the place called Golgotha, they offered him wine to drink, mixed with gall; but when he tasted it, he would not drink it.

[*Unaccompanied Solo: "They Crucified My Lord" (2 stanzas). The singing of the solo is accompanied throughout by slow, deliberate blows of the hammer on the cross.*]

[*Music Group continues humming additional stanzas of "They Crucified My Lord" as necessary throughout the narration and casting of lots for Jesus' robe.*]

[*The blows stop when the Music Group begins to hum, and the soldiers come to center with Jesus' robe. They dicker around a bit about who gets it, finally deciding to roll dice for it. The winner holds it up to see if it fits him. Then all sit down to watch. The humming stops when the soldiers sit down.*]

NARRATOR. And when they had crucified him, they divided his garments among them by casting lots.

JESUS. Father, forgive them. They don't know what they are doing.

NARRATOR. Then they sat down and kept watch over him there. And over his head they put the charge which read, "This is Jesus, the King of the Jews." Two robbers were crucified with him, one on the right and one on the left.

[*Caiaphas and Joshua saunter by from stage left and pantomime the speeches of the chief priests and elders.*]

And those who passed by derided him, wagging their heads, and saying, "You who would destroy the temple and build it in three days, save yourself! If you are the Son of God, come down now from the cross." And so also the chief priests and elders mocked him, saying, "He saved others; he cannot save himself. He is the King of Israel; let him come down now from the cross, and we will believe in him. He trusts in God; let God deliver him now, if he wants him. For he said, "I am the Son of God."

One of the criminals who were hanged railed at him, saying, "Aren't you the Messiah? Save yourself, then, and us, too!" But the other rebuked him, saying, "Do you not fear God? We've been condemned justly for our crimes, but this man is innocent. Jesus, remember me when you come in your kingly power." Jesus said to him:

JESUS. Truly I say to you, today you will be with me in Paradise.

NARRATOR. Standing by the cross were Jesus' mother, and his mother's sister, and Mary Magdalene.

[*Music Group sings two verses of a hymn mourning the death of Jesus.*]

NARRATOR. When Jesus saw his mother and the disciple whom he loved standing near, he said to his mother:

JESUS. Woman, look. There is your son.

NARRATOR. Then he said to the disciple:

JESUS. Look. Your mother.

NARRATOR. And from that hour the disciple took her to his own home. [*Pause.*]

Now from the sixth hour there was darkness over all the land until the ninth hour.

[*Music Group hums one verse of the last song.*]

NARRATOR. And about the ninth hour, Jesus cried with a loud voice:

JESUS. My God, my God! Why have you forsaken me?

[*Music Group hums one verse of the last song.*]

[*Drum roll starts very quietly as Narrator begins, and crescendos to very loud after the speech ends. The Centurion falls on his knees. There is a moment's pause after the last echo of the drum dies away.*]

NARRATOR. And behold! The curtain of the temples was torn in two from top to bottom, and the earth quaked, and the rocks were split.

When the centurion and those who were with him keeping watch over Jesus saw the earthquake and what took place, they were filled with fear. And the centurion said, "Surely, this was a son of God!"

And the crowds who assembled to see the sight, when they saw what had taken place, returned home beating their breasts.

[*Music Group sings one additional verse of the same song.*]

[*The crowd disperses slowly. They are in various states of mourning, shock, awe. Jesus' mother and friends go back stage to the cross and stay the longest. Mary Magdalene and Salome exit last, so that as the song ends they have just left the stage.*]

EPILOGUE

NARRATOR. Now there was man named Joseph from the Jewish town of Arimathea. He was a member of the council, a good man, who had not consented to their purpose and deed, and he was looking for the Kingdom of God. This man went to Pilate and asked for the body of Jesus. Then he took it down, and wrapped it in a linen shroud, and laid him in a rock-hewn tomb, where no one had ever been laid. It was the day of the Preparation, and the Sabbath was beginning. The women who had come with him from Galilee followed and saw the tomb and how his body was laid. They returned and prepared spices and ointments. On the Sabbath they rested, according to the commandment.

[*Music Group sings, mourning yet celebrating the death of Jesus.*]

Suggestions for Discussion

1. Analyse how each episode sheds light on Christ as suffering servant: Judas's betrayal; Peter's denial; the people's choice to have him crucified and Barrabas freed; the mock coronation; the verbal abuse while Jesus hangs on the cross; his forgiving the murderer; and his last gesture of love for Mary and John.

2. In groups of six, have each person assume the viewpoint of one of the characters in the play: Judas, Peter, Mary, John, Caiaphas, Pilate. Relate what happened from the perspective of that character, and defend your actions. Be ready for questions from other members of the group. After you have all had a turn, change roles. At the end, discuss the effect of this exercise.

Other Workers for Peace

Throughout the centuries, many people have turned to Christ as an example of righteous living and have sought to apply his teachings: "Love your enemies, do good to those who hate you; bless those who curse you and pray for those who maltreat you." "Be compassionate, as your Father is compassionate." "Do to others what you would have them do to you." The plays in this section portray people who followed these commandments. All four plays are linked in that they show historical peacemakers with an active faith who explore non-violent measures to resolve conflict.

The first two plays are set during the Revolutionary War in America. This was a trying time for the historic peace churches. The Pennsylvania Assembly was pressuring the Brethren and Quakers to support the defense of the colonies through tax monies and military service. At a time when frequent conflicts with the Indians and the Revolutionary War threatened the settlers, many non-pacifist neighbors deeply resented those who refused to join the militia for defense purposes. In addition to these problems, the Anabaptist communities had to cope with some of their own members' breaking away from the church. All along, of course, people were also struggling with individual crisis, trying to apply their convictions about nonviolence to interpersonal conflicts.

"Winds of Change" deals with peacemaking on all these different levels: individual, communal, and societal. How do we handle a personal offense, like the stealing of our property? How can we best relate to people who endanger the church community by supporting a divisive faith stance? Can a Christian contribute to war preparations by paying taxes or enlisting? The play reveals the answers found in a Brethren community under the leadership of George Miller, minister-in-charge of the Big Swatara congregation.

"William's Pruning Hooks" relates how a Quaker from Nantucket refused to hand over weapons because he could not in good conscience contribute to the war effort. As in the first play, peacemaking involved a creative individual initiative. It was not so much a matter of "not taking sides" in a certain conflict, but rather of taking a clear stand consistent with one's beliefs. The play shows that pacifism is far from passive; in fact, peacemaking requires courage, commitment, and willingness to suffer the legal consequences of one's actions.

Carie, the main character in the next play, was a missionary's wife in China before the war. One day she faces an angry mob that wants to kill her. Instead of fearing for her life or seeking some form of escape, she literally disarms her enemies by speaking to them and offering them her hospitality. The play shows that Christian love of neighbor is a better means for "defense" than any weapon could provide.

"A Man in the Loin Cloth" explores the possibilities of non-violent civil disobedience. Under Gandhi's leadership, the people of India were on the verge of ending British imperialist domination. The spinning wheel in every home had become a symbol of the growing movement in India to seek economic and political independence. The scene depicted in "A Man in a Loin Cloth" includes the training for non-violence and the message of carrying out civil disobedience in a spirit of love. The actions of Gandhi are faith-centered, a faith that is crushed neither by the pain over the dissent of one of his closest allies, nor by the devastating sense of failure near the end when the demonstration turns violent. Gandhi combined great leadership with humility, and strict discipline with kindness toward others. Like many peacemakers before and after him — such as Christ, members of the early Christian church, the radical Anabaptist, M. L. King, and Archbishop Romero-he was persecuted, ridiculed, and ultimately killed because his methods so completely contradicted the commonly accepted standards. But his death like that of the others was a tribute to a humanity which is powerful even in its powerlessness. The teachings live on, and with them the hope for peace.

WINDS OF CHANGE

by Evelyn M. Frantz

CHARACTERS

MICHAEL STEWART, *non-German neighbor of George Miller.*

GEORGE MILLER, *age 54; minister-in-charge of Big Swatara congregation; should wear Brethren-cut coat; beard; broad-brimmed hat.*

CATHERINE MILLER, *early 50's; should wear hair up on her head and a prayer covering that ties under her chin; long dress of light or dark material, no bright colors.*

MARGARETTA SMITH, *no older than 14; dress similar to Catherine; should wear hair in one or two braids; no prayer covering.*

ELIZABETH ETTER, *early 60's; a tall, gaunt, severe-looking woman, with a dazed air about her; dressed similarly to Catherine.*

JACOB METZGER, *member of Big Swatara congregation; 35-40; more impetuous in speech and manner than George; dressed in similar manner.*

SAM FRANTZ, *middle 20's; does not wear Brethren coat; dressed in Colonial style, but plainly, as a farmer would.*

HENRY ALBRECHT, *middle 40's; German Lutheran neighbor of George Miller; dressed similar to the other men.*

PRODUCTION NOTES

Both the cold weather and making bed coverings are important to the play. Anyone entering or exiting from the left entrance should put on or remove outdoor clothing: scarves, gloves, coats, etc.

Whenever the women sit down, they should pick up their sewing — darning or patching is permissible; fancy work is not; their main sewing, however, should be patchwork or quilt piecing. Colors should be dark and patterns simple, with material being coarse or heavy rather than light. Margaretta's pattern should be simple four or nine patch.

BIBLIOGRAPHIC INFORMATION

Stories told in the play, as well as the story on which the play is based, can be found in the following books:

M.G. Brumbaugh, *History of the German Baptist Brethren in Europe and America* (Mt. Morris, Illinois: Brethren Publishing House, 1899); Donald I. Smithers, ed., *Lower Paxton Township, Pennsylvania 1767-1967* (Harrisburg, Pennsylvania: Triangle Press, 1967); *History of the Church of the Brethren of the Eastern District of Pennsylvania,* Committee appointed by the District Conference (Lancaster, Pennsylvania: New Era Printing Co., 1915); and Harold E. Frantz, Reuben Frantz King, and Laura Frantz Pfautz, *Genealogy of the Matthias Frantz Family of Berks County, Pennsylvania* (Lebanon, Pennsylvania: Boyer Printing and Binding Company, 1972).

ACT ONE

SCENE 1

A Saturday afternoon in early January, 1776, on a road in Mount Joy township.

This should be played in front of the curtain or a backdrop that suggests a winter road.

Michael Stewart enters, holding a rope and looking around furtively as if he doesn't want to be seen. When this is established a man's voice is heard singing or whistling a hymn tune. A recording of a hymn sung in German would be ideal. On hearing this, Stewart becomes even more irresolute, undetermined whether to go forward or back, acting as if he has something hidden just out of sight, finally apparently deciding to brazen it out. A faint tickle of a cowbell is heard.

The singing grows louder and George Miller enters, still singing or whistling, carrying a small valise, walking with a staff. When Stewart recognizes him, he becomes even more agitated, seeking escape. Finally he drops the rope and steps on it. During the conversation he tries to swagger at the same time that he is stepping on the rope.

Finally Miller notices Stewart and stops singing, pausing in the road.

MILLER. [*Mildly*] Why, good evening, neighbor Stewart. It's a cold afternoon to be out, isn't it?

STEWART. Oh . . . Oh . . . h—hello there, M—Mister M—Miller. Y—Yes, it is a cold day. [*A little bolder*] I . . . I didn't expect to see you so far from home. [*Mockingly*] It's not Sunday, is it?

MILLER. No, it's not Sunday. I've been over to Conestoga to a meeting of our church leaders. There were some problems we had to discuss.

STEWART. [*Harshly*] Oh, yes. I can imagine your "problems." You *Dunkards* still trying to get out of doing your duty as citizens? I heard about your petitioning the assembly so you won't have to help defend us against our enemies.

MILLER. [*Still mildly*] We're not trying to get out of our duty as citizens, neighbor Stewart, but we have pledged our first loyalty to Jesus Christ, as I'm sure many of the English-speaking churches have done also. [*The rope jerks.*]

STEWART. [*Trying to keep his foot on the rope and maintain his bravado, but speaking bitterly*] Well, I wouldn't know too much about that, but I do know that *some* of the church people around here ain't afraid to protect their families. Even if those families go hungry while the men are up in Canada with Capt. Smith's company.

MILLER. [*Concerned*] I'm sorry to hear of people in need, neighbor Stewart. Would you please let us know about such people, so we can help?

STEWART. Oh, we . . . I mean . . . they'll manage all right, without any help from those that have to run to the fat, rich Quakers in Philadelphia for protection. [*The rope jerks again and he executes some fancy steps.*]

MILLER. [*With more concern*] Neighbor Stewart, can I help you in some way?

STEWART. [*Desperately*] No! I mean no . . . thank you . . . Preacher Miller. Ev . . . Everything's all right. It . . . it was nice talking to you.

MILLER. [*Still puzzled*] Well, it'll be getting dark before long. I'll be going on my way. I wish you a safe journey home. God bless you. [*Stewart starts visibly at this last sentence. Miller moves in front of Stewart and past the bushes, exiting, beginning his humming or whistling again.*]

STEWART. [*Grabbing the rope and registering great relief*] What a narrow escape! I've got to get this ox off this road! Why in thunder did he have to come along just then? Nothing makes me madder than a pious, blockheaded Dutchman pretending to love his fellow man. C'mon, you tough old critter. Let's get out of here. [*He exits as the bushes move slightly and the cow bell is heard again.*]

CURTAIN

SCENE 2

Two hours later, in the living room of George Miller's home.

The room should be simple and plain as befits a Brethren home of 1776. There is an interior door and an exterior door. Necessary furniture includes fireplace with simulated fire since it is the source of heat; table; chairs; chest or bookcase or cabinet for holding papers and a King James Bible, preferably a large family Bible. A spinning wheel would be appropriate, but is not necessary. Coats hang by the door. During this scene the lights should go down, to indicate the coming of evening. As curtain rises Catherine and Margaretta are seated, sewing.

CATHERINE. [*Inspecting Margaretta's sewing*] No, no, no, Margaretta. You must watch what you're doing! Keep the edges together! And don't take such big stitches! They must be small and even. Otherwise Cousin Sam will pull hard on the quilt some cold night and it'll come apart in his hand.

MARGARETTA. [*Giggling*] Oh, Grandmother, that's funny! Then he'll be cold in the middle.

CATHERINE. Well, it won't be so funny if the quilt's on your bed. Here, you'll just have to take this out and do it over. I'm sorry, Margaretta, but you must pay attention. You can't do patch-work and look out the window at the same time.

MARGARETTA. I'm sorry, Grandmother. I want to do it right, like you and Aunt Elizabeth. It's just so hard to sit still all after-noon. [*A sound is heard off stage, like moving furniture.*]

MARGARETTA. [*Cautiously*] Grandmother, I've been wanting to ask you. Why do I feel the way I do about Aunt Elizabeth? I try to like her, but . . . she's . . . different. Sometimes I think her body is here, but she doesn't know it is.

CATHERINE. We have to be patient with Aunt Elizabeth, Margaretta. She's had some very hard experiences. She needs us to love her right now.

MARGARETTA. This place she talks about—the Cloisters. What is it?

CATHERINE. It's a community in Ephrata, near Lancaster.

MARGARETTA. Is she really my aunt?

CATHERINE. No, she's really my cousin. But your mother always called her Aunt Elizabeth, I guess because she called my sisters Aunt when we all lived at Conestoga and she knew them.

MARGARETTA. If she's your cousin and Sam is a cousin, are they related?

CATHERINE. He's her . . . nephew. His mother died in [*stops suddenly*] a long time ago, and his father died later and he came to live with us, and now we think of him almost like our own son. He keeps us company now that most of our own children are gone.

MARGARETTA. Ten children is a lot, Grandmother!

CATHERINE. They've been good children to us all our lives, just like you must be a good daughter to your mother.

MARGARETTA. [*Seriously*] Oh, I want to, Grandmother. Can't I go home and see her soon? It's nice to be here, but . . . I miss her, and Papa too.

CATHERINE. [*Briskly*] You can go soon enough, but you should finish your patchwork first and take it along to surprise her. Watch there, now; keep the edges together. Don't let them get uneven.

MARGARETTA. Oh, I'm sorry. I'll try, but my hands are getting cold.

CATHERINE. [*Rising*] I'll poke up the fire a little. We must have it warm when your Grandfather comes. [*Adds wood to the fireplace.*]

MARGARETTA. Oh, I wish he'd come soon. I want to hear all about the meeting at Conestoga. Do you think he saw my friend Anna?

CATHERINE. This wasn't like the love feast, Margaretta. This was just for the leaders and elders.

MARGARETTA. My, it's an honor for Grandfather to be invited, isn't it?

CATHERINE. [*Sitting down to her sewing again*] Well, since he's the main preacher for the Big Swatara congregation, he should be in on these meetings. You know how he does: he waits until everyone else has had a say; then he sums it all up and puts in his opinion and the decision is almost always the way he wants it.

MARGARETTA. I don't understand, Grandmother. Why are they worried about the Assembly?

CATHERINE. Grandfather can explain it better than I, Margaretta. We want the Assembly to leave us in peace and respect the fact that we can't help them in their wars.

MARGARETTA. Is that what we asked in the petition? I like the sound of those big words, but I don't understand them too well.

CATHERINE. Yes, the petition that our churches took to the Assembly last November asked them to recognize that we can't fight because of our religious beliefs.

MARGARETTA. Did the Brethren really take this petition all the way to Philadelphia and read it before the General Assembly? Wasn't that a scary thing to do?

CATHERINE. Why, yes, Sander Mack and Christopher Sower and some others took it to the Assembly. We have as much right to do this as anyone else.

MARGARETTA. But do you thing the Assembly will grant our request? Sam says his friends are talking about war with the English. What would happen to us then?

CATHERINE. [*Sighing*] I don't know, Margaretta. I just don't want to think about it. And I wish Sam wouldn't spend so much time with the young men around here. He should go back to Conestoga and be with the other Brethren. But we couldn't get along without him here, when your Grandfather is gone to preach so much.

MARGARETTA. I like to hear Grandfather preach. But why does he have to go to so many different places?

CATHERINE. This congregation is called Big Swatara, but we have several meeting places. The Brethren live too far away to come to the same meeting place in the winter time. We only get together for the love feast. But Grandfather must preach at Conewago and Spring Creek and Paxton.

MARGARETTA. But wouldn't the people give him some dinner? Why does he have to walk all the way home without eating?

CATHERINE. Of course they would give him some dinner! They'd consider it an honor to feed him after the service. He just wants to get home quickly and on these short winter days. It's a good thing he does start home immediately.

MARGARETTA. But fifteen miles without any dinner, especially after that long church service! [*Elizabeth enters.*]

ELIZABETH. Well, I got the loom threaded up for Brother Miller; I hope he doesn't catch his death on this trip, so he'll be able to finish that order for Mrs. Stroehner. I'm sure I don't know why he doesn't want me to help him with his orders. We did beautiful weaving at the Cloisters and I did my share.

CATHERINE. [*Soothingly*] I know you did, Elizabeth, and Brother Miller does too. It's just that he's proud of his reputation as a good weaver, and he feels he should earn the living.

ELIZABETH. [*Self-righteously*] Of course, it does seem very strange to be working on the seventh day instead of resting and worshipping. After all those years . . .

CATHERINE. [*Interrupting with some asperity*] Elizabeth, you know we told you you're free to have your worship on the seventh day if you choose. We're not asking you to work.

ELIZABETH. Oh, I know, I know. But it's very hard to meditate when everyone else is working. [*As if noticing Margaretta for the first time.*] Are you still here, child? Isn't it time for your afternoon chores? [*Margaretta looks at Catherine questioningly.*]

CATHERINE. I believe it is time, Margaretta. It'll get dark early tonight.

MARGARETTA. All right, Grandmother. [*Puts down her sewing; puts on outside clothes.*]

CATHERINE. I hope you find some eggs. The hens just don't lay in this cold spell. [*Margaretta exits.*]

ELIZABETH. [*Sitting down to her sewing*] I don't see why you

52

keep that child here, Catherine. She should be at home with her mother. She's certainly old enough to be there now when her mother needs her.

CATHERINE. [*Firmly*] We've gone through this before, Elizabeth. Her mother wants her here. After losing so many babies and having such a hard time she doesn't want Margaretta there this time.

ELIZABETH. She's too old to be shielded that way. Young people today don't know what trouble is. Why, I could tell her stories . . .

CATHERINE. Please *don't* tell her those stories, Elizabeth. She'll have to hear them soon enough. [*Sound of voices and stamping feet.*] Oh, I do believe the men are back. [*She rises as George Miller and Jacob Metzger enter.*] Oh, Geo —, Brother Miller, I'm so glad you returned before dark . . . And Brother Jacob, it's good to have you come on such a cold day. How's sister Hannah?

METZGER. She's tolerable well, Sister Catherine. This cold and damp doesn't help her lumbago, but she's up and about. How is everyone here? Any news from your daughter?

CATHERINE. No, not yet. We're eager to hear, but it may be awhile yet. [*She bustles about, poking up the fire, taking their coats.*]

MILLER. Thank you, Catherine. This fire feels good. Well, sit down, Brother Jacob. Sister Elizabeth, how are you today?

ELIZABETH. [*Stiffly*] As well as can be expected, thank you.

CATHERINE. [*Bringing lighted candles*] Brother Jacob, I didn't realize you were going with George. You must be cold and tired. [*She returns to her sewing.*]

METZGER. Oh, I didn't go with him, but I just couldn't wait to learn what they did at the meeting. I was coming over to see what had happened when I met him coming.

MILLER. I'm not sure what happened, Brother Jacob. I don't believe the Brethren at Conestoga feel the effects of the war fever the way we do here on the frontier. They have more Quakers in Lancaster and I don't think they realize the seriousness of it.

METZGER. They've never had the Indian trouble that we have. The Quakers have been friends with the Indians in that area, and the tribes from the West who have been stirred up by the war with the French don't go as far east as Lancaster.

MILLER. Well, I believe our worst troubles are going to come from the settlers, not the Indians.

METZGER. Why do you say that? We sent the Assembly our petition last November. And last June the Assembly recognized those of use who couldn't join the war effort.

MILLER. Yes. I know. But that isn't stopping the war fever or the criticism that's being stirred up against us.

METZGER. But, Brother George, how can they forget William Penn's charter? It promised that no person in this province shall be molested because of conscience, nor compelled to worship other than conscience allows, or to do anything contrary to religious persuasion!

MILLER. Ach, yes, I know, Brother Jacob, but that was written in 1701. This is 1776. The Quakers have lost control of the legislature and many people have come to Pennsylvania who don't share our views or those of William Penn. Great changes are coming, perhaps sooner than we think! After all, even by the time Alexander Mack and the first Brethren came, we had to declare loyalty to King George.

METZGER. Well, that wasn't hard to do, as long as they let us live in peace.

MILLER. Of course not. But even that was moving away from Penn's charter. And now the people in the East are even more rebellious. Since that battle in Massachusetts colony last April, war fever against the British is rising higher all the time. Did you know that the day after we presented our petition to the Assembly last Novemeber they ordered an investigation to determine how much money we've given to support the Army?

METZGER. Ach, no; that's the trouble with living out here in the West, so far away from the Capitol in Philadelphia. Whatever will we do about that?

MILLER. It was reported today that Elder Sower has said he will mark his subscription to be used for the wives and children of the poor.

METZGER. I guess we could do that. After all, Elder Sower has been urging for years that we should voluntarily tax ourselves to support the Indians so they wouldn't fight us. If we're forced to pay taxes now, we could insist that they be used for peaceful purposes. Having done that, we really can't be responsible if they don't obey our wishes.

MILLER. Of course not. We're told in the New Testament to be subject to the governing authorities. We have much to be grateful for to King George.

METZGER. Grateful to King George and to God Almighty! We must remember where our strength and eternal protection lies. Well, I must be going. It's dark already yet and Hannah will be looking for me. [Sounds offstage; Margaretta comes bursting into the room from left.]

MARGARETTA. Oh Grandfather, Grandfather! Wait till you hear . . .

MILLER. [Mildly] Margaretta, is this any way to act? You interrupted Brother Metzger. Can't you . . .

ELIZABETH. Mercy me! Hasn't anyone told her that children should be seen and not heard?

MARGARETTA. [*Breathlessly*] Oh, I'm sorry! How do you do, Brother Metzger? Oh, Grandfather, I have such terrible news! The ox is gone! Cousin Sam and I looked all over for it, and couldn't find it anywhere. [*Sam enters.*] Didn't we, Cousin Sam? Tell them what happened.

MILLER. Sam, is this true?

SAM. It's true. The gate is open and the ox is gone.

CURTAIN

ACT TWO

SCENE 1

One week later; evening, in the barn on George Miller's farm. This could be played in front of the curtain or with a spotlight off the main stage, with just enough props to suggest a barn. Sam and Margaretta, wearing outdoor clothing, are seen. Sam is whittling or repairing harness. Wind noise is heard as scene opens.

MARGARETTA. Oh, it's warmer here in the barn, away from that wind. It seems like it's been cold forever. [*Pauses*] Cousin Sam, I'm so relieved that Grandfather doesn't blame us for the ox being gone. He doesn't, does he? I really didn't go near his stall that afternoon.

SAM. Uncle George doesn't blame you, Margaretta. He knows we had nothing to do with it.

MARGARETTA. But it's a bad thing to be without the ox! How will you get the ground plowed in the spring? Do you think it will come back?

SAM. No, I don't. It didn't go away by itself and this time of year it will be kept in a barn, so it won't have a chance to come back.

MARGARETTA. What do you mean, Sam? What are you saying? Did someone take it?

SAM. The ox was stolen, Margaretta; didn't you know?

MARGARETTA. Why no! How can you tell? Who would do that?

SAM. The rope was cut, not worn in two. And didn't you see the tracks?

MARGARETTA. No; what tracks?

SAM. You remember the sun was shining that afternoon? Even though it was cold, the ground had softened enough there by the gate that there were tracks — a man's tracks leading the ox away.

MARGARETTA. My goodness, I didn't see them. How did you learn to notice things like that?

SAM. [*To himself*] I learned that when I lived with the Indians.

55

MARGARETTA. You lived with Indians? I didn't know that! Tell me about it.

SAM. [*With reluctance*] I . . . I thought you knew, Margaretta. I . . . I don't talk about it very much.

MARGARETTA. But why did you do that? Wasn't it scarey? Aren't the Indians dirty — and mean?

SAM. [*More forthrightly*] Yes, they were mean. But don't you see how they feel? The settlers have taken their land, built fences, made laws. The Indians had lived here for hundreds of years and there was enough land for all of them. Now they're being pushed away. Besides that, the French got them all stirred up against us. They are mean to the settlers sometimes because they think they have to be, but they weren't mean to us. They . . . treated us well enough. [*He seems to be lost in memories again.*]

MARGARETTA. Cousin Sam, what do you mean? Were there others who lived with the Indians?

SAM. [*He doesn't want to talk about it.*] Yes . . . for a while . . . then they let us go again. We were glad to come back, but I did learn much from them, like the tracks. [*Firmly again*] That's why it makes me so mad when the godless people here on the frontier treat them so mean, like the Paxton Rangers did in '64.

MARGARETTA. Why, what did they do?

SAM. Oh, I forgot you don't know about that. Well, some day . . .

MARGARETTA. [*With sudden spirit*] Cousin Sam, don't you tell me that! I get so tired of people talking in riddles and telling me I'm too young to understand!

SAM. Well, I suppose you do. But you'll be sorry you asked!

MARGARETTA. Well, tell me anyway. I'm not a baby.

SAM. It's hard for me to understand, Margaretta, I guess because I can see it from different sides. The French and the Indians have been fighting with the English for a long time, especially out in the west, at Fort Duquesne. That makes the Indians on that side of the Susquehanna River restless and suspicious of all white people. The Quakers and the Germans have lived for a long time in Philadelphia. Most of them won't fight anyone, especially the Indians. Elder Sower has always said we should give money to support the Indians. And here in the western part of Lancaster County the Scotch and' Irish and Presbyterians live. They don't mind fighting. They're afraid of the Indians and they hate the Quakers, who are rich and don't understand the dangers of living on the frontier. And we Germans who have moved in here from the East are right in the middle.

MARGARETTA. Well, yes. But what about the Paxton Ra — what did you call them?

SAM. [*Sighing*] Yes, I was afraid you weren't going to forget that. Well, in '64 the Paxton Rangers were restless and angry. The Quakers had put some good Indians in the workhouse in Lancaster in order to protect them, but one night the Rangers went over there and got the Indians out of the workhouse and . . . and killed them.

MARGARETTA. Oh, Sam, that's terrible! The Indians had trusted the white men and then other white men betrayed them. Weren't the Rangers punished?

SAM. Oh, there was a great to do about it. The Quakers were furious and the settlers around here marched on Philadelphia to try to convince the Assembly what it was like here on the frontier, but no one was ever prosecuted.

MARGARETTA. Sam, are they really having a war with the British?

SAM. [Seriously] I guess so, Margaretta. One of the first companies in the colonies was raised near here last summer by Captain Matthew Smith. The Easterners are getting awfully tired of paying taxes and taking orders from England. It'll be a bad day for us Germans if the war fever spreads.

MARGARETTA. Why do you say that? Do our neighbors think we're enemies?

SAM. They'll think we are if we don't fight with them. If we don't join the Associators, people will think we're helping the Tories, who are loyal to England.

MARGARETTA. I don't understand the Associators, Sam. What are they?

SAM. Last year the Assembly asked all the white men in the colony to associate for defense. That means they get together to practice marching and shooting. They're supposed to protect us against the Indians and the English both, I guess.

MARGARETTA. But what about us Brethren, who don't believe in fighting?

SAM. The Assembly asked everyone to let us alone and respect our beliefs, but that's pretty hard to do when they might get shot and we benefit from their battles. The Assembly also asked us to pay taxes and to help the Associators in any way we can.

MARGARETTA. But how can we do that? Isn't that helping them to fight? I don't understand.

SAM. [Desperately] Oh, I don't either, Margaretta. I keep going 'round and 'round in my mind about it. That's why I haven't joined the church. I know Uncle George wants me to, but if I do I'll have to promise not to fight, and I don't know if I can do that. Some people say we can help the families of the Associators if they are in need. It seems to me that Brethren are pretty good at helping people in need, but they're not so good at seeing both sides of the picture.

CURTAIN

SCENE 2

Living room. Catherine and Elizabeth are sewing. Left door opens. George Miller and Jacob Metzger enter, removing their coats and hanging them up. Catherine rises to meet them with greetings. Miller and Metzger sit down to the fire, continuing a conversation begun outside.

MILLER. I'm glad you came over again, Jacob. I found some papers when I unpacked from the meeting at Conestoga. Catherine, could you get them for me? [*Catherine gets the papers from the chest and hands them to George.*] Thank you, Catherine. You remember we were talking the other night about paying the tax? [*Catherine returns to her chair.*]

METZGER. Yes, I've been giving it a lot of thought.

MILLER. Well, I have a letter here to Alexander Mack, Jr., from Jacob Stoll in Conestoga. It was written last September after Sander Mack had asked how the Brethren in Conestoga were handling the tax money. Here it is. [*Hands him the letter.*] They decided that to refuse the whole payment would be too risky; instead, they gave the money to the Committee with the request that it be used for the needy. They then obtained a receipt stating that their request would be granted.

METZGER. Well, that satisfies my mind. If that's what the Brethren in Conestoga are doing, I think we should do that, too. Brother George, it grieves my heart to ask this, but I have to. Are any of the Brethren joining the Associators?

MILLER. [*Sighing*] Well, Brother Jacob, I guess we have to expect that some will fall away from the faith and join.

METZGER. But what are the churches doing about it?

MILLER. There is little we can do other than keep loving them. I understand that Brother Cornelius Nice has lately withdrawn from Sander Mack's congregation after he put his name on the list for the drill. He no longer wants to be addressed as "Brother" and also refuses our customary kiss of greeting. But he did allow Brother Mack to keep praying for him.

METZGER. Ach, it's a sad time, and I'm afraid harder times are coming.

ELIZABETH. [*Starting nervously*] I . . . I heard something! Is someone outside? [*Voices outside; door opens and Henry Albrecht enters, followed by Sam and Margaretta.*]

MILLER. [*Rising to greet Albrecht*] Well, neighbor Albrecht. This is a pleasant surprise. Let me take your coat . . . Sit here by the fire. Our January cold spell is really hanging on this year. [*Sam and Margaretta remove their wraps; Sam sits down and begins to whittle; Margaretta joins Catherine and Elizabeth and picks up her sewing.*]

ALBRECHT. [*Greets all the adults and sits down.*] Thank you, Preacher Miller. This feels good. Yes, we're really having a hard winter.

MILLER. I'm glad you came over. I was just telling Brother Metzger about my trip to Conestoga last week.

ALBRECHT. Yes, well, I didn't come just to talk. I have news for you.

MILLER. Oh?

ALBRECHT. Yes. I found out who stole your ox. [*Quickened interest from all but George and Catherine.*] It was Michael Stewart!

MILLER. [*Calmly*] Yes, I know.

MARGARETTA. You know, Grandfather? How did you find out?

ELIZABETH. Margaretta! Children should be seen and not heard! [*Margaretta grimaces and picks up her sewing again.*]

MILLER. These things are not so hard to find out, Margaretta.

ALBRECHT. But . . . but what are you going to do about it?

MILLER. Nothing.

ALBRECHT. Nothing! But you should take him to law! We can't have this kind of thing going on.

MILLER. The New Testament says, "If any man take away thy goods, ask them not to return them again." [*Teasingly*] You're a good Lutheran, neighbor Albrecht. You should know that!

ALBRECHT. [*Sputtering*] Well, I . . . I know. But . . . but you just can't let him go. It . . . it's not safe for the community! The rest of us care about our property, even if you don't.

MILLER. [*Mildly*] Oh, I care about my property! I'm going to miss that ox, especially when plowing time comes. [*firmly*] But I'm not going to take Mr. Stewart to law.

METZGER. Perhaps Mr. Albrecht doesn't understand our beliefs. Have you heard the story about Elder Christopher Sower? You know, the printer in Germantown?

ALBRECHT. [*With asperity*] Of course I know Christopher Sower! There isn't a German in the colony that doesn't read Sower's newspapers and almanacs. Are you talking about Christopher Sower, Sr.?

METZGER. No, this is the present Christopher Sower. We call him elder because he is a minister and elder in our church. His father never joined the Brethren.

ALBRECHT. Well, what's the story?

METZGER. Several years ago a man came to Germantown and asked Elder Sower to loan him money to help get started in a business. Elder Sower did. Not long after that the man happened to come to meeting and heard Elder Sower preach on the evils of going to law. The next week the man went to see Elder Sower and asked if he believed what he had preached. Of course he said he did, because that's what we're taught in the Bible. So then the man said he wouldn't repay the money unless Elder Sower sued him.

MARGARETTA. Oh, my goodness! [*Elizabeth frowns at her and Margaretta goes back to her sewing.*]

ALBRECHT. Why, that scoundrel. I hope Sower taught him a lesson!

METZGER. Of course not. He said that since the man wouldn't pay he'd just have to cancel the debt, which he did.

ALBRECHT. But that's letting the scum get off scot free! How can you ever get along in this world living like that? Of course, I understand Christopher Sower has done very well.

MILLER. But not from that man's money. Brother Jacob, didn't you ever hear the rest of that story?

MARGARETTA. Oh, is there more? Please tell it, Grandfather. [*All are very interested.*]

MILLER. [*Enjoying the limelight*] I heard it the last time we had love feast. Didn't I tell you, Catherine?

CATHERINE. No, I don't think so. Go on.

MILLER. Well, last year, about a year ago now, the man appeared at Elder Sower's printing shop one morning with the money. [*Exclamations from the others.*] Elder Sower insisted the debt was cancelled and the money was no longer owed, but the man said, "That money has been a constant source of trouble to me. I cannot rest till the debt is paid."

ALBRECHT. Well, that's more like it. I hope Sower charged him plenty of interest!

MILLER. No, Elder Sower refused to take the money, because he had cancelled the debt, but he saw that the man was really serious, so he told him to give it to some poor people that he knew of in Philadelphia.

ALBRECHT. Well, I never! I don't know what it is about you Dunkers. But with the present situation the way it is, I just hope your beliefs don't get all of us Germans into trouble.

MILLER. [*Seriously*] That's been troubling me, too, neighbor. We are concerned about the state of affairs, and if the agitators can't tell the difference between Brethren and Lutherans, and get all the German-speaking people in trouble, we shall be extremely sorry.

ALBRECHT. I just wish things could be as they used to be. As long as the Quakers were in power we Germans could live in peace.

METZGER. It was the Germans that kept the Quakers in power. Don't you remember the election of '55? Christopher Sower had been telling the Germans how to vote for years, but we almost lost that one. And it was only a year later that all the Quakers resigned because the governor declared war against the French and Indians.

ALBRECHT. You see, that's what I mean about you non-Associators! Oh, I'm sorry. I didn't mean to sound so harsh, but couldn't the Quakers have kept their seats instead of resigning in a body? They could have done some real good in the Assembly by staying in there and influencing it to take a more moderate course, instead of resigning in a huff. Now they have only a minority to protect their own interests.

METZGER. But then they would have compromised their witness against war. Resigning in protest was the only way they could keep their position clear.

MILLER. [*In a conciliatory manner, as host*] It's hard to say after twenty years what would have happened. Even back in the '40's there was a lot of opposition to the Quakers and resentment that the Germans were keeping them in control of the Assembly. But I think you're overly concerned, neighbor Albrecht. I have a copy here of a statement issued by the Lancaster County Committee of Inspection and Observation. They issued it last April after the battle at Concord, Massachusetts, when the mobs were so riled up. [*Hunts among his papers.*] Here it is. It talks about violence against the non-Associators and it says, "The Committee . . . " where is it? Oh, yes, here it is: "The Committee . . . proceeds to discourage such mob spirit."

ALBRECHT. [*Groaning*] "Discourage such mob spirit!" Neighbor Miller, do you really think that phrase is going to keep some of these wild young bucks at home some night when they've had too much to drink at their Associator's meeting and want some excitement? Captain Smith's company is in Canada this winter. When word comes back that they've suffered casualties the feeling will run pretty high against the non-Associators.

CATHERINE. Oh, it wouldn't come to that, would it?

SAM. It might, Aunt Catherine. Mr. Albrecht is right. There's a lot of feeling against us.

MILLER. I can't say what a group of our neighbors might do some night, Neighbor Albrecht, but I do know that I have to put my trust in Almighty God. You're a believing man. Can't you do that too?

ALBRECHT. [soberly] I don't know. I'm afraid I don't have the faith that you have, Neighbor Miller. I'm also afraid for the safety of my family. That's why I think you ought to take this opportunity to put one of the trouble makers out of the way, where he can't be stirring up trouble against us.

METZGER. But when they listen to reason, we can make them understand our position. Do you know the story of Christopher Sower, Senior, the father of Elder Sower? Back during the expedition against Fort Duquesne he was accused of treason against the King because he had printed a broadside against the expedition. He was summoned to a court martial because of this. This was in 1758, the year that he died, and he didn't have the health to answer the summons. His son, Elder Sower, met General Forbes, who had ordered the court martial, at an inn on Lancaster Street in Philadelphia. They say that in three minutes Sower proved to the distinquished General that they were not enemies of the King, but enemies of war, because war is an enemy of the Savior.

ALBRECHT. Oh, I don't doubt that! When you Dunkards start quoting Scripture the rest of us have to take a back seat. But people like General Forbes are gentlemen enough to stand still and let you convince them with your arguments. I fear the people in this area aren't that polite. They're too likely to take things into their own hands. Well, I must be going. It's getting late, and Mrs. Albrecht will worry. [Rises, puts on coat.] You're sure you won't change your mind about the ox thief?

MILLER. [quietly, but with conviction] I can't take him to court and still be obedient to the New Testament, neighbor Albrecht.

METZGER. [rising, reaching for coat] I must be going too, Brother George, I'll walk along aways with Neighbor Albrecht. Good night, Sister Catherine, Sister Elizabeth, Sam. [The others rise; general chorus of farewells.]

[Albrecht and Metzger exit.]

MILLER. Well, it is getting late, and I want to finish that weaving tomorrow. It's time for worship and then we must all get to bed. [Picks up Bible and opens it to Matthew 25. All draw their chairs into a circle.] Did you know that Elder Sower's third edition of the Bible will be ready this year? Sam, will you read tonight?

[*Sam seems reluctant, but takes the Bible and reads Matthew 25:31-40, as Margaretta holds the candle for him to read by. At the conclusion, all murmur "Amen," rise and kneel at their chairs.*]

CURTAIN

ACT THREE

SCENE 1

Four days later, in the living room of George Miller's home. Elizabeth and Catherine are sewing patchwork pieces.

ELIZABETH. Where's Margaretta?

CATHERINE. She's out in the barn helping Sam. She's been so pale these last few days I thought it would be good for her to get out in the cold and stir up her blood.

ELIZABETH. She won't learn to manage a house or do her patchwork if she's out with Sam all the time.

CATHERINE. I guess she misses her father.

ELIZABETH. Well, I'm glad she's out for a little while. I've been so unsettled in my mind these last few days and she does get on my nerves, with all her questions.

CATHERINE. [*Mildly*] Well, it's a good thing for children to want to learn.

ELIZABETH. I suppose so, but it's just not what I'm used to. Why, we used to go for days at the Cloisters without saying anything when we were in meditation. And when we did talk, it was only to glorify God, not to discuss worldly things.

CATHERINE. [*Determined to be non-commital*] Oh?

ELIZABETH. That conversation the other night just set my nerves on edge. It made me realize how *safe* I felt in the Cloisters. The walls were so thick and high. And surely no one would ever bother people whose only aim was serving and praising God, who never participated in any of the evil of the world. Besides, once Conrad Beissel began to preach, you just forgot everything else. Did you know he didn't even use a Bible? He just closed his eyes and preached so fervently, [*getting carried away*] sometimes people couldn't even stand to be in the same room with him. There just was never anyone like Brother Conrad.

CATHERINE. [*Sternly*] Elizabeth, our adoration should be reserved for our Savior Jesus Christ. No *man* is worthy of worship!

ELIZABETH. Oh, I know, Catherine, I know. That's what Conrad Beissel was always telling us. And we would get so wrapped up in our devotion that we were hardly aware of our surroundings. People think we had a hard life, sleeping and eating so little and working so hard, but Catherine, you can't know what it was like to sing Brother Conrad's music unless you have done it. But [*sighing heavily*] it'll never be the same again. Everything changed after he died. So many of the members fell away and I got restless too. I know it was sinful, but I began to wonder what it was like out here in the world I had left.

CATHERINE. Oh? [*Margaretta appears in the inside door and then steps back. The women do not notice her, but the audience knows she's there. She becomes more agitated during the conversation.*]

ELIZABETH. [*Agitatedly*] And now I'm here and I think maybe I shouldn't have left, but I don't want to go back with everything so different. But all that talk the other night, when Brother Jacob and neighbor Albrecht were here frightened me so. I . . . . I thought the Indian troubles were settled down, and now there's this talk of war with the English, and . . . and Mr. Albrecht thinks . . . the Germans will be persecuted . . . [*She is unable to go on, burying her head in her hands.*]

CATHERINE. [*Reaching out to Elizabeth*] Elizabeth, we must trust God and have *faith*.

ELIZABETH. [*After a few seconds*] Catherine, I . . . I've never said this to anyone . . . I've never dared to say it to myself, but do you know the . . . real reason why I went to the Cloisters?

CATHERINE. [*Gently*] No, Elizabeth.

ELIZABETH. [*Speaking under great strain*] I . . . I was so frightened after Mary was killed . . . I never . . . wanted to see Blue Ridge Mountain or Little Swatara Creek again. What good did it do to live so close to Fort Henry if it couldn't protect us? Father always said we were safe there, but we weren't and poor Mary . . .

CATHERINE. Please, Elizabeth, you mustn't think of it.

ELIZABETH. She was my little sister, Catherine! Murdered by those savages! If we had only been able to get the children back, so I could have cared for them in her stead! But when the men came back without the children, something in me died too. I just wanted to get as far away as I could, away from the mountain and the frontier, somewhere that was safe.

CATHERINE. Elizabeth, you mustn't blame yourself. We do what we have to do.

ELIZABETH. [*Not hearing her*] And then when Sam and the others did return, I was so confused. I thought I should leave the Cloisters and help to raise them, . . . but they were older then . . .

and I thought they'd be different . . . and Brother Conrad didn't want us to leave . . . [*Margaretta sobs and exits.*] Oh, someone's coming. I must go; no one must see me like this. [*She rushes off.*]

MARGARETTA. [*Bursts into room, horror written in her face*] Grandmother! Grandmother! I . . . I heard what Aunt Elizabeth said! Tell me, what was she talking about? You said that Sam is her nephew. Was his mother killed by the Indians? He said he lived with them once, but he didn't explain . . .

CATHERINE. [*Sadly*] Yes, Margaretta. Elizabeth's sister married John Frantz. They lived in Berks County near the mountain. One morning, in June of 1758, when John was away . . . the Indians attacked . . . killing Mary and . . . and capturing the children. A few years later all the children except the youngest came back. Sam doesn't like to talk about it.

MARGARETTA. Grandmother, is . . . is *my* mother going to die? I . . . I know she's going to have a baby and . . . and I know they've all died except me, . . . but . . . is *she* going to die?

CATHERINE. [*Swiftly gathering Margaretta into her arms*] Margaretta, we must trust God, and pray. [*To herself*] We have . . . so much . . . to pray for. [*They hold the embrace for a moment, until there is a loud knock and commotion at the door. Reluctantly they pull apart. Margaretta rushes and attempts to control her feelings. Catherine, blowing her nose and struggling to regain her composure, slowly goes to the door and opens it. Henry Albrecht bursts in.*]

ALBRECHT. [*Abruptly*] Where's Mr. Miller?

CATHERINE. Why, he's weaving. I'll call him. Let me take your coat.

ALBRECHT. No, no, I can't stay. I must see him at once. [*He is very agitated, pacing the floor. Catherine exits. Sam enters. He greets Albrecht, who pays no attention to him. Sam stands quietly inside the door.*]

CATHERINE. [*Enters*] Brother Miller will be right in. Won't you sit down? It's so cold again today, isn't it?
    [*Albrecht pays no attention, but continues to pace agitatedly. After a long minute George enters.*]

MILLER. [*Offering his hand*] It's good to see you again, neighbor Alrecht. Sit down by the fire.

ALBRECHT. [*Ignoring the greeting*] Preacher Miller, I didn't want to be the one to tell you, but they said I had to do it, since it was my idea.

MILLER. [*Calmly*] What is it, neighbor?

ALBRECHT. You've got to understand, we did it for your own good. Yours, and ours, too. The rabble around here have to be taught a lesson. We just can't have such lawlessness. They have to respect us and our property, even if we are Germans.

MILLER. But what is it you've done?

ALBRECHT. The neighbors all got together — we all know who stole your ox — and we gave information to the authorities and now they've got Michael Stewart in jail in Lancaster!

MILLER. [*Stunned*] But . . . but *no!*

CURTAIN

SCENE 2

Early morning, three days later, in the living room of the George Miller's home. As the curtain rises George is seated at the table, going through some papers. The Bible is open on the table. He has a distracted, worried air. Catherine enters, carrying a bowl covered with a cloth.

MILLER. Oh, there you are, Catherine. Can you talk for a minute? Seems like we seldom have a chance to talk between just the two of us.

CATHERINE. [*Sets the bowl down by the fireplace and comes to stand beside him at the table.*] It does seem as if a lot has been going on lately, doesn't it?

MILLER. Yes, and there's something I've been wanting to ask you. Why have you started calling me "Brother Miller?" We've been married all these years and you always called me "George," at least here in our own home. Why have you changed?

CATHERINE. [*Looks around guiltily*] Oh, I . . . I don't know, George. I guess I'm self-conscious in front of Elizabeth. I don't know if she approves.

MILLER. If *she* approves! Since when is Elizabeth your standard of behavior? You know we believe marriage is a sacrament, or-dained of God. You're not getting some of those Ephrata ideas about celibacy, are you? [*Reaches for her hand*]

CATHERINE. Of course not, George. I wouldn't have given up my life with you for anything. But I feel sorry for her. She's so confused. The whole church was upset when those people were breaking up our families and congregations with false doctrines and strange practices. Now their leader is dead, the community is thrown into confusion, and the members are as mixed up as the rest of us were years ago.

MILLER. Well, you know I find it hard to be as tolerant as that, Catherine. You're the one that has the burden of her being here, and I admire your patience. Just don't let your sympathy change your own convictions. [*Yawns*] Oh-h-h, I'm tired. I didn't sleep well again last night.

CATHERINE. I know you didn't. You're still worried about Michael Stewart? [*She sits down at the table.*]

MILLER. [*Soberly*] Yes, Catherine, I am. I can't be easy in my mind about it. It never occurred to me that the neighbors would lodge charges against him if I didn't.

CATHERINE. Well, he *did* steal the ox and that *is* against the law.

MILLER. I know it. If he had stolen Mr. Albrecht's ox I wouldn't think anything about their arresting him. But it was my ox and the New Testament says we must not go to law. Here it is, right here in First Corinthians six. [*He reads vs. 1-8.*]

CATHERINE. I know that, George, but how can you get him out? You can't pretend he didn't do it!

MILLER. I know! I've gone around and around about it.

CATHERINE. Well, I know you'll find the answer. You usually do. [*Rising*] Right now I've got to set the bread or it won't be ready by dinner time. [*Picks up bowl and exits. George abstractedly continues going through the papers. Sam enters, stamping his feet and blowing on his fingers. Wind noise is heard.*]

SAM. It's really cold out there! I can't remember when a cold spell has hung on as long as this. Can you, Uncle George?

MILLER. [*Worriedly*] It's still cold, is it? No sign of moderating?

SAM. [*Warming his hands at the fire.*] None that I can see.

MILLER. [*Staring into space*] Cold . . . it must be cold. [*Rousing himself*] How's everything at the barn? Animals all right?

SAM. Yep, they seem to be.

MILLER. That's good. Don't know what I'd do without you, Sam. [*Wistfully*] You don't understand how I feel about this ox steal-ing business, do you?

SAM. Well-l-l-, no, not exactly..But I'm sure you must be right, you being the minister and all. [*Catherine enters, puts bowl down by the fireplace and sits down, picking up her patchwork.*]

MILLER. [*Ruefully*] I guess that isn't enough right now. I need to feel that you approve.

SAM. [*Uncomfortably*] But Uncle George, why do you need my approval? Everyone looks up to you.

MILLER. Well, they shouldn't. I make as many mistakes and have as many temptations as anyone else. But I've got to keep trying. You see, if we cannot keep peace at home and practice love of neighbor, how can we expect peace in the world at large? If we are not willing to suffer, we will soon lose peace and quarrel or fight to defend our interests. Don't you think that's right, Sam? [*Sam has been pacing the floor uneasily.*]

SAM. [*Miserably*] I don't know, Uncle George. I just don't know. I'd like to feel that way. I'd like to really believe it, the way you and Aunt Catherine do. I've really tried. But I'm just not sure I can.

MILLER. [*Gently*] None of us are sure we can, Sam. It's a step we have to take by faith. And our faith grows as we act on what little we have.

SAM. [*He is moved by this and wants to get away; he buttons up his coat and moves toward outside door.*] I . . . I don't think I watered all the stock. I . . . I'd better go see. [*Exits*]

MILLER. [*Watches him go and sighs deeply*] Oh, Catherine, I love that boy like my own son. I want so much for him to make the right choices in life.

CATHERINE. I know you do, George. Sometimes we just have to wait.

MILLER. [*Absentmindedly again*] I suppose so. He says it's still so cold. [*As if noticing her sewing for the first time*] Catherine, what are you sewing?

CATHERINE. This? Why, it's patchwork for a quilt. We can't let anything go to waste, you . . .

MILLER. Do you have a lot of quilts? More than we need? Will you get these done soon?

CATHERINE. Well, I believe there are a couple in the chest that I haven't gotten out yet. I always want to have enough.

MILLER. But even if we don't have enough, at least we have a fire. We could find something to keep us warm.

CATHERINE. George Miller, what are you talking about? [*Elizabeth appears in doorway. George and Catherine do not notice her.*]

MILLER. It's cold, Catherine. I'm sure the Lancaster jail doesn't have a fireplace. It probably doesn't even have enough blankets. That man is cold, Catherine.

CATHERINE. That man! You mean Michael Stewart?

MILLER. Yes, I mean Michael Stewart! You know what Jesus said: "I was in prison, and you came unto me; naked, and you clothed me." The least I can do is take him some blankets.

CATHERINE. George Miller, you surely aren't going to walk to Lancaster in this weather! It's twenty miles! And what if it storms? Or you have an accident? As cold as it is you could freeze to death before anyone found you!

MILLER. I'd stay on the main roads, Catherine. And I don't believe it's going to storm. I doubt if anything'd happen to me.

CATHERINE. Except you'll catch your death of cold. George, you can't leave now. We're waiting to hear news from Barbara. We need you here!

MILLER. Catherine, I'm not a midwife. If Barbara does need help, I can't do anything but carry firewood. She'll have plenty of help for that.

CATHERINE. But, George . . .

MILLER. I haven't decided anything yet, Catherine. I'll have to think about it awhile. Speaking of firewood, I'm going out to chop some. Maybe the exercise will help me clear my mind. [*Puts on outside wraps and exits. Elizabeth enters.*]

ELIZABETH. Well, I never! [*Picks up sewing and sits down*]

CATHERINE. [*She doesn't want to discuss it, but she can't have any criticism of her husband.*] He has to do what he believes is right, Elizabeth.

ELIZABETH. But your quilts, Catherine? How can you let him take them? They'll get *dirty* and . . . and . . . you never know *what* they might pick up in a place like that! All kinds of things!

CATHERINE. Well, I wouldn't expect to get back anything I sent. But it's out of the question. He surely won't do it! He'll listen to reason. Won't he?

ELIZABETH. I wouldn't be so sure. George Miller's a mighty determined man. If he does go through with it, give him a horse blanket or something. Don't send anything you'd use yourself.

CATHERINE. [*On the other side of the fence again*] A horse blanket — certainly not! If Michael Stewart is worth risking George's life for, he's worth a decent covering. Not my best, maybe, but at least a clean warm one.

ELIZABETH. You'll be lucky if he doesn't take one to everyone in there!

CATHERINE. Now that's where I draw the line! You've got to stop somewhere! But I'd better go punch down that bread. I feel like punching something. [*Exits with bowl*]

[*Elizabeth seems troubled. She tries to sew, can't continue, walks around the room; with some hesitation she picks up the Bible, sits at the table and reads, half to herself and with troubled pauses, Matt. 25: 41-46. Catherine appears in doorway holding bowl, during the end of the reading. She waits quietly when Elizabeth finishes reading and stares into space, her lips moving. Finally, Elizabeth rouses and notices Catherine, who enters quietly, puts down the bowl by the fireplace, and picks up her patchwork.*]

ELIZABETH. [*Begins quietly but becomes more agitated during this conversation*] Catherine, we didn't read that passage very often at the Cloisters — we spent more time reading what Brother Conrad wrote — but the other night when Sam read the first part at worship I thought there was more. I see now why Brother Miller feels he must do this, since the Brethren have always put so much stock in this section. I . . . I remember back . . . before I entered the Cloisters, this was a favorite text of the preachers at Conestoga.

CATHERINE. Yes, many's the time we've heard sermons preached on this text. It's really a Brethren belief.

ELIZABETH. A Brethren belief, but is it mine? Have they been right all this time and I've been wrong? Their emphasis was on helping people wherever they found need and ours at the Cloisters was on withdrawing from the world and spending all our time in comtemplation. [*More agitatedly*] Were we wrong,

Catherine? Have . . . have I given my life to . . . the wrong thing? Is it too late to . . . to change?

CATHERINE. [*Going to Elizabeth at the table*] Elizabeth, we can't know these things. We have to act on the light we have. You mustn't condemn yourself. The Brethren don't have all the truth. There must have been some good in the Cloisters even if we couldn't see it. It was hard for the Brethren to think charitably of the Cloister leaders because they broke up so many of our families and congregations.

ELIZABETH. Oh, I know, Catherine and maybe that wasn't right. I suppose there's no point in dwelling on it now, but it's so hard to find the right way, and so hard to think I may have been wrong all those years.

CATHERINE. What's important, Elizabeth, is doing the best we know now, and trusting God to take care of the past.

ELIZABETH. Yes . . . I suppose so. I thank Him for your patience, Catherine. You and Brother Miller have been so kind to me. I haven't any right to criticize your kindness to another. I . . . I must do some things in my room now. [*Exits*]

CATHERINE. [*To herself*] I didn't know it was decided we were going to do it, but I suppose by this time George has convinced himself. Well, I suppose it's time to make that bread into loaves. [*Exits with bowl. Margaretta enters and sits down with her patch-work. Sam enters removes his outer clothing and warms himself at the fireplace.*]

SAM. It's still cold outside. Isn't warming up a bit.

MARGARETTA. I know. I was helping Grandfather carry firewood awhile ago. Sam, is . . . is he really going to take some covers to that man who stole the ox?

SAM. I wouldn't be surprised, Margaretta. You know how stub... determined Uncle George is when he makes up his mind.

MARGARETTA. But it's so far to Lancaster! He doesn't have to do it, does he, Sam?

SAM. Of course he doesn't! No one else would! Everyone else would say it served the man right, to suffer a little, after committing such a crime.

MARGARETTA. But isn't it the right thing to do? [*Wind noise is heard offstage.*]

SAM. [*Desperately*] Margaretta, I don't know what is the right thing! The winds of change are blowing away our world and the life we've known, just like the real wind is blowing outside today, and all Uncle George can think of is one man who's cold.

MARGARETTA. Maybe that's the way it should be, Sam. Maybe doing the right thing for a person in need is all we can do in a world that's blowing away.

SAM. [*Shaking his head*] I don't know. It sounds a little too simple to me.

MARGARETTA. I think it's the right thing, but . . . can I tell you something?

SAM. Sure. What is it? [*He moves closer to her.*]

MARGARETTA. I must be very bad of me, but . . . but I'm glad I don't have my patchwork done yet. Since it isn't done, I don't have to give it to that ox thief.

SAM. [*Laughing and pulling her braid*] You're all right, Margaretta. There aren't many people as honest as you.

MILLER. [*Enters, carrying a burlap bag and stamping his feet*] Catherine! Catherine, where are you?

CATHERINE. Yes, George, what is it?

MILLER. [*Briskly*] I think I ought to go as soon as possible. I want to start now in the middle of the day.

CATHERINE. You're going today? Can't you at least have something to eat first?

MILLER. No, I'm not hungry and I want to get started, now that I've decided this is what I should do. Can you get me some quilts?

CATHERINE. [*Resignedly*] All right, George, just a minute. [*She exits. Miller warms his hands at the fire. Sam seems uncomfortable, starting several times to speak, but never bringing himself to it. Margaretta watches, wide-eyed. Catherine returns with two comforters. Obviously they were not far away.*] Here you are, George.

MILLER. Thank you, these will be just fine. I brought this gunny sack to carry them in. [*He stuffs them into the bag. Catherine exits as Elizabeth enters.*]

ELIZABETH. Brother Miller, here . . . here's a pair of socks I just finished knitting. Maybe Mr . . . the man can wear them. [*To Sam*] I planned to give you two pairs for a Christmas gift, but I didn't get these finished in time. I . . . I hope you don't mind.

SAM. [*Trying not to laugh*] Why, of course not, Aunt Elizabeth. The ones you gave me were very nice.

CATHERINE. [*Enters with package*] Here, George, if you're not going to eat first, at least take this with you. The new bread isn't baked yet, but it's the last of the old bread, and some meat from supper last night. I wish you'd eat it, but if I know you, you'll still have it when you get to the jail and that man will get the quilts and the bread too!

MILLER. [*Smiling at her*] You're a good woman, Catherine. Thank you very much. Well, I've got to go before it gets any later. I'll stay with Brother Weaver in Lancaster tonight and probably come back tomorrow. Don't worry.

CATHERINE. Well, we *will* worry, George, but God go with you.

SAM. [*Taking a scarf from the clothes he had removed when he came in.*] Here, Uncle George, this is for you. [*With emphasis*] Maybe another scarf will keep the cold away a little better.

71

MILLER. [*A meaningful look passes between him and Sam. Miller extends his hand and Sam takes it; they shake hands.*] Thank you, Sam, I appreciate it. [*During this time, Margaretta has been folding up a small square of patchwork. Now she runs forward with it.*]

MARGARETTA. Here Grandfather, I . . . I didn't get this done yet, but maybe Mr. Stewart can use it on his pillow or wrap his feet in it.

MILLER. [*Gravely*] Thank you, Margaretta, that'll be just the thing. [*He puts it in the bag and puts on the scarf, with Catherine's help. She also hands him the lunch package and his staff. Sam gives Margaretta a questioning look.*]

MARGARETTA. [*Apologetically, in an aside to Sam.*] Well, that was all the blocks I had sewed together. And those were my first ones. They weren't very good. [*Sam puts his arm around her shoulders and ruffles her hair as they turn to wave goodbye.*]

MILLER. Well, thank you all. I know God will bless you for these gifts. I really have to go in order to be in Lancaster before it gets too late. [*He turns and exits, amid a chorus of "Goodbye" and "God bless you." All watch as he leaves.*]

CURTAIN

Suggestions for Discussion

1. Divide into groups of four to six and focus your discussion on one of the following topics: how to resolve interpersonal conflict, how to deal with divisiveness in the church family, and how to witness through war tax resistance. Choose among the three topics according to your own preference.

   a. Conflicts on the individual level
      - Do you think that the conflict over the stolen property was well handled? Explain why or why not.
      - Would you have acted like the Lutheran neighbor who resolved not to tolerate this injustice, or like George Miller who was most hurt but nonetheless remained determined not to sue, or like Sam Frantz who hesitated to be as extreme in his forgiving and peacemaking? You may wish to roleplay this using a debate format. Speak first as the character you most identify with; then switch and speak from the viewpoint of the one you understand the least.

72

b. Divisiveness in the church family
   - Give some examples of how divisions come about.
   - What are some potentially divisive issues your church has to deal with today?
   - Brainstorm on reactions that would aggravate the conflict. Then think of as many reactions that you feel might help solve it.
   - What would we do about these issues if we followed the example of George Miller? What would we do if we followed the example of Christ?

c. War tax and military service
   - The Conestoga congregation, we learn in the play, demanded that their taxes be used for the needy rather than for military purposes. Which avenues are open to us today to witness for peace when we pay our taxes?
   - As in Sander Mack's days, many people pay the military portion "in order to be safe." Which "safety" is endangered? Listen to a war-tax resister about the consequences for our safety if we *do* keep paying billions for weapons while people are starving and suffering all over the world.

2. Which historical facts about peace churches did you learn from the play that you had not been aware of before? For further information, you may wish to read the following books which were used as sources for the play: Rufus D. Bowman, *The Church of the Brethren and War* (Elgin, Illinois: Brethren Publishing House, 1944); and Donald Durnbaugh, *The Brethren in Colonial America* (Elgin: Brethren Press, 1967.)

WILLIAM'S PRUNING HOOKS

by Luise Van Keuren

CHARACTERS

Members of the committee from the General Court:

JOSEPH HAWLEY, *major in the Colonial Army*
NOAH GOODMAN, *a captain*
JOHN BLISS, *a major*
TWO NON-SPEAKING MEMBERS
NATHANIEL, *a young man, and court clerk*
MARTIN PIKE, *a merchant of New Bedford*
A LAWYER
A SOLDIER
A WOMAN IN THE CROWD
WILLIAM ROTCH, *a merchant of Nantucket, a Quaker*
TRISTRAM FINCH, *a sailor*
BLACKLEDGE, *a captain of a Colonial vessel*
JEDIDIAH SPOONER, *a chairman of the Committee of Safety*
OBADIAH JACKSON, *a fisherman*
DEGRACY, *a militia colonel*

Watertown, near Boston. Late summer, 1777. A committee room in the offices of the General Court of the Massachusetts Bay Colony. The room is a plain, pale-colored chamber, equipped with benches and wooden chairs, forming a semi-circle open to the audience. A rectangular table parallel to the right wall provides a station for the committee. Two chairs stand at the table; four stand in a row behind it. At the left, facing the large table is a small table, providing a station for petitioners, claimants, witnesses, and their lawyers. In the upstage wall are two uncurtained and many-paned windows revealing an outline of the town: a steeple, roofs of red brick and white trim buildings, a few weathervanes. There are two doors: one behind the committee's table, leading to an interior room; and a second door, left of center in the upstage wall, leading to the stairs and ground floor. At left is a fireplace, empty at this season of the year.

At curtain the crowded room is in a hubbub. The committee is in session. Major Hawley, the chairman, sits calmly and wearily at

74

the table, pounding the gavel. On the table before him are a large gilt-edged book, a stack of papers, inkwells and quills, a bell and an hourglass. The other members of the committee sit behind him, in a flurry of comment among themselves. The members all wear variants of the Colonial uniform. In differing degrees of consternation, the persons who make up the crowd of petitioners and their associates are a portrait of outrage. Cries of "It's a shame," "Is there nothing to be done," "Poor Martin!," "Lost his cargo?," "It's an outrage!," and such exclamations, are heard from the men and women filling the room. Nathaniel, the youthful clerk, repeatedly calls out "Silence!" He stands upstage of the committee table, where his record of the proceedings lies open before him on the table. He picks up the bell and rings it.

HAWLEY. [*Banging the gavel*] Enough! Enough!

NATHANIEL. Silence! Silence!

HAWLEY. [*Addressing a man in merchant's dress at the center of the group*] We have heard your petition, Mr. Pike —

PIKE. [*Waving his fist*] I protest!

HAWLEY. And have made our decision.

LAWYER. Will the committee —

HAWLEY. [*Raising his voice over the din*] The committee will not. [*Bangs gavel*] The decision of the General Court of the Colony of Massachusetts Bay is upheld. [*Bangs gavel*] Your cargo remains impounded, Mr. Pike. And your sloop, too, till the fine is paid.

PIKE. [*Furious*] What do you Boston men know of New Bedford? You with your silk slippers and your French puddings! [*The clamor continues.*]

HAWLEY. [*Banging the gavel and attempting to go on to further business*] The next matter, Nathaniel!

NATHANIEL. [*Calls out, over the noise*] William Rotch!

HAWLEY. [*Unable to find the proper document among his papers*] Once again, Nathaniel?

NATHANIEL. [*Leaning towards him and handing him the correct papers*] The Nantucket man, Sir.

LAWYER. Gentlemen! I beg you —

HAWLEY. William Rotch, merchant, of Nantucket!

LAWYER. One word more, Sir!

WOMAN IN THE CROWD. Turnip-pullers! Farmer-judges! Thimble-seller-magistrates!

HAWLEY. [*Banging the gavel*] Silence!

PIKE. Thieves!

HAWLEY. Mr. Pike. We are at war in this country. And the very question of our having a country at all depends upon the law. Without that no country can exist. Smuggling is still smuggling, Sir, even in New Bedford. [*Calls out, holding up a document*] William Rotch! [*Clamor continues.*]

75

NATHANIEL. [*Leaning over to him*] He's downstairs, Major Hawley. I'll have him summoned.

HAWLEY. [*Rising immediately, turning to his colleagues*] Gentlemen, shall we have our tea or whatever we're drinking instead of tea these days? [*The committee exits through the door, ignoring the shouts of the group remaining.*]

[*Grumbling among themselves, the group withdraws through the door. Nathaniel busies himself tidying the desk. He then straightens the chairs. As the last of the crowd leave, a soldier enters, escorting William Rotch. Rotch is a tall man with dark eyes, his straight hair worn long and plain. He dresses simply in a gray waistcoat, black coat, and plain white neckcloth. He wears a high-crowned black hat. He is 43 years of age. His speech is quiet but firm; he is gentle, but earnest.*]

SOLDIER. [*Motioning Rotch to a chair next to the small table*] Sit there. They'll be back in a while. Yer not under arrest, so you can just sit there yerself. [*Rotch sits. A young sailor, in irregular and colorful garb, rises from an obscure corner in the back.*] But you are! Sit down and stay quiet, or I'll march ye back to the jailhouse!

FINCH. Pardon me —

SOLDIER. Sit!

FINCH. [*Quickly sits*] Yes, yer honorship. Can ye tell me when they'll be calling me, if I may trouble ye?

NATHANIEL. [*Coming forward, officially*] Mr. Tristram Finch, sailor?

FINCH. Aye, that's myself, yer honorship.

NATHANIEL. He may suitably be put near the front now. [*Nods to the soldier*] The Committee is in short recess and will reconvene in [*consults pocket watch*] seven minutes. [*Nods towards Finch*] If you will be seated [*indicates a seat in back and to the left of Rotch*] there.

SOLDIER. [*Gesturing with his musket*] Sit over there. [*In a warning tone*] Watch yerself. I'll be waitin' at the door.

FINCH. [*Rising to change his seat*] Glad to oblige, yer honorships. But, [*addressing Nathaniel*] if I can ask yer honorship, when they'll call me, if ye know, I'd be obliged.

NATHANIEL. [*Nodding toward Rotch*] This gentleman is to be called next. Mr. William Rotch, merchant, of Nantucket Island. After him, Mr. Tristram Finch, sailor, of Barnstable.

FINCH. [*Pleased*] That's myself, yer honorship. [*Sits near Rotch*] Tristram Finch, sailor.

[*Nathaniel retires to his duties at the table. Upon finishing, he goes to the door and waits for the return of the committee. He will stand with his back to the audience.*]

FINCH. [*Leaning toward Rotch*] Merchant of Nantucket, is it, Sir?

ROTCH. William Rotch.

FINCH. [*Introducing himself*] Tristram Finch, sailing man. As you yerself are, and a whaler, if yer a Nantucketer, for they're one and the same, any sailor knows.

ROTCH. [*With a smile*] Correct, my friend.

FINCH. Ye wouldn't be a smuggler, would ye, Sir?

ROTCH. Nay, though there's an appeal in it for many! I can understand that, in these times. Scarcely a branch to put on the fire, nor a soup to fill the stomach.

FINCH. Not that I'm a smugglin' man, Sir. [*With an eye on the soldier; softly*] These Provincials are a sore lot when it comes to smugglin', and the King's men, no less. [*Importantly*] Myself, I'm a petitioner! How else is a man to live with this rebellion on. Smugglin', petitionin', delegatin' — an man has to be quick in findin' a way 'round things, if ye gets my meanin'. Look at me. I'm a sailin' man. Been so since I was able to climb stairs up and down. I'm tryin' hard to continue to be one, but 'taint hardly possible with this war, not without some — "flexibility," Sir. Flexibility!

There I was, sailin' out o' Plymouth, Sir, on the Thundercloud; a fine little schooner she is, Sir. Headed for the Falklands, that is till the King's brig — no, privateer she was, that's right, *Caroline*, took us. So, there we were off to Halifax, or headed so. Got captured by the Provincials again, though I'm one of'em myself — more or less. The *Delight*, a brig. Then the Britishers — the *Red Bird* — refugees they were. Set her guns on us, she did. Then some Provincials again — near to New York we was, too. Course, then nobody knew who anybody was. No, not uncommon, Sir, though it sounds uncommon enough. My third time 'fore Major Hawley. Go with the winds, I say. Flexibility. That's a sailing man's motto: with the winds, Sir.

ROTCH. [*After a pause*] When I sail, I keep my eye on the compass needle, Friend Finch. If winds change, I turn my sails about, pull in a line here and there, and hold tight against the wind. Keep my eye on the needle, and small as it is, yet it guides me home across the great sea. But it's in the storm a sailor needs that little turning needle most — to keep him true to his course.

FINCH. [*Thoughtfully*] Aye, that's right, too, Sir — as far as sailin' goes.

[*The committee returns. Major Hawley sits at the table, Nathaniel at the end of the table. Hawley turns over the hourglass, and Nathaniel prepares to ring the bell. A few interested bystanders come in and take their seats. Captain Noah Goodman, of the committee, sits to Hawley's right, behind him. Major John Bliss sits left of and behind Hawley. Two other members are farther left behind Hawley.*]

FINCH. [*Quietly to Rotch, as the members take their seats*] Ye haven't been a touch too flexible yerself, have ye, Sir?

ROTCH. Not yet. It's a certain matter of trade — a commodity I could not supply the Provincials. That's what troubles them.

77

FINCH. Be ye Tory or Patriot, Sir?

ROTCH. Neither.

FINCH. [*Surprised*] Not on any side?

ROTCH. Not on those thou hast mentioned, but on the Lord's side, that is, on the side of peace.

FINCH. No wonder yer in trouble, Sir. [*A few prospective petitioners enter and sit down.*]

NATHANIEL. [*Ringing bell*] Silence, please.

FINCH. [*Quickly, to Rotch*] Take my advice, as a vet-rin petitioner. Don't let yerself get uppity. Tell yer story straight as ye kin.

ROTCH. I intend to. [*Smiles.*] Thank thee.

NATHANIEL. This committee of the General Court of the Massachusetts Bay Colony, one of the thirteen free and independent American Colonies, is now in session. Major Joseph Hawley, Chairman. [*Sits and takes notes.*]

HAWLEY. [*Wearily wiping his brow and looking through his papers*] What was it again?

NATHANIEL. [*Softly, to him*] The Nantucket Man, Sir.

HAWLEY. [*Finding the pertinent paper*] Ah, yes, William Rotch, Merchant, of Sherburne, Nantucket. [*Looks up at Rotch*] That is you, I take it, Sir.

ROTCH. I am William Rotch.

HAWLEY. Evidently, Sir, as you are the only man here wearing a hat, and [*consulting the paper*] as this man Rotch is from the island of Nantucket, which I understand to be chiefly populated by the people called Quakers: a folk peculiarly adverse to the removing of hats.

ROTCH. Adverse to the trappings of distinction among people whom the Almighty intended to be equals.

HAWLEY. [*Studying him*] Yes . . . no doubt. [*Studying the report*] Let me remember. It was a matter of some supply order refused . . . the merchandise . . . yes, an order of bayonets . . . bayonets. [*Looks up*] Is Captain Blackledge here?

BLACKLEDGE. [*Jumps up and begins speaking*] I can inform the committee very well about this man. In the fall of 1774, before I assumed command of the brigantine *New*—

HAWLEY. [*Firmly*] You are Captain Blackledge?

BLACKLEDGE. Yes, I—

HAWLEY. That was my question, Captain. Would you come forward? [*Blackledge, in uniform, comes to center and stands before the committee table.*] Thank you. [*Reading*] "whereas, on the fifth day of the month of—etc. etc.—should the court deem fit—my testimony of—etc.—the foregoing merchant—hmm hmm—in the glorious cause, etc." [*Looks up at Blackleldge*] Captain, I wonder if you might outline—in brief—your experience in the matter? [*As Blackledge takes a preparatory breath*] In brief, Captain.

BLACKLEDGE. A privilege, Gentlemen. In September of the year 1774, while my merchant vessel the *Henry B.* was refitted — later, I might add, to serve gloriously in the service of the great colony of Massachusetts — [*Hawley taps slowly and quietly with his gavel.*] I made visit to the island of Nantucket in the company of an associate, later chairman of the Committee of Safety on Cape Cod, Mr. Jedidiah Spooner —

HAWLEY. [*Nodding to a man smiling broadly*] Mr. Spooner?

JACKSON. Obadiah Jackson, if you please, Sir, petitioner for a cod fishing permit out of Marblehead, Sir —

HAWLEY. [*Wearily*] Codfish — yes, sit down for now, Mr. Jackson.

NATHANIEL. Sit down, please.

BLISS. [*Leaning over to Hawley and whispering*] Spooner. [*Points to a meek, obsequious individual near center*] Committee of Safety.

HAWLEY. Mr. Spooner?

SPOONER. [*Bowing slightly*] Jedidiah Spooner, Committee of Safety, Falmouth.

HAWLEY. Thank you, Mr. Spooner. Please sit down for now.

NATHANIEL. Sit down, please.

HAWLEY. Continue, Captain . . . Captain Blackledge.

BLACKLEDGE. In short —

HAWLEY. As much so as possible, Captain.

BLACKLEDGE. I went to this man Rotch [*gestures toward Rotch*] — to his store, to buy a musket, intending to do some quail hunting which I understood to be quite commendable on the island.

GOODMAN. Quite good it is.

HAWLEY. [*Turning to his colleague*] Noah.

BLACKLEDGE. I chose one — a musket — which happened to be equipped with a bayonet. Yet the man — this Rotch — refused to let me have the bayonet. He took it from me and would sell nothing but the musket only, despite my insistence.

HAWLEY. [*To Rotch*] How is it that a man of your persuasion came to deal in muskets with bayonets, Mr. Rotch?

ROTCH. [*Standing at his place*] The arms came to me from a Boston merchant who died insolvent and owing an extensive debt to me. Numerous goods came to me from his merchandise, among them these muskets; some with bayonets; some without.

HAWLEY. Thank you. [*Rotch sits; to Blackledge*] Continue.

BLACKLEDGE. I was later informed that this man Rotch had kept back a store of these bayonets, holding them in his warehouse. Others on the island had bought muskets of him for much the same purpose as myself. All *without* bayonets.

HAWLEY. Are you suggesting to the committee that the bayonets in question were intended for the King's men?

BLACKLEDGE. I leave the committee to decide that question, Sir.

HAWLEY. So, you managed to hunt quail without bayonets?

BLACKLEDGE. [*Slightly disconcerted*] Yes . . . Yes. Then, lately, being in acute need of armaments, I happened to think on those bayonets and mentioned them to Mr. Spooner. [*Spooner rises again, smiling, with a little bow. Nathaniel motions him down again.*]

HAWLEY. [*Also nodding Spooner down*] Yes, yes, Mr. Spooner. We remember.

BLACKLEDGE. And he, as he will no doubt tell you himself, informed the supply officer of the supposed location of these bayonets.

HAWLEY. Yes, these bayonets of which you personally saw a specimen some . . . uh . . . three years ago, Captain Blackledge?

BLACKLEDGE. That I learned of the bayonets? Yes, three years ago, Major.

HAWLEY. Three years is a fair number of pages in a merchant's day book, Captain. Did you ever see the entire store of weapons rumored to be in Mr. Rotch's possession?

ROTCH. I can clarify this matter, if I may. [*Stands*]

HAWLEY. Mr. Rotch?

ROTCH. When I received the order for the bayonets, I, indeed, had quite forgotten them. If I remember rightly, it was some thirteen years ago that I first received the muskets from Boston: 1764. And I had sold them all over a period of years. In truth, I had to go over to the old warehouse and see if they remained there, for I had removed to another store since Friend Blackledge visited me. The bayonets were there, amongst some rubbish, forgotten and neglected, except, of course, by the Committee of [*glancing at Spooner, with some irony*] Safety.

HAWLEY. [*A pause*] I see.

GOODMAN. So, you admit you had the bayonets still?

ROTCH. I did have them.

SPOONER. [*Jumping up*] Major Hawley, Sir?

HAWLEY. Yes?

SPOONER. I have prepared a statement in my capacity as chairman of the Falmouth Committee of Safety, concerning my report of the matter to Coloney DeGracy, of the Militia —

HAWLEY. [*Consulting his record*] Ah, yes. You informed the supply officer that the "aforesaid armaments are available at the aforesaid merchant's establishment in Sherburne, Nantucket Island; whereas, etc." Yes, I see.

SPOONER. That was in April of the present —

HAWLEY. Thank you, Mr. Spooner. You may sit down.

NATHANIEL. Sit down, please.

SPOONER. [*Holding his report*] But I've prepared —

HAWLEY. [*Firmly*] Thank you.

GOODMAN. [*Indicating a man holding his hat nervously at left; softly to Hawley*] Colonel DeGracy — of the Militia.

HAWLEY. Colonel DeGracy?

DEGRACY. Yes, Sir.

HAWLEY. It was you who placed the order for the bayonets which Mr. Rotch refused to comply with; is that correct? [*DeGracy nods.*] Have you anything to say concerning this matter?

DEGRACY. I think everything concerning me's been said, if you please, Gentlemen.

HAWLEY. Nothing to add?

DEGRACY. Can't think of anything, Sir.

HAWLEY. Thank you, Colonel. [*Warmly*] Thank you. So, as I understand it, an order for a supply of bayonets was placed with Mr. Rotch's firm. He has declined to acknowledge it. [*Pause*] Now, if everyone else will be seated, Mr. Rotch, I believe that matter can best be cleared up if you will honor us with a full explanation.

NATHANIEL. [*Standing up and motioning to the group*] Sit down, please. Sit down.

HAWLEY. Nathaniel, will you kindly sit down?

NATHANIEL. Me, Sir?

HAWLEY. Please.

NATHANIEL. I — Of, course. As you wish, Sir. [*Sits*]

HAWLEY. Mr. Rotch? [*Rotch stands and moves a step forward. Hawley consults his papers.*] According to the report and these witnesses, you have refused to comply with the supply order which Colonel DeGracy transmitted to you. Is that a true statement?

ROTCH. True.

GOODMAN. [*Reminding him*] You already admitted to this committee that you still had the bayonets when you received the order.

ROTCH. Oh, the weapons had been quite well known on Nantucket — famous, if I may say so. Many bought a musket of me since I first obtained them. The time then came upon me to test whether I would follow the testimony of Friends against war and all manner of contributing to war, or to abandon that testimony. I could not hesitate which to choose, and, therefore, denied each applicant. Several left me much dissatisfied, especially since the hostilities threatened to encroach upon us. Oh, it made a great noise in the country then. My life was even threatened.

BLISS. [*Hotly*] Yet you refused to supply us with these instruments, even though they were not but rubbish to you to be thrown in a heap in the corner?

GOODMAN. [*Jumping up*] Are you not aware that we are at war, Sir? [*Hawley urges him to sit, taking Goodman's arm.*]

ROTCH. I am aware that thou art.

HAWLEY. You mean to say that you are not, Mr. Rotch?

ROTCH. And hope never to be, with God's help.

BLISS. Don't you people claim not to cause any trouble?

ROTCH. Trouble is quite a different thing from war. No, I never heard one of us say such a thing. On the contrary, if a man intends to hold out to the last for a life of honesty, justice, and love for all of God's creatures, he fully intends to cause a great deal of trouble. Men call us neutral because we espouse neither their own cause nor their opponents'. Yet we are as partisan as any. We have our cause, and I fancy it humankind's as well as the Lord's.

BLISS. You're doing this colony a great deal of harm, Sir, by refusing us these necessary supplies. [*Stands up*]

ROTCH. 'Twas harm I hoped to avoid, Friend. As the instrument in question is purposely made and used for the destruction of human life, I could put no weapon into a man's hand so that he may destroy a fellow being, none that I could not in conscience use myself.

GOODMAN. Come, Sir. We are fighting for liberty. I dare say you have no principles against liberty. [*Stands by the table*]

ROTCH. What sort of liberty would that be, Friend? The liberty for every man to believe exactly as thou dost?

HAWLEY. You have a point there, Mr. Rotch. [*To Bliss*] John, please. [*Bliss sits, agitated; to Goodman*] Sit down, Noah. Now, Mr. Rotch, I hope there is no one here who finds war pleasant. Only a madman would do so.

ROTCH. Yet, you find it — war — acceptable.

HAWLEY. Acceptable?

GOODMAN. [*Gruffly*] Under certain conditions —

ROTCH. Thou dost accept it.

BLISS. Sir, the war was not our personal invention —

HAWLEY. Yes, acceptable. Our actions, these very gold buttons, show that. But, after all, we are not wicked men, either, though our principles are different from yours. We only want peace.

ROTCH. [*Quietly*] No, Friend. Thou seekest victory, not peace.

HAWLEY. [*Acknowledging this*] Victory . . . yes . . .

ROTCH. The man who seeks victory intends to harm — his enemies, and whomever among his own ranks may be required to overcome and render powerless his adversary. Perhaps, once, thy people hoped to threaten and frighten England. But the war means more than that. Look around thyself and tell me if any one will take harmony with England — without victory — now. [*Hawley is silent.*] The man who seeks victory seeks war. The man who seeks harmony seeks peace.

GOODMAN. Peace, but at what cost, Sir?

ROTCH. At great cost. Infinite patience, understanding, cooperation, mercy.

BLISS. You are wrong, Sir. Peace is impossible without the defeat
of one's enemies.

ROTCH. I pray thou art wrong, Sir. Consider the cost of victory.
Is it so cheap? Thousands of men dying in ships sunken by you
and the King. Men dying in miserable prison ships, dying of
fever, cold, neglect. And innocent victims grieving, dying, from
illness, from want of food, fuel, and shelter, a child playing his
drum into battle. A price thou art willing enough to pay. But the
time may come when no man can afford the price of victory,
and then the price of peace may seem more reasonable to more
of us than a few cranks like myself.

BLISS. [*Quietly*] You realize we can easily send a detachment to
take the bayonets by force?

ROTCH. No, thou canst not.

·GOODMAN. Major Hawley, I move we make a recommendation
to that effect to Mr. Spooner of the Committee of —

ROTCH. To no purpose, Friend Goodman.

HAWLEY. Do I understand the bayonets are no longer in your
possession, Mr. Rotch?

ROTCH. They are not.

GOODMAN. He's buried them.

BLISS. We'll find them out. It's not a great island, as I understand
it.

HAWLEY. Since you certainly would not have sold them to anyone else, either, what did you choose to do with them, Mr.
Rotch?

ROTCH. I would gladly have beaten them into pruning hooks, but
being unable to do so, I loaded them into a dory . . . and rowed
myself out to sea, beyond the south shoal.

HAWLEY. And?

ROTCH. Threw them into the sea, every one. [*Bliss jumps up. Exclamations among the onlookers. Hawley pounds the gavel.*]

FINCH. [*Leaning towards a neighbor*] Dumped them in the drink?

NATHANIEL. To the bottom of the sea?

FINCH. That's pluck!

HAWLEY. [*To Rotch*] The bayonets in question are now at the
bottom of the sea?

ROTCH. That is where I put them. I have been ever glad that I did
so, and if I am in the wrong I am to be pitied. I did it from
principle.

HAWLEY. [*Puts his quill down and closes his book*] I see.

BLISS. Then your principles are passive obedience and non-re-
sistance.

ROTCH. Active obedience and passive suffering.

GOODMAN. [*A sigh*] At least the King's men won't have them either.

HAWLEY. I dare say . . . Sunk them in the sea.

NATHANIEL. [*To the onlookers*] Silence, please.

BLISS. [*To Hawley*] What do we do now, Major?

HAWLEY. Gentlemen, we have an odd case here. Our soldiers have ransacked many a farm and storehouse, and I recall many a case of a man's trying to do what he could to keep the goods for himself or for the Tories. But never do I recall a man destroying his property precisely so that no man might use it, not even himself. [*To Rotch*] I am sorry we could not have had the bayonets, for we could have used them.

ROTCH. Precisely.

HAWLEY. [*Understanding his meaning*] Yes.

ROTCH. But art thou sure the instruments would have ended the life of a Loyalist? [*Indicating Finch*] Here is a man, a sailor, who has been bandied about from the King's ships to thine own and back again, as though a man were no more than a barrel of whale oil. If a man, why not a bayonet? Which man here might have perished from one of the bayonets now lying at the bottom of the sea?

HAWLEY. [*Studying Finch*] Is that you, Fitch?

FINCH. Finch, Sir.

HAWLEY. Back again?

FINCH. 'Fraid so, Sir, a spoil o' war, ye might say.

HAWLEY. Where's Mr. Finch's petition, Nathaniel?

HAWLEY. [*Examining it*] Halifax . . . New York . . . And where will you be off to now, Finch?

FINCH. The *Alexander's* headed for the Guinea coast tomorrow, Sir.

HAWLEY. [*He has started writing a release.*] Well, see you keep your eye on the compass this time.

FINCH. My eye on the compass. I will, Sir. I'm ever grateful, Major Hawley, gents. I'm heartily sorry to get myself captured twice over, yer honorships, an' I promise to keep a good lookout in the future an' keep myself loyal to the thirteen colonies, Sir. An' my old mother in Barnstable'll be ever so grateful for yer kindness, as the old lady has none but me to care for her, an' I'll be off and sending her something what to live on right off now. All due to yer graces, Sir.

HAWLEY. [*Hands him a paper*] There you are. And your shipmates will be freed as well. [*To Nathaniel*] Did you get that, Nathaniel?

NATHANIEL. The important parts, Sir.

FINCH. My eye on the compass, Sir. But, if I may ask, yer honorship. What about the Nantucket Man?

HAWLEY. [*Looks up at Rotch*] I believe Mr. Rotch has given us a candid account, and every man has a right to act consistently with his religious principles. I hope we can still afford that. It is clear he meant no harm — [*a pause as he realizes the meaning of his words*] — no harm. [*To Rotch*] I would like to inquire more about your principles, Mr. Rotch. As a man at war, as I am, Sir, I learn more of peace every day.

ROTCH. And I, too, Friend. I see now that peace does not happen by itself. It is not merely something left over when war has finished. Peace has to be worked for mightily, worked for and held onto with an effort of love.

HAWLEY. Go home to Nantucket, Mr. Rotch, and attend to your pruning hooks. We may need them. [*Bangs gavel*] Court is in recess until tomorrow morning at eight o'clock. [*All seated now rise. The onlookers depart slowly, murmuring among themselves. The committee members leave through the door, except Hawley, who opens his book to make a final note. Nathaniel carries his journal and the bell off. Finch hurries out, with a parting wish to Rotch whom he gives a hearty pat on the back. Nathaniel returns for the inkwells and papers and goes out again. The last one to depart, Rotch turns back at the doorway, studying Hawley.*]

ROTCH. Art thou a quail-hunting man, Friend?

HAWLEY. [*Looking up from his book, smiling*] I have been known to be. [*Pause*] I may be again, when this war is over.

ROTCH. The birds are especially fine on our island. And we have our secret places, we islanders. I should be pleased to have thee visit among us when thou are finished soldiering.

HAWLEY. [*Closing his book*] Then I am not irretrievably wicked because I wear this uniform.

ROTCH. [*Taking a step toward him*] I confess to a natural repulsion when I see thy military colors. I have long been prepared to feel so. Yes, I feel strong concern for thee because thou choosest to wear it . . . Thou art a worthy man, Friend. I am fortunate. Another may not have treated this affair of the bayonets so — thoughtfully.

HAWLEY. In all candor, Mr. Rotch, I have felt myself on trial here today. [*Stands and walks toward Rotch*] I wonder, Sir . . . I wonder if peace is possible. Or is it colossal error? An invitation to slavery?

ROTCH. Are not men slaves that must be ever warring — of *necessity?*

HAWLEY. Dear heaven, this war is a vicious thing! [*He goes over to the window, looks out from time to time, then looks back to Rotch.*] A pestilence! Yet men have fought wars since antiquity and show no sign of giving it up.

ROTCH. Thou art a doubting man for a soldier.

HAWLEY. A tired one, my dear sir. That is all. [*He gazes out the window a moment.*] In the end, Mr. Rotch, I'm afraid we may be too small for peace. We have far, far to go if we are to learn it. A man can't take up your principles in a day, can he?

ROTCH. Indeed, I am still learning them. Yet I question if we have ever truly tried peace. Our practice in war is ancient, as thou hast said. But have we ever had peace — made peace — or have we merely supposed that we had it?

HAWLEY. This I have observed, Sir, that the making of it is labor, indeed. How easy it would have been for you to pack up your bayonets and send them to us, never to have thought of them again. What you did took courage, but it was only a small, small moment of peace. Oh, yes. War takes bravery, immense bravery. But to face this world with nothing but your honesty and good will, yes, and your faith . . . I sometimes think it would destroy things only, not people . . . a weapon that would destroy other weapons, property, in short, our defenses, and leave us naked as God made us. Is that why He made us so, after all — so that we might one day realize how frail we are in truth — no great jaws like the whale, no claws, thick hide or fur, no poisonous bite? Naked and helpless, without our machinery of war, we might be compelled to settle our differences.

ROTCH. [*A pause*] Yet peace has its risks.

HAWLEY. [*Admitting this*] Yes.

ROTCH. Friend, ask the people of Nantucket. Our men are dying by the hundreds. Our people starve and freeze. Plundered from both sides, we have but few provisions left. Men drag a single branch miles to heat their cottages. Not a ship will survive this war — not one — and we had . . . we had many. Our whole way of life will be changed utterly, never to return again. And we are not even fighting.

HAWLEY. [*Taking a few steps toward Rotch*] War is an evil I don't want to accept. Yet I feel I must. You are right that war is acceptable to me, but peace? I don't know, truly.

ROTCH. Friend, I did what I did not because it was easy but because there was no other choice.

HAWLEY. No acceptable choice.

ROTCH. No. No choice. [*Hawley sighs. He starts to go out, stops and turns back.*]

HAWLEY. Perhaps, I shall come quail hunting when the war is done. Good day to you, Mr. Rotch.

ROTCH. Thou hast asked if peace is possible, Friend. Yes, I believe humankind will have it, when we want it, peace more than any other thing — more than victory. When we demand it.

HAWLEY. [*At the doorway*] When will that be, I wonder? [*He exits.*]

ROTCH. [*Pausing a moment before he exits*] In time, I pray. *As the curtain closes, we see the hourglass, the sole remaining object on the table, its sands running down.*]

Suggestions for Discussion

1. Clarify why Rotch is summoned to appear in court.

2. Rotch makes a distinction between fighting in war and "causing trouble." Why is the latter acceptable or perhaps necessary for a Christian? Rotch says: "If a man intends to hold out to the last for a life of honesty, justice, and love for all of God's creatures, he fully intends to cause a great deal of trouble." Do you agree? Can you think of Christians today who are this type of partisan for their faith?

3. What consequences do people today face who refuse to build, use, or pay for instruments used for the destruction of human life? If possible, refer to people you know who have witnessed in such a way.

4. Talk about the "cost of victory." What feelings does victory provoke in the defeated? Rotch prophetically says that "the time may come when no man can afford the price of victory." What would that price be in human terms if we used our weapons today?

5. Toward the end, Rotch mentions the devastating effects of the war on his people of Nantucket even though they were not fighting in it. Show how economic suffering among many today could be alleviated if we spent less money on war preparations.

6. Hawley admits that he himself has felt on trial during the hearing. Can you explain why?

CARIE

by John Ferguson

*This is written as a monologue. The actress playing Carie must play
so that we see the other characters without them appearing. The
story is a true one. Carie was a missionary's wife in China before
the War. It is after dark.*

CARIE.
Still no rain.
Dear Christ, how hot it is, how dry and parched!
A haze of dust cloaks the air, stifles and strangles us,
clogs up our pores, our nostrils, lays
its heavy blanket on our mouths.
Still no rain.
The doors and tables crack with dryness, exploding
like pistols at our heads. The flowers wither
in the garden, the crops in the fields.
The farmers wait for the rain for the rice.
But no rain comes.

[*She sings.*]
"He sends the springs into the valleys
    which run among the hills.
They give drink to every beast of the field:
    the wild asses quench their thirst.
He waters the hills from His chambers:
    the earth is satisfied with the fruit of your works—"

[*She breaks off.*]
But he doesn't—it isn't . . .
O God! What little faith!

[*She drops to her knees.*]
Lord Jesus, forgive my weakness.
You are Lord of all. Even the winds
and waves obey you.
Give us rain.

[*She rises.*]
I wish Andrew were here. But he has to do
the Master's work up in the hills.
They do not come to our chapel any more.
Not one last Sunday. They say the gods are angry.
They say that never was there a drought like this.

They say that never before have foreigners lived
in their city. They say that we have drawn the people
from the worship of the gods. The gods are angry.
Wang Amah told me not to go into the street
for fear of the people. I am not afraid,
but I have stayed with the children. And then I heard —
I thought I heard — a voice outside the window:
"Kill — kill — kill. Tonight we'll force the doors.
Their blood shall flow — and then the rain will flow.
Kill the foreigners: the favour of the gods
will return. Kill — kill — kill."
I am not afraid, not *afraid*. "Perfect love
casts out fear" — the beloved disciple says it.
The Master says it again and again:"Be not afraid."
When the storm swells on the lake:"Be not afraid."
When blazing glory shone round him:"Be not afraid."
When they tried to kill him:"Be not afraid."
Kill — kill — kill. Be not afraid. Be not afraid.
Be not afraid.
So the children are in bed, and I have sent
Wang Amah to walk about and find
what they intend to do. She's coming now.

[*We are to imagine Wang Amah, the Chinese servant,
arriving in a panic.*]
Why, Wang Amah, whatever's the matter.
You look as if you've seen a ghost. I thought you
Chinese never showed your emotions. Don't be afraid.
Jesus is with us at all times.

[*Wang Amah speaks.*] I see.
They're coming any moment now to kill
us all . . . Very well . . . We shall be ready for them.
Go and wake the children and dress them.

[*Wang Amah goes out. Carie stands for a moment quietly with
head bowed. Then she shakes herself into action, and busies herself
getting out tea-things for a large number of people. She moves over
to the organ and lets her fingers play over the keys; then returns to
her job. As she works she sings.*]
Other refuge have I none.
Hangs my helpless soul on Thee:
Leave, ah! leave me not alone.
Still support and comfort me.
All my trust on Thee is stayed.
All my help from Thee I bring:
Cover my defenceless head
With the shadow of Thy wing.

[*Then she picks up some sewing, and sits quietly with it. Wang Amah comes back with the children.*]
There you are, darlings. It's a funny day, isn't it?
But we're expecting visitors, and you must be here
to welcome them. Why don't you play
quietly on the mat for a little? Wang Amah,
put out the cakes, and boil up the kettle
ready for tea.

[*She goes on sewing, singing as she does so.*]
And thou most kind and gentle Death,
Waiting to hush our latest breath,
    O praise him, Alleluia!
Thou leadest home the child of God,
And Christ our Lord, the way hath trod —

[*She breaks off, and speaks to herself.*]
I am persuaded that neither death nor life,
nor angels, nor principalities, nor powers,
nor things present nor things to come,
nor height, nor depth, nor any other creature
shall be able to separate us from the love of God,
which is in Christ Jesus our Lord.
He has overcome death. He can overcome
those who threaten death.

[*She pauses, listening.*] They are coming.
It is time.

[*She puts her sewing aside.*]
Wang Amah, please make the tea.

[*Carie picks up an oil-lamp, turns up the wick, goes to the door and opens it and hangs the lamp there. She calls outside.*]
Will you please come in? . . .
Come in, friends, neighbors, I have tea prepared.

[*They begin to come in. We must picture them, militant, angry working-men with sticks, clubs and knives. She presses a cup of tea on the leader.*]
Will you come and drink tea for yourselves?
Please sit down. I am sorry my humble home
has not enough seats for you all, but you are welcome
to what I have. Welcome, one and all.

[*She goes to the table and busies herself.*]
Oh, and do leave your sticks by the door,
if you like. [*To the children*] It's all right, darlings.
These are our friends and neighbors. They've come
to see what we look like. They've never seen
Americans before. Isn't that funny?

I expect they think you've got a funny face.
There's nothing to be afraid of. Why don't you go and
play with them?

[*Catching a remark from one of the crowd*]
Why do you say it's strange I'm not afraid?
Why should I fear my neighbors, my friends?

[*She goes round among them filling tea-cups, passing cakes, showing them the curtains, furniture, the children's toys. She moves
over to the organ.*]
Do please let me fill your cup . . . And yours.
Have another cake . . . another cake . . . another cake.
How about you? . . . Yes that curtain
has a lovely feel, doesn't it? . . . The chair
folds up like this. It's easier for carrying . . .
That's one of the children's toys. Wind it up
like this . . . and it runs along of its own accord . . .
I've taken Arthur's favorite toy, so he wants
to play with your finger . . . That's right . . .
Yes, he does pull hard for a boy of his age . . .
I'm glad you think he's a game little fellow . . .
Excuse me a moment . . . Let me show you
how to work the organ. Let me sit here.
I'll press with my feet. Now you push that note down.
Boom! That's right. Did it make you jump?
Try this one. Peep! Very different, isn't it?
Boom!
Peep!
Now let me play and sing you something.

[*There is absolute silence as she plays and sings.*]
Jesus, lover of my soul,
Let me to Thy bosom fly,
While the nearer waters roll,
While the tempest still is high.
Hide me, o my Saviour, hide,
Till the storm of life is past,
Safe into the haven guide,
O receive my soul at last!

[*As she finishes she catches a muttered remark.*]
That's right. There is nothing here — only
these women and these children. Must you
be going? Thank you, friends, neighbors, for calling.

[*She gets up from the organ, picks up her youngest child in her
arms and goes to the door to see them off.*]
Make sure you haven't left anything behind.
That's right, darling, give them a big smile

and a wave. Thank you for coming. You must forgive
my poor hospitality. Thank you, thank you, thank you.

[*To the leader, who is the last to go, handing him a scroll*]
Thank you for coming to see us, and for bringing
you friends. Let me give you this. It says:
God is love.
Good-night.

[*She stands for a little at the door, with the little boy in her arms, so
that they turn back and see her so. She gives them a smile and a
wave as they do so. Then, after a few moments longer, she puts the
child down, shuts the door, and brings the lamp back to the table.*]
Wang Amah, did you hear what he said?
"There is nothing more to do here. I'm going home."

[*She laughs, almost hysterically, then controls herself.*]
I must sit down. I'm feeling a little faint.

[*She does so.*]
But, Wang Amah, it's cooler. A breeze has sprung up
while we've been talking. I'll sit quietly
for a little here.

[*She picks up her sewing.*] Wang Amah, take the
children upstairs to bed again. Good-night, my
darlings, my dear, dear darlings. You've been good,
strong, brave boys. Good-night. God bless you.

[*They go out. She sits sewing, then looks up.*]
Lord, you are God, who made heaven
and earth and sea and all that is in them.
By the mouth of your servant David you said
"Why did the heathen rage and the people
imagine vain things? The kings of the earth rose up
and the rulers took counsel together
against the Lord and against his Christ."
So the people gathered against your holy child
Jesus. In all their threatenings grant you servants
that with all boldness we may speak and live out
your word, and that signs and wonders may be done
by the name of your holy child Jesus.

[*She turns again to her sewing. Then suddenly*]
What is that sound, like tapping on the roof?
Light-fingered yet . . . now striking
like the hammer-blows of fists.
The rains have come. Blissful, blessed rain!
Thank God!
Thank God!

Suggestions For Discussion

1. How does Carie prevent the bloodbath? Describe her method of dealing with aggression.

2. What other reactions would have been possible? Consider Wang Amah's for example. What would have been the most likely result of showing fear? Of trying to run away? Of barricading herself?

3. What is the role of the children? How do they become part of the peacemaking process?

4. What is the source of Carie's strength? What can we learn from her?

A MAN IN A LOIN CLOTH

by Jay Gurian

HISTORICAL NOTE

The events are a composite of two situations that took place in early February 1922. Mohandas K. Gandhi had returned from successful civil disobedience campaigns in South Africa in 1915 to an India divided by regionalism, religion, caste, colonialism and language. The British still held fast to the greatest treasure in their Empire. Quickly, Gandhi began to rally divided Indians to the cause of direct action nonviolence. With laser insight, he understood that Indians must learn or relearn village self-sufficiency to fight the British exploitation of their economy: the spinning wheel became the instrument of this insight. That is why Gandhi is spinning when the play begins.

Gandhi designed a limited civil disobedience action for the Bardoli area near Bombay to impress the British "Raj" with the readiness of Indians for a greater measure of independence. The setting of this play, then, is Bardoli on February 8, 1922.

The situations in the play are historically accurate because they are taken from the records left by Gandhi himself, by his secretary Krishna Das, and by such able biographers as D. G. Tendulkar and Louis Fischer. Much of the dialogue is fashioned from the speeches and writings of Gandhi and those who worked with him.

GLOSSARY

1. *SATYAGRAHA — Satya in sanscrit means "truth" and agraha means "force." Truth or Soul Force is based on the belief that love, as universal energy, underlies all nonviolence, and that self-suffering (even unto death if necessary) is the duty of the satyagrahi, who may never hate the "enemy" and must only regard enemies as opponents. Satyagraha is thus an ideology and a set of strategies for enactment.*

2. *KHADI — homespun cloth. In 1919 Gandhi hit upon the idea of returning Indians to the age-old, pre-British practice of spinning their own cotton into crude yarn, then manufacturing their own clothing with it. Following the example set by Gandhi and his followers, Indians everywhere began to defy the British ban on the manufacture of cloth goods. Village economics hurt the cotton mill industries back in England and became a powerful force in later negotiations with the British government.*

3. THE ROWLATT ACTS — Legislation enacted in 1919 that continued the civil liberties restrictions imposed on India as a measure for the Empire's protection during World War I. Indian nationalists were enraged. The Acts became a focus for protest.

4. "GANDHIJI-KI-JAI" — the chant thrown up in reverence by Gandhi's followers and supporters. Most people by 1922 had come to consider him more than a man, something akin to what in the western world is called a "saint." This roughly translates to "Gandhi, the exalted, above all!"

5. "BAPU" — father, but as with so many words used in India, expanded in the case of a figure like Gandhi, or later Nehru, to mean "father of us all," "father of the motherland," etc.

6. SAREE — the outer garment worn by most Indian women, consisting of a simple blouse, an inner and ample length petticoat and six or nine yard of colorful cloth. During the Gandhi period, women followers adopted the practice of wearing khadi sarees, an off-white, the color of homespun cotton.

7. SWADESHI — the broad concept of which "khadi" was a particular expression. Gandhi himself defined swadeshi as "that spirit in us which restricts us to the use and service of our immediate surroundings to the exclusion of the more remote," including everything from religion to clothing.

8. ASHRAMITE — a person who lives in an ashram. Ashrams are whole life communities in India (now also in America) fulfilling spiritual as well as familial and physical needs. After returning to India, Gandhi became the focus of two ashrams. Louis Fischer has described the ashram at Sabarmati as "the navel of India," from which satyagrahis launched many of the great nonviolence campaigns including the March to the Sea in 1931.

PRODUCTION NOTES

The western world view is linear. The Indian world view is circular. For Indians, ultimate reality is neither the seen nor the scientifically "proved." Reality is what is believed to be, primarily by intuition or "knowing." The durability of Indian civilization suggests that the circular view, with its assumption of infinite dimensions and hospitality to contradiction is more "truthful" than the linear western view. The West looks forth to self-extermination.

As a consequence of their world view, Indians do not usually speak with the steel-shaft directness of Englishmen or the bluntness of Americans. Both pace and direction of speech are less angular, more fluid, more lilting. To the impatient modern ear, Indian English often sounds stilted. It always sounds sing-song. And laughter is an integral part of communication, even during the most serious moments. This play tries to preserve the flavor of actual Indian English while bringing it somewhat nearer American English than it actually is.

There are several easily found 16 mm. films that project the time, place, language and "ambience" depicted in this play; for example, CBS's 27 minute "Gandhi" narrated by Charles Kerrault. Gandhi's voice has been preserved on disc. Some of these media resources should be consulted before production.

The full-length play from which this scene has been taken dramatizes the non-violent struggle spearheaded by Gandhi between 1916 and 1922.

CHARACTERS

MOHANDAS K. GANDHI, *age 52*
MUKRAM BANERJEE, *former calcutta attorney, now a satyagrahi*
ANAND NARASIMHAIAH, *former Central Government Education Minister, now a satyagrahi*
SYED MOHAMED ALI, *former wealthy merchant, now a satyagrahi*
KASTURBAI, *Gandhi's indomitable wife, about 45 years old*
LAKSHMI, *an untouchable caste girl "adopted" by Gandhi*
BETTY HURLEY, *a British reformer in her thirties, now a satyagrahi*
SIR MICHAEL O'DWYER, *British Governor*
MADAME KAOOSJI, *a wealthy Bombay Parsi woman in her forties*
INDIAN SOLDIER

The stage should consist of a raised platform with open-wing exits to the sides. In the Indian manner, the platform should be covered by white sheeting. Potted trees and plants should be distributed on stage. If possible, a flat depicting an Indian rual/town setting can be set up along part of the rear.

A simple room facing an open space to the rear, in Bardoli District near Bombay, February 1922. Gandhi sits on the floor, cross-legged, spinning on a typical small spinning wheel, or charka. He is in his early fifties, dressed in both a loin cloth and long jacket, both made of homespun. Mukram Banerjee paces nervously back and forth, a former Calcutta attorney now in his forties, hawk-like; also in khadi clothing.

BANERJEE. Gandhiji, this Bardoli campaign is going to be tragic.

GANDHI. [*Sweetly*] My dear old friend Banerjee, all I have done is notify the Viceroy of India that here, in Bardoli District, we are going to demonstrate the readiness of Indians for a greater measure of self-rule. That is not food for tragedy. That is food for celebration.

BANERJEES. [*Accusingly*] You wrote the Viceroy, at the same time, demanding that he free the press from Government control, right?

GANDHI. The unjust government control imposed in 1919 by the Rowlatt Acts, yes. Banerjee, you have been with me since 1916. Once you were a finicky Calcutta attorney dressed in the finest London wear. Now you are a man of satyagraha. Surely you must respect — you must worship — the freedom of the press. A freedom John Milton of London sang about. John Stuart Mill of London wrote about. A freedom invented in the Viceroy's own England!

BANERJEE. But invented over centuries, Gandhiji. You would have it with the stroke of a Viceroy's pen! As if that were not enough, somehow you demand —

GANDHI. [*Gently again, wagging his finger, with humor*] In the name of 87,000 citizens of the Bardoli district —

BANERJEE. [*Somewhat stentorially*] As I look around Bardoli at this moment I do not see even 87 citizens demanding the release of all the non-cooperating prisoners — another of your "demands!" I see only you!

GANDHI. [*Spinning again*] But the 87,000 are aware of constant government repression — and you know it.

BANERJEE. The Viceroy objects to the word "repression."

GANDHI. [*Wagging his head, Indian fashion, side to side*] Of course. In my letter I apologized for having to offend him —

BANERJEE. That at least, was sensible —

GANDHI. Offend him, with truth —

BANERJEE. [*Frustrated*] Then you offended him with insult!

GANDHI. And have not his police and soldiers offended us with repression?

BANERJEE. That word again!

GANDHI. [*More gently than ever*] I shall change it at your pleasure.

BANERJEE. Thank you.

GANDHI. "Oppression."

BANERJEE. Two weeks ago, while the Prince of Wales crossed Bombay, the very citizens you addressed turned our khadi rally into mayhem. I say violence is worse than repression. You can live repressed, even oppressed. Violence destroys even these possibilities.

GANDHI. [*More seriously, but still spinning*] I deplore violence.

I live in its terror. But my dear, dear friend, we must test ourselves continually, right? The demonstration in Bombay was a failure. Can we not also look back on successes? [*He stops spinning.*] So you remember the simple soldier I told you about, at the railway siding in Patwal? [*Blackout. Gandhi immediately lies sideways, hands under head, as if on a third class wooden railway seat. If possible, sounds of a train whistle repeating in distance. Lights up as an Indian soldier complete with lathi — polished stick for keeping order — enters briskly.*]

INDIAN SOLDIER. You are Mohandas K. Gandhi?

GANDHI. Yes, soldier, I am.

SOLDIER. I have a written order forbidding your entrance to the Punjab. [*Shows order.*] "Your presence is likely to result in a disturbance of the peace." You are to disembark in my company.

GANDHI. My ticket is in order. I am a free citizen intending to travel the Punjab in response to a pressing invitation.

SOLDIER. If you do not come out, I shall have to force you out.

GANDHI. I understand the problem this order poses for you.

SOLDIER. The problem is yours.

GANDHI. [*Sitting up*] The problem seems to be, if I refuse to leave this car, you will be placed in the awkward position of doing violence to my body. Which, as we know from the Vedas, is your body as well. Isn't it?

SOLDIER. I am well-trained to do my duty!

GANDHI. I am sure you do your duty with excellence. But can you respect another kind of soldier, equally well-trained to do another kind of duty?

SOLDIER. What kind of soldier is it who calls on his troops to make mayhem?

GANDHI. But is not a call to military battle equally a call to mayhem?

SOLDIER. A military battle is organized!

GANDHI. I am willing to grant that nonviolence is not so organized as violence.

SOLDIER. That is not what I meant!

GANDHI. But that is what you said. [*Stands*] Please to use me according to your conscience and your duty. A satyagrahi knows how to suffer.

SOLDIER. Do not make me lay a hand on you.

GANDHI. Then let us go together. [*Puts a hand on the soldier's shoulder*] You will guide me. [*They start off. Suddenly the soldier drops to Gandhi's feet.*]

SOLDIER. Mahatma-ji, I cannot! [*Blackout. Soldier off. Gandhi sits up and begins spinning again. Lights up.*]

GANDHI. If there is one such soul in Bardoli, today we cannot fail!

BANERJEE. Your politics are beyond utopian, Gandhiji! They are not rational! In Bombay we marched for khadi, for the spinning wheel, for swadeshi. And what we got was —

GANDHI. You are questioning the swadeshi program itself. Swadeshi means only to wear Indian khadi, only to use Indian products. Swadeshi means self-respect.

BANERJEE. From the office windows of New Delhi, swadeshi means riot!

GANDHI. Because our Indian people need more discipline, yes. You would countenance the flogging of innocent brothers in jail, rather than discomfit the colonial oppressor — that is not non-violence. That is embracing their violence as if it were your due.

BANERJEE. [*Falling to his knees before Gandhi*] I beg that you cancel today's plans. Before we find ourselves surrounded by 87,000 kinds of mayhem. Before you force government to arrest not only the rest of us, but the Mahatma himself.

GANDHI. I have always found prison a place to grow in spirit.

BANERJEE. Your wife is barely able to walk. How could she bear prison now?

GANDHI. No one soul, if studying to be pure, would wish to stand in the way of justice.

BANERJEE. The Viceroy cannot legislate justice!

GANDHI. With the stroke of his pen, the Viceroy could abrogate the Rowlatt, give us back our freedom to publish, return our rights of assembly, grant amnesty to our protestors —

BANERJEE. It was your activities which forced him to invoke the Rowlatt measures in the first place!

GANDHI. The nature of his response to our just demands is his problem!

BANERJEE. And you are a political child!

GANDHI. [*Passionately*] I will never be otherwise! At this moment in all the capitals of the world your political adults are slashing each others' throats. They have no sense of the people, only their deadly games of power. They play for wars, cooing over battlefield statistics. They nauseate god. They enrage the decencies of the few decent men — the political children whom they lay on Abraham's altar. Only these Isaacs are not spared — they are bayonetted on European battlefields, or machine-gunned in our own cities. You ask me to be realistic about what a man of power can do — and I say to be "realistic" I would have to cancel not only the Bardoli campaign. I would have to send all our workers home. I would have to tell the untouchables, "Go back to your toilets! Forever!"

BANERJEE. Of course.

GANDHI. I would have to close the ashram itself.

BANERJEE. If the alternative were bloody streets, wouldn't you close it?

GANDHI. Only a man who lacked faith could ask that question.

BANERJEE. The Viceroy can no more grant amnesty, or cancel the Rowlatt —

GANDHI. Than we can tolerate them!

BANERJEE. He cannot give.

GANDHI. But we can?

BANERJEE. We must! Because he is government, and we are —

GANDHI. Anarchists, terrorists, revolutionaries — ?

BANERJEE. I would have hesitated —

GANDHI. Just short of that.

BANERJEE. Just somewhat short of that. You have asked the Viceroy to order a change in the political arrangements of men — which is most basic of all.

GANDHI. Then the state precedes the individual?

BANERJEE. I would split the difference with Aristotle: At least, the individual does not precede the state.

GANDHI. If you truly believe this, you cannot believe in satyagraha. The force of truth is to change people's hearts so that they may change the nature of the state that people themselves have created.

BANERJEE. The state has its own nature —

GANDHI. Look out there — the Bardolis are beginning to gather, alight with the challenge. The Viceroy did not respect our deadline with an answer and now they come to prepare complete satyagraha. True opposition includes love of all that is opposed. I shall insist they love the British, even the Viceroy. But you no longer love our cause, and I must ask you to leave.

BANERJEE. [Unbelieving] We have spent six years together —

GANDHI. [Coldly] I am not sure of that.

BANERJEE. You now reject me, bapu?

GANDHI. You have rejected us.

BANERJEE. I did not expect —

GANDHI. [Angrily] What did you expect?

BANERJEE. Have you so little faith that you fear my lack of it? [Offstage sounds of a gathering crowd begin.]

GANDHI. [Standing] There they are, Mukram. I give them to you. If you do not choose to leave Bardoli, my next request is that you speak out against my plan as strongly to them as you did to me. Abuse me in the bargain if you will. Try to make them return to their huts and their everyday duties.

BANERJEE. [Hesitating] This is not fair. [Syed and Narasimhaiah enter.]

NARASIMHAIAH. The road from Bombay is overrun with villagers. The entire district seems to be coming.

SYED. Whole families are crossing the field, chanting and dancing. This should be a day!

GANDHI. You'll have your audience, Mukram.

SYED. I've listed the speeches thus —

GANDHI. Please to place Mukram's name at the head—

BANERJEE. [*Hurt*] Why do you use the cold name "Mukram?"

NARASIMHAIAH. At the head, Gandhiji?

GANDHI. [*Crossing away*] He wishes to speak to Bardoli.

BANERJEE. I have not said that!

GANDHI. [*Angrily*] Are you afraid to lead them away?

BANERJEE. [*Furiously*] Why do you dare me thus? ·

GANDHI. [*Turning on him*] Why do you dare *me* thus?

SYED. Banerjee first, then—

BANERJEE. [*Starting to leave*] Banerjee not at all!

GANDHI. You cannot have it both ways! That I cannot allow!
[*Banerjee breaks into sobbing, and leaves. Off-stage shouting
begins: "Mahatma-Gandhiji-ki-jai" repeated three times.*]

GANDHI. [*To Syed and Narasimhaiah*] Have you prayed today?

SYED. Since sun-up.

NARASIMHAIAH. I have faith, Gandhiji. [*Off-stage call repeated*]

GANDHI. I am master of knowing others' faith. Is it possible my
own may falter? They need us so much. They want us. Why am
I stuck to the ground? Why is my soul in my stomach?
[*Narasimhaiah and Syed cross to him, and he throws his arms
over them; they shield him.*] In Bombay, something failed. That
blood is on my head.

SYED. Gandhiji, have you prayed today?

GANDHI. [*Trying to pull away*] I must speak to God! [*Off-stage
call repeated*]

NARASIMHAIAH. The Bardolis are too impatient. It is now or
not at all!

GANDHI. Then not at all! [*As he pulls away from them in terror,
Kasturbai enters, helped by Lakshmi. They face each other.*]

LAKSHMI. Bapu, she would not stay in bed.

NARASHIMHAIAH. [*To Kasturbai*] We left you at the ashram!

LAKSHMI. She would come only.

KASTURBAI. [*With gentle humor*] Since I have foresworn the
beef tea and pulses, you see I am much stronger. [*Gandhi lets her
hold him.*] The doctor wrote solicitations, begging to know if I
was yet alive. I had an ashramite with gift of pen write him
answer. The satyagrahis are waiting.

LAKSHMI. We begged her to stay in bed.

KASTURBAI. [*Crossing*] It is a good crowd of the faithful, isn't it?
[*The crowd offstage renews its shout. Kasturbai namaskars to
them. They shout for Gandhi again. Narasimhaiah and Syed
cross, namaskaring. The crowd again shouts. Betty enters hur-
riedly.*]

BETTY. When I heard Mrs. Gandhi had started for Bardoli, I hur-
ried—But she's doing quite well, isn't she?

GANDHI. She's India, my dear.

101

BETTY. Then God help England! [*Betty crosses over and namask-ars. The crowd again shouts for Gandhi.*]

SYED. [*Gesturing for silence*] Bardoli satyagrahis, listen! The Viceroy has ignored the ultimatum! [*Offstage shouts joined in by Narasimhaiah and Kasturbai: "Outrage! Outrage!"*] The Crown has left us no choice! [*They all join: "No choice! No choice!"*] The thousands are starved and flogged in prison! The newspapers are muzzled! Khilafat workers are plucked off the streets and thrown in dungeons! There is no time left for words! [*Repeated shouts by those off-stage and on-stage. Those on stage turn to Gandhi during the chant: "Mahatma-Gandhiji-ki-jai!" Gaining strength, and clutching Lakshmi, Gandhi crosses as the shouts build to a roar. He steps in front of the others.*]

GANDHI. Brothers, sisters, children of God. My tears of joy and faith cannot stop the words I must speak. The Government is cowardly, thus it believes we are afraid of its jails. Let us welcome the possibility of prison as if it were a health resort! [*General laughter. Off-stage shouts throughout his speech: Wa, Wa!" "Tell us!" "Yes, Gandhiji!"*] The bond of the slave is snapped the moment he truly considers himself to be a free being. It does not matter if he grovels in prison in chains. His being will plainly tell the master: "You may kill me if you like. But if you keep me alive, I am your slave no longer. And if you throw me in a ditch and cover me with earth, I am equally your slave no longer!" The people of Bardoli are slaves no longer! [*Great cheers*] Now while we pray for the strength of our intentions, the resolution that you have drawn will be read. If anyone finds a condition in this resolution repulsive to his nature, he must withdraw from the satyagraha. And if one withdraws, the others will clap him gently on the back, wish him well, name him their brother, love him at all times. [*Gandhi sits in lotus, praying. The others on stage sit also, in prayer. Syed stands reading.*]

SYED. "Having fully understood the conditions essential for mass civil disobedience, the inhabitants of Bardoli resolve that for the redress of India's grievances, unity among Hindus, Muslims, Parsis, Christians and all others is absolutely necessary."

GANHDI. Let God hear your prayers.

SYED. "That non-violence, suffering and love are the only remedy for such grievances. That the use of the spinning wheel in every home, the wearing of hand-spun and hand-woven garments only are indispensible for India's freedom."

GANDHI. Know in your hearts if your bodies can be satisfied thus.

SYED. "That freedom is impossible without complete removal of untouchability!"

GANDHI. You are prepared to embrace all your brothers, to share their water. Be sure!

SYED. "That for the attainment of freedom, we are ready to suffer imprisonment — and if necessary to lay down our lives in the service of truth!" [*A great shout of approval. Gandhi leads everyone in a brief section of "Bande Mataram," the Indian national anthem. A recording may be used, or an actor come onstage to accompany with either a sarod, sitar or harmonium.*] But satyagrahis have a choice; it is satyagraha, the gift of God. The satyagrahi will harbor no anger. He will suffer the anger of his opponent. [*Turning to Narasimhaiah*] You are a dirty Hindu dog, an Indian pariah, and I spit upon you! [*He spits. Narasimhaiah recoils, brushing the spittle away.*]

NARSHIMHAIAH. Gandhiji!

GANDHI. In such suffering, he will put up with assaults from the opponent — I did not say "enemy," for the satyagrahi pledges never to believe the man before him is an "enemy." You do violence to your enemies. The satyagrahi never does violence. The satyagrahi will put up with any assault from his opponent. [*He pushes Syed away, and as Syed starts forward, Betty pushes Syed into Gandhi, who pushes him back into Betty. Syed turns on Betty angrily. As suddenly, Syed drops his arms, places his head down. The crowd cheers, as do those on stage. The crowd laughs during the satyagrahi demonstration. Demonstrators may be solicited from the audience.*] When any person in authority seeks to arrest a civil resister for disobeying an evil law. . .[*Betty grabs Syed as if to arrest him.*]

BETTY. "I have here the Crown's order for your arrest on charges of violating the law against public assembly!" Will you come?

GANDHI. . . . the satyagrahi will voluntarily, he will joyously, submit to his arrest.

SYED. Indeed, officer, it is my pleasure. But what is the name of the health resort? [*Laughter*]

GANDHI. A satyagrahi will undertake the suffering of his opponent upon himself.

NARASIMHAIAH. [*Crossing to Betty*] May we help you to arrest us, please?

GANDHI. Non-retaliation excludes swearing and cursing —

BETTY. [*To Syed*] The Crown shall eat you for breakfast. You are a filthy-cow protector. You are a savage Musselman. Fire erupts from your snout when you try to speak. You abuse five wives. You trample your Bedouin horses over you children. You worship a false god, and you revel in the offal of the Caliph himself!

SYED. [*As if beginning to assault her*] You are a sterile, puerile, simpering, stupid — [*Gently*] I thank you for these opinions.

GANDHI. And if anyone should insult an official or assault him, the true satyagrahi will protect such officials . . . [*Narasimhaiah makes as if to assault Betty. Syed steps between, receiving the*

103

blow intended for Betty, slumps to the ground and assumes the arms folded, head down position of passive resistance. The crowd cheers.] . . . from insult or attack, even at the risk of his life! For the satyagrahi, there is only love. And if the soldiers come to take you in, what will you do?

EVERYONE. We shall love!

GANDHI. And if the soldiers and the police strike you with lathis, or aim their rifles at your heads. What will you do?

EVERYONE. Sit!

GANDHI. And pray!

EVERYONE. And pray!

GANDHI. And if they strike you again, drawing blood?

EVERYONE. Suffer!

GANDHI. And love!

EVERYONE. Suffer, and love!

GANDHI. Satyagraha means full surrender—to love, which is God. To God, which is force. To truth force, which is satyagraha!

EVERYONE. Satyagraha! Satyagraha! Satyagraha!

GANDHI. As a sign of my ever more total commitment to Satyagraha, henceforth I shall be satisfied with nothing more than a loincloth! *[Offstage shouts: "Mahatma-Gandhiji-ki-jai!" Gandhi strips to his loincloth. Michael O'Dwyer enters.]* Sir Michael!

O'DWYER. How do you do, Mr. Gandhi?

GANDHI. When I see my people in such joy, I do splendidly.

O'DWYER. The Viceroy sent me.

GANDHI. To know our intentions. See the laughter, the small talk, the colorful sarees, and the hope that swadeshi brings to the people? To the peaceful and generous people of India, Sir Michael!

O'DWYER. May we count on that?

GANDHI. You may tell the Viceroy that I guarantee the good behavior of my satyagrahis and my friends.

O'DWYER. But what of your enemies?

GANDHI. *[Playfully]* They are all in your hands, right?

O'DWYER. Precisely my question.

GANDHI. When we first met at Benaras, there was tension. I wish to erase that with brotherliness. *[He rises and holds out his hand.]* If ever you find it necessary to arrest me, we shall remember this moment and be kind to one another. *[O'Dwyer leaves. Gandhi stands downstage on the platform. A great crowd roar: "Mahatamaji-jai! Jai hind!" Gandhi waits, head down.]* And now, satyagrahis who have lighted up the skies, and brought new faith into my heart, now we must proceed to march to the office of the revenue collector. We must gently and with love inform him that since the government of Great Britain denies us our liberties, guaranteed to men in the common and civil law of Great Britain herself, we henceforth deny the government the sweat of our brows, the earnings of our labor. We will not pay taxes, though all the laws of Parliament demand it! Go Syed, Narasimhaiah, Betty, please. Lead the joyous and loving procession! [*The three go off, and Gandhi, Kasturbai and Lakshmi stand singing "Bande Mataram" as the crowd takes it up. Kasturbai puts a colorful shawl over his head.*]

GANDHI. Do you remember the first march we led, in Africa?

KASTURBAI. I was then more frightened.

GANDHI. You are not frightened now at all.

KASTURBAI. But you are.

GANDHI. Lakshmi darling, do I look frightened?

LAKSHMI. No, but I am.

GANDHI. Did you pray when I said to?

LAKSHMI. I prayed, but I was frightened. What if God didn't hear?

GANDHI. [*Laughing broadly*] That is really impossible!

LAKSHMI. [*Stepping forward and pointing*] What is happening there?

KASTURBAI. [*Looking off*] Doubtless some confusion in the rear of the procession only.

LAKSHMI. But I see some policemen beginning to run from the people —

KASTURBAI. [*Straining to see*] Oh, they are only hurrying to the police station. It must be tea-time, isn't it, bapu?

LAKSHMI. Then what are the shouts for?

KASTURBAI. That must be the shouts of the happy marchers.

LAKSHMI. But the marchers are gone past the police station. Those are not happy shouts. And look how the people are running while they shout — and they are surrounding the police station!

KASTURBAI. Oh, that must be a puja. It is festival time, no doubt! [*Narasimhaiah rushes on stage.*]

NARASIMHAIAH. Gandhiji! A mob of stragglers behind the march have done battle with soldiers and police! They have overturned police cars! [*Rushes off*]

SYED. [*Dragging in wounded Indian*] A mob has trapped the British soldiers and police in the station and they have set it on fire!

GANDHI. [*Shouting in utter rage*] Must I throw myself on that fire, to stop you! Must I sacrifice myself!

BETTY. [*Entering dissheveled, helping Madame Kaoosji onstage*] They have gone mad! Fifty men are trapped in the building, burning to a crisp! This woman was caught, her car overturned, her driver hacked to bits. [*She helps Madame to a lying position. Gandhi rushes to help her.*]

MADAM. I knew it would come to this, Mohandas Gandhi! You

105

meant it to come to this, Mohandas Gandhi!

O'DWYER. [*Rushing to stage*] So this is your guarantee, Gandhi? Mayhem!

GANDHI. The rioters are not our satyagrahis, I swear!

SYED. Some of them are—

O'DWYER. They are all what you are—dirty, loathsome, savage, barbaric Indians! [*Calling off*] Sergeant, charge the entire crowd! Blast them down! [*Off*]

NARASIMHAIAH. [*Helping in the Indian soldier, mortally wounded*] They are dying everywhere! The smell of burning flesh fills Bardoli to suffocation!

GANDHI. [*Kneeling by the soldier*] Bring him water!

LAKSHMI. I'll find water. [*Off*]

GANDHI. Soldier, where is the wound? Your face—somehow it shames me.

INDIAN SOLDIER. Is this what you intended for us? At the siding in Patwal, I fell at your feet. Now I am at your feet again. What does it mean? [*He dies.*]

GANDHI. [*A great cry, lurching downstage. Blackout. A single spot builds on Gandhi, prone, his legs drawn up under him. A lonely raga is heard from offstage. Kasturbai comes to kneel behind him, and Lakshmi is at his feet.*] I will take—water—only.

Suggestions for Discussion

1. Read about Ghandi's life and philosophy. Prepare to share this information.

2. With a partner, roleplay a physical or verbal conflict like the ones shown in the drama. Play first the role of the provoking person, and then that of the person provoked. React in a completely non-violent fashion.

3. Discuss the activity above. Which role did you find more difficult to act out? How did it feel to abuse/be abused? What did you learn?

4. In the particular situation depicted in the play, the protest did not remain peaceful. Who or what was responsible for this failure?

5. Can you condone any form of violence? If so, what kind?

6. Ponder the question of ends and means. Are any means justified if the end is good? Is the end irrelevant as long as the means are ethically sound? Give examples for both approaches.

PROBLEMS FACING PEACEMAKERS TODAY

Idolatry

The problems peacemakers face today differ little in essence from those of our forefathers. The question is still whether we see all people as brothers and sisters whose lives are a gift from God and in whom we can find God potentially incarnate or whether like Cain we see them as enemies, competitors, and potential threats to our self-interest whom we therefore threaten to defeat or kill. The question still is whether to worship a God of love and justice or rather to follow idols like the nation state, military or financial power, and a high standard of living.

All the problems we face ultimately rest on idolatry: worship of a false God. Once we approve of shedding human blood for the flag, for oil, for profit, for any "system" be it capitalism or communism — we have strayed from the path of righteousness and turned to idol worship by justifying wicked means. Militarism and worship of the nation state are probably the most blatant forms of idolatry today. In pounds per person, the world has more explosive power than food. Every three weeks, we are spending on arms what it would take to feed the world's hungry for a whole year. This is seen as justified because the survival of the nation state has become an absolute for which any act, no matter how inhumane, appears good.

In the process of idol worship, everyone is victimized. Fear, hate, obsession, apathy, guilt, and hopelessness characterize the worshipper of the idol; hunger, poverty, persecution, and the threat of war burden the oppressed. Those who wrong others deny in themselves the God of love and justice and are therefore punishing themselves. We who build weapons, for example, thereby sacrifice social services and contribute to the world's misery now as well as later. In doing so we deny God and are in the process of killing our own souls.

The tasks for peacemakers today seem overwhelming. How do we deal with the continuing arms race, constant new and old political crises, poverty and hunger, human rights violations, increase in crime, depreciation of human life in general? But although there are many tasks, we lastly have only one fatal error to remedy: worship of a false God. "I am a jealous God," says the Lord. "You shall have no other gods before me." Jesus reemphasized this when he said that we cannot serve two masters. Once we turn to a Creator God, and one that became incarnate in a human being, the ethical choices become clear.

THE MIDDLE MAN

by Celia Lehman

CHARACTERS

W, *People of the World, first speaking choir*
G, *People of God, the second speaking choir*
MM, *The middle man, a young man standing between the two choirs*
V, *Individual voices within given choir*

When the scene opens the PEOPLE OF THE WORLD stand to the right of the stage. Behind them is a U.S. flag and a sword. To the left are the PEOPLE OF GOD. Behind them is a cross and an open Bible. The MIDDLE MAN faces the two choirs. He is seeking to understand both viewpoints.

INTRODUCTION

W. [*A strong voice announces that everyone should stand and pledge allegiance to the flag. Hand is placed over heart and in unison the PEOPLE OF THE WORLD say the Pledge. The PEOPLE OF GOD do not pledge allegiance. The MIDDLE MAN looks both ways and doesn't know which position to take.*]

MM. [*Addressing PEOPLE OF GOD*] You weren't pledging allegiance. Aren't you grateful for America? Have you no loyalty?

G. [*Stand and face cross and Bible. They pledge these words:*] "I pledge allegiance to our Lord Jesus Christ and the everlasting kingdom of which He is Lord and King, one universal nation of every kindred, tribe, and land, moving under God to the end of the age with liberty and salvation for all who receive the Good News."

MM. [*Scratching his head and looking confused*] I'm confused. A Mennonite teacher taught me the flag salute in the school down the road and also led the Lord's prayer. Tell me, what is your objection?

W. [*In unison, shaking heads scornfully.*] Yes, tell us, what is your objection? Isn't America founded on Christian principles?

V-1. Our forefathers came here to worship God.

V-2. Our nation laid its foundation and developed its political and social structure by these spiritual religious ideals.

V-3. The beliefs in God are inscribed on the great public buildings and monuments . . .

V-4. . . . as well as in our historic documents. The Declaration of Independence called on the protection of Divine Providence.

V-5,6,7. Churches were built in order to worship.

V-8. There are chaplains in Congress. Recognition of God and appeal for divine assistance has been accepted procedure for our presidents and leaders.

V-1,2,3. On all our coins are inscribed the words . . .

All. . . . "In God We Trust."

SCENE 1: Glories of America

MM. [*Looking for an answer from the PEOPLE OF GOD*] Say, I thought for a moment I was getting my sides mixed. I thought I was hearing your speech. Can you do one better? Or don't you grab that one either?

G-V-1. I am a natural born citizen of the United States, not by choice but by God's divine leading. I consider it a privilege to be an American. [*PEOPLE OF GOD nod their approval. V-1 looks at MM and W and continues his speech.*] We share your freedoms:

V-2. Freedom of worship. We may gather in peace and worship God the way we choose. The government does not interfere.

V-3. Freedom of speech. We may say what we think. Also we have freedom to print whatever we will.

V-4. Freedom of conscience. Those who find it impossible on the basis of religious convictions to participate in war are exempt from military service. For that I am grateful.

V-5. Freedom of enterprise. Except for Big Business taking over, anyone in America has a chance to venture out and be successful.

V-6. Freedom of fear. Our land has enjoyed a measure of peace. War has not ravaged our land.

V-7. Freedom of family life.

V-8. Freedom of travel.

V-2,3,4. Our country affords a variety of climate, natural wonders, places of attraction.

V-1,5. Our universities offer a diversity of specialized skills.

V-6,7. Our medical system has made tremendous advances in the last decade. With the newest medicines and surgical skills, many people have a new zest for living.

V-8,1. Our schools aim to teach all children, of any race, color, or creed. There may be problems, but efforts are being made to overcome them.

V-2,3,6,7. America is a melting pot, a refuge center. Many people want to immigrate.

V-1. [*Loud and clear*] There is freedom, prosperity, beauty, and opportunity.

ALL. America has given us a good life. The blessings have been many. We are glad to live in America!

MM. [*Getting very excited and waving to both choirs*] Hey, this is great! Just great! I don't see any difference between the two kingdoms. I think you're married. [*With this the young man sings or leads the audience in singing such songs as "My Country 'Tis of Thee," "God Bless America," "This Land is Your Land," or "Mine Eyes have Seen the Glory of the Coming of the Lord."*]

SCENE 2: Civil Religion

G-V-1. Do you know what you have just done?

MM. Who me? Tell me. Did I do something wrong?

G-V-1. It's what we call Civil Religion.

MM. Civil Religion? What's that?

G. Civil Religion is a cloak of righteousness to cover evil deeds.

V-1. You have combined the church and state into one. A religion such as this takes on a form of godliness but denies the power and lordship of Jesus Christ. In it lie many dangers.

MM. Dangers? [*Looking around as though something would spring at him*] What kind of dangers?

G-V-1. I'll try to explain. You say America is Christian?

MM. I always thought so.

G. That means America is great because she is good.

MM. Well, why not?

G-V-1. That makes America the new Israel of God. God helped the Israelites to overcome their enemies . . . the Hittites, Amorites, Moabites, Canaanites, Jebusites . . .

MM. . . . and the Perizittes.

G-V-1. [*Laughing*] Exactly. With God on *our* side we have a right to get rid of *our* enemies . . .

V-2. . . . the American Indian. [*Everyone groans.*] The treatment was shameful.

V-3. . . . We tramped on the Blacks . . . and are still having problems . . .

V-4. . . . destroy the Vietnamese and Cambodians . . .

V-5. . . . fight the Communists and Bolsheviks . . .

V-6,7,8. . . . and are justified in doing so . . .

V-1,2,3,4. . . . because we are right . . .

V-5,6,7,8. . . . and the rest are wrong . . .

V-5. . . . because God is on our side.

MM. [*Agreeing, clarifying G's point of view*] I get it. It's just like on television. If a bad guy gets in the way, get rid of him!

G. Civil religion is a cloak of righteousness to cover evil deeds!

V-7. Have you listened to a politician trying to drum up votes? He will get sentimental nods if he uses the name of God even if he himself does not claim the Lordship of Christ.

111

MM. Yes, I remember Grandma listening to the political speeches to make sure the candidate mentioned God's name. If he didn't [*shakes a finger*] he wouldn't get her vote!

G. Taking a form of godliness but denying the power of God is a dangerous thing.

V-8. This combination of politics and religion using the Bible and Cross is a potent force to exploit and get support for the political system.

MM. Sorry, you lost me on that one. Would you repeat that?

G-V-8. [*Repeats*] This combination of politics and religion using the Bible and Cross is a potent force to exploit and get support for the political system.

MM. I guess I'm dense. Can you give me an illustration?

V-7. One example would be we gained free labor by capturing the African blacks, making them second-rate citizens to work our good plantations and they did not receive their portion in return. The more slave labor there was the bigger the plantations grew.

MM. [*Whistles*] Wow!

G-V-6. A more recent example may be the mineral resources discovered in the ocean. Should it not be shared with poorer countries? Should the rich get richer, and the poor poorer?

MM. If I understand you, you are saying we use Christianity to justify our own ends. A kind of push-over victory over our enemy? [*Pauses*] That makes us sound greedy.

G. Civil Religion is a cloak for petty interests and ugly passions.

SCENE 3: Defining Positions

W. A question. Aren't you a bit harsh? Tell us, where would you be without a government?

MM. [*Shrugs shoulders and looks to the church for an answer*]

G-V-1. A government has a right to exist. The governing authority with its symbol of order [*Points to sword and flag*] is appointed by God to keep order and is a threat only to those who do evil.

W. [*Looking smug and shaking heads in agreement but adding sarcastically*] There is no king but Caesar!

G-V-1. You are forgetting one thing. Who was it that made Caesar? [*Pause*]

V-2. Men should always give God first place in their lives. He is Supreme Ruler of history and deserves our unqualified obedience.

V-8. It was not God's original intention for people to have a king. It was man's sin and rebellion and insistence on his own way that made a place for earthly kings.

G. The Lord is God, He is our King.

V-6. Romans 13:31. Rulers are not a terror to good works, but to the evil.

W. But people need security.

V-1. What would you do with transgressors of the law? Would you let someone come and kill your wife and children?

ALL. And not stand guard?

V-1. Evil deeds deserve punishment . . .

ALL. [*With finality*] . . . and *DEATH*. [*Pause*]

V-4. We protect the good. [*Silence*]

G-V-1. Jesus said, "My Kingdom is not of this world." His main concern was to be faithful to God by which he formed a new kingdom characterized by a new life, loyalty and methods.

V-7. In this kingdom is persuasion,

V-8. forbearance,

V-2. patience,

V-3. non-violence,

V-4. forgiveness,

ALL. and LOVE.

MM. Love even my enemy?

G-V-4. In the Old Testament people went to battle against their enemy. When Jesus came he said, "A new commandment I give unto you, That ye love one another."

V-6. In the Sermon on the Mount he taught that we were to love even our enemy.

MM. Even Caesar? [*Looking at the PEOPLE OF THE WORLD*]

G-ALL. Yes, even Caesar.

V-3. In Romans 13 we read that we are to pay to Caesar the things which are Caesar's and to God the things which are God's, to pray for our government, and respect those in authority.

V-4. Honor and respect, yes. Show reverence? no. Show gratitude and loyalty?

ALL. Yes.

V-4. Worship?

ALL. No.

V-10. When coercion, force, violence, vengeance and killing are norm, we cannot be a part of it.

V-11. Christ forbade his disciples to enforce justice. "Vengeance is mine, I will repay," says the Lord. "It is righteousness, not military power, that exalts a nation."

ALL. We take the teaching of the Bible as our norm.

MM. What does the Bible say?

V-3. I John 2:15,17. Love not the world, neither the things that are in the world . . . and the world passeth away, and the lust thereof: but he that doeth the will of God abideth forever.

V-4. Colossians 1:18. For God is the head of the body, the church: who is the beginning, the firstborn from the dead; that in all things he might have the preeminence.

V-5. I John 4:4. Ye are of God, little children, and have overcome them: because greater is he that is in you, than he that is in the world.

V-6. James 4:1,4. From whence come wars and fightings among you? Come they not hence, even of your lusts that war in your members? Ye adulterers and adulteresses, know ye not that the friendship of the world is enmity with God?

MM. I've been taught that you pay, pray, and obey our government. Are you suggesting you have no connections to these people [*He points to the PEOPLE OF THE WORLD.*] over there?

G-1,4. The Schleitheim Confession of Faith as believed by the **Anabaptist forefathers 450 years ago said, "Ways of the government** are ways of the flesh. . . . Have no part with them."

ALL. Our citizenship is in heaven.

V-1. The Sermon on the Mount found in Matthew 5, 6, 7, does work. For 20 years William Penn lived peaceably with the Indians. The Quakers practiced these non-violent methods and the Indians knew they did not carry weapons. Not one person was injured during his rule. But when the white men came with guns, the scalping began.

A solo voice stands and sings, "I'm a Pilgrim, I'm a Stranger," or the group may sing any song emphasizing heaven as our goal. "I Love They Kingdom Lord," "Wayfaring Stranger," etc.]

SCENE 4: Conflicts

The scene changes from quiet to that of conflict, clashing as tension builds. A drum beat with strong militaristic beat is heard. Flags start waving, a real celebration is in the making within the PEOPLE OF THE WORLD. Money flows freely for things to celebrate.

At the same time the PEOPLE OF GOD become more and more apathetic. They do not really listen or participate in the celebration but they lose their vitality. This is evident by having them turn their back. Their prayers are hypocritical.

This dual play leaves the MIDDLE MAN in a state of confusion. He looks one way, then the other, but only gets more confused. At the end he sits down and puts his hand over his head and is crushed by it all.

W. [*As the drum beats people clap and cheer. They march in time to the music, donnings flags, all in a very festive mood.*]

V-1. Behold our country's heroes!

V-2. George Washington, Father of Our Country!

ALL. Yea, Man.

V-5. First in war, [*salute*] first in peace, [*finger in V signal*] First in the hearts of his countrymen. [*Hand over heart*]

ALL. First in war, [*salute*] first in peace, [*finger in V signal*] First in the hearts of his countrymen. [*hand over heart*]

V-1. Abraham Lincoln.

ALL. Yea, man.

V-5. Saved our country.

ALL. Yes, he did.

V-5. Saved the Union.

ALL. Yes, he did. Yea-a-a MAN!

V-6. Patrick Henry, fearless patriot spoke out boldly against England.

ALL. Yea, man.

V-6. Urged colonists to defend their rights and freedom.

V-7. "Give me liberty or give me death."

ALL. "Give me liberty or give me death."

V-8. Robert E. Lee, humble leader.

ALL. Ah, man. [*In more subdued tones*]

V-8. With sword and Bible led his people to victory in spite of defeat.

ALL. V-I-C-T-O-R-Y [*Spell it out, then speak.*] VICTORY! [*Cheer and yell*]

G. We must not listen to them. It is not right to worship heroes, making them equal to Jesus Christ. It is God alone who deserves our worship. [*PEOPLE OF GOD turn face from the world and bow heads in act of prayer. The world clamors for attention but only an echo of defense is heard from the hypocritical prayers.*] [*In sing-songy tones*] Thank you, God, for your blessing, Mashed potatoes, turkey, dressing, OOdles of noodles, giblets and gravy, Cranberry salad to tickle the palate. Sassafras tea with pie a la mode.

W. We need you, man. [*Pointing to the MIDDLE MAN*] You're our style. Fight in the army. Make life worthwhile.

MM. Me? [*Shrugs shoulders and puts hands to chest*]

G-V-6. Thank you, God we're not like the radicals who do not respect their country, or themselves. . .

W. We need youth. We need power. Defend our country in this hour.

G. Thank you God, we are not like the world. We honor and praise you . . .

W. See the world with Uncle Sam.

G-V-3,4. God's people cannot take up arms to fight.

W. We take care of our people

V-1. Titles I, II, XI

V-7. Medicare for the aged

V-8. Old age pension

V-2. Social security and welfare

115

V-5. Child abuse programs

V-8. Red Cross

V-10. Aid for disabled veterans

ALL. We take good care of our people.

MM. [*Palms up*] So? [*Looking to PEOPLE OF GOD with no response.*]

G. Thank you for our large families. And that you have caused us to prosper.

V-4,5. And we've been so blessed since we sent Grandma to the old people's home. We're so glad she's got a nice place to live.

W. [*Very sarcastic voice*] . . . and if she doesn't live to long you can inherit her farm! Pray she doesn't live long . . .

G-V-1. Thank you for the social security check and that our children who can't find jobs can be on unemployment compensation . . .

V-3. Thank you that we can pay taxes for schools, roads, and not for suicidal world conflicts . . .

W. Vote for the new president . . . New blood will make a new nation . . .

G-V-5,6,7. **Thank you, God, that the mask was torn off, showing corruption.**

Watergate and the truth was exposed.

W-V-4,5,6,7. We got to have courage. We got to be brave. Never give up, never give up, never give up!

V-1,2,3,8. Our country is the world power. Let's keep it that way.

V-1. We are the first.

V-2. We are the best.

V-3. We got to fight to win.

ALL. Never give up, never give up, never give up!

G. And about the telephone tax, Lord. It supports war. You have noticed we haven't been paying it?

W. We have the right to eat more protein. We're the ones that produce it.

G. The world feels so little shame to be so selfish . . . to kill others . . . help us not to be that way . . .

W. [*Becoming annoyed by the church's apathy. Addressing PEOPLE OF GOD*] What happens when good men stand idly by? Don't you see the crisis?

V-1. Smothering smoke and smog, [*coughing and clearing of throats*]

V-2. People clawing each other because of busing orders, [*fist fights*]

V-3. Discrimination against women, [*Women hold up hands in protest.*]

V-4. Chicanos living in the ghettos,

V-5. Violence in the city, [*screaming*]

V-6. Assassinations, [*Gun shots and screams are heard.*]

V-7. Hospitals full of disabled veterans, and mentally
V-8. Theft because of drug addiction,
V-9. Alcoholics sleeping in the gutter,
V-10. Unemployment, poor housing, people moving, eve
V-11. Abortions, gonorrhea
V-12. The continuing exile of our promising young men in Canada
V-13. Property being destroyed in vandalism
V-14. Prisons full and overflowing
ALL. We gotta fight it with *violence*. They gotta learn who's boss.
G-V-6. Thank you for the comforts of life, for amusements . . . for **my dear wife and lovely family** . . .
MM. [*Near tears*] What about it? What are you going to do about it? [*He looks both ways but no one pays any attention to him. At this point he slumps to a sitting position, hands over his head. Looking up briefly*] Where can I turn? Who has the truth? [*All become deathly silent.*]

SCENE 5: Call to Repentance

A voice is heard over the loud speaker as though it could be the voice of God. It should be a strong, forceful, older voice, clearly enunciated words. The MIDDLE MAN gradually raises his head, looks both ways and eventually up. During this time the lights become dimmer and dimmer and a spot light appears on the MIDDLE MAN at the end of the speech.

Oh, evil men, your transgressions rise before me like a wall so high I can no longer see your good works. I cannot stand to hear your songs. I hate your show and pretense.

What have you done? Two terrible evils characterize your lives. You love ease and luxury and you lack love and mercy. You worship at the shrine of Materialism. This is your God. Where have you denied yourselves one thing you wanted in order to give more?

Woe to you who are secure in the United States of America who put security first in armaments and governments of men!

Woe to you who love to sit by your stereos and TV's more than to kneel in prayer and study my Word!

Woe to you who eat three meals a day, and demand morning and midnight snacks, with little concern for the starving and hungry world!

How have you returned to the Lord for bringing you into a good land? By taking its goodness and godlessness to yourselves.

Know this, you will be crushed by your comforts and conveniences. The perils of plenty shall devour you.

I want holy living, not lukewarmness. I want truthful living, not nicely worded resolutions.

I have heard it all. But know this. While it is day decide to repent. Only then will judgement be stayed. And let justice roll down like waters and righteousness like a mighty stream.

During the reading of the above script the PEOPLE OF GOD begin to show penitence, and turn to face the audience and once more ban together as one group. The PEOPLE OF THE WORLD are now subdued but turn their backs to the audience to show they do not accept the need for repentance, except for a very few who repent and move toward the PEOPLE OF GOD who embrace them and they become a part of their group. When the spotlight appears on the MIDDLE MAN, he picks up the Bible, opens it and reads II Chronicles 7:14.]

MM. If my people, which are called by my name, shall humble themselves, and pray, and seek my face, and turn from their wicked ways, then will I hear from heaven, and will forgive their sins, and will heal their land.

G-V-8. Surely God was in this place!

V-1,2. The Holy Spirit is moving among us to rise up at a time like this.

V-3,4,5. Lord, what is it you want us to do?

[*The PEOPLE OF GOD get out their Bibles and begin to search the scripture. Various people find verses and read them. The rest listen and agree.*]

G-V-2. Acts 5:29. We must obey God more than human beings.

V-5. Joshua 24:15. Choose you this day whom ye will serve;

ALL. We will serve God.

W-V-1. Kissinger was urging all Americans for increased support so the U.S. would stay first in world power. He said, "I don't want to live in a world where we are second best."

W-ALL. We agree! We must stay in first place at any cost.

G-V-6. [*Pointing to the new members*] Here is a verse for you. Ephesians 2:19. Now therefore you are no more strangers and foreigners but fellow-citizens with the saints, and of the household of God. [*There are gestures of acceptance.*]

V-3. This is a long passage. I will take a few thoughts to share from Romans 12:1-21 [*Others turn to it and share ideas.*] Be kindly affectionate to one another with brotherly love . . . not slothful in business;

V-8. patient in tribulation; constant in prayer . . .

V-1. distributing to the necessity of saints; given to hospitality.

V-4. Bless them which persecute you.

V-3. Recompense to no man evil for evil. Provide things honest in the sight of all people.

V-7. *Therefore if thine enemy hungers, feed him, if he thirsts,*

V-5,6,7. give him drink;

V-2. And the last part of verse 21 . . .

ALL. Be not overcome of evil, but overcome evil with good.

[*As they read a spirit of unity and understanding is beginning to form within the group. They give knowing glances what is happening to them.*]

G-V-1. Isaiah 6:8. I heard a voice of the Lord saying, "Whom shall I send, and who will go for us?" Then said I, "Here am I, send me."

VARIOUS VOICES. Lord, send me. Lord, send me. And me. And me. [*A solo voice may sing "So Send I You," "It May Not Be on the Mountain High," or another missionary song.*]

MM. May I ask where all of you are going?

G-V-1. A good question. It's time we stop to see who we are and what we have.

W-V-3,4,5. Ask those people who live under Communism what it's like in Viet Nam . . .

V-5. . . . Angola

V-6. . . . Cuba

V-3. . . . Cambodia

V-7. . . . Poland or Czechoslovkia

W-ALL. Would you want Communism to take over our country?

G-V-1. Certainly not! But we believe there are ways of combatting it.

[*The PEOPLE OF GOD look at each other for a moment then begin to move about until they find their interest groups. Various leaders emerge bearing signs they can see but the audience cannot. As they move into place they sing, "They Will Know We Are Christians by Our Love," or another service-oriented hymn. As each group gets ready to share they turn the sign for the audience to see and begin their speech. Much enthusiasm is shown in the projects, with much gesturing.*]

MM. I believe they are trying to say something. What are you doing?

GROUP I. [*Raise a sign FOOD*] We are the farmers. We produce the food.

G-ALL. Food?

V-5,6,7. Food is one of the major exports of the United States. It must not be used as a weapon of foreign policy.

V-2. Mark Hatfield said that we consume 40% of the world resources but have only 6% of its population. If this food would be equally distributed there would be no hunger. Equal distribution is the only thing that will save our nation. I say, "Start right here at home."

119

V-4. Edgar Stoesz, in the World Hunger Conference, reported that Americans use 40% more food than a child in the third world. 2/3 of the world goes to bed hungry every night.

V-3. If the world now has 4 billion people you can imagine what the needs of the future will be!

G-ALL. Yes, farmers. You're at the right spot. Hang in there. Develop the agricultural resources.

W-V-1. Easy for farmers to talk about food. They always have food to eat.

V-2. Any other ideas?

MM. Here comes another group.

GROUP II. [*Erect the sign A SIMPLE LIFE*] We are the consumers.

V-1. We confess we have been guilty of affluence at the expense of our less fortunate brothers.

V-2. We have decided we could take a lesson from our Amish neighbors. They are not slaves to progress. They respect nature, work with vigor, live a simple life style, and are surrounded by loyalty of family.

MM. And ride a buggy?

V-2. What they lose in time they make up in fellowship.

V-3. We need to return to the thought pattern of our Anabaptist forefathers.

MM. And what is that?

V-3. To be content with simple needs. The rest must go to relieve suffering, enrich humanity, to build the spiritual kingdom.

V-4. I could do with a few less pounds. [*Pointing to stomach.*]

ALL. We all could.

W-All. [*Angrily*] You quiet sheltered people. What do you know about the threat of nuclear annihilation?

V-6. If we depended on you for progress where would America be today?

G-V-5. Did you know that in the United States we use more gasoline for leisure than most countries do on essentials?

V-6. I heard about a boy in India who when asked what he wanted most replied, "A meal today and to go to school tomorrow."

V-1. I'm a realist. I'm sticking to my job. But I'll include the church in my will. That will help.

V-2. [*Combatting the statement*] Did you know you could give your money to church-related institutions now and let them do the worrying about the taxes? They use it to promote education, medical work and the things you yourself want to sponsor. You live off the interest.

V-1. We should all work together in these benevolent causes.

V-3,4,5. Look, we made a slogan.

REST. Go ahead, tell us.

V-3. I found this slogan and posted it by my kitchen sink. It says: "Make it do. Wear it out. Use it up. Do without."

REST. Very good. Say it again so we can learn it.

V-3. [*Says one line — all repeat, etc.*]

W-V-1. Pat yourselves on the back! Liz Taylor alone gives millions to benevolent causes. You aren't the only people who give.

MM. A simple life style isn't such a bad idea; I'm getting tired of the "Rat Race" myself.

GROUP III. [*Raise the sign FREEDOM FOR THE OPPRESSED*] To many people freedom has not yet come. We have decided to identify with the enslaved.

MM. Oh, oh, a crack in the Liberty Bell!

V-1. We'll try to reach men, women and children who need to be fed, clothed and educated.

V-2. Alcoholics should no longer be anonymous. They need to be redeemed. They need Christ but they also need jobs. As Christians we will receive, hire, and try to help them.

V-3. There are juvenile offenders. We will seek to provide a resource of trained staff geared to work on their problems.

V-4. The radicals. We'll listen to them as individuals. They are saying something we need to hear.

V-1,2,3. We'll redeem and restore offenders to the church and society in all ways possible. Forgive them and show them there is a better way of life.

V-1,2,3,4. We will build bridges of acceptance!

G-ALL. We'll help you. We can all show love and compassion. [*They sing "They Will Know We are Christians by Our Love."*]

W-V-5. Good idea. Let's see what you do with people who preach something you disagree with!

MM. Maybe the next group will have an answer to that one.

GROUP IV. [*Come with the sign EVANGELISM*]

MM. Um. You're busy. What are you doing?

V-1. Preaching the Up-Side-Down Kingdom.

MM. Up-Side-Down Kingdom?

V-1. Yes, the concept of love and meekness Jesus talked about could reform the world.

V-2. If violence breeds violence, then love should produce love.

V-3,4. It is the work of the church to preach the gospel of Jesus to those who have never heard it.

V-5. Before we go out to the world we need to establish what we believe, teach our own children, and live a life beyond reproach.

MM. That sounds like a difficult task to me.

V-3. We confess we do not always live as we should, but with God's help we mean to direct our energies to the service of the Prince of Peace.

MM. How will you do that?

V-3. Through discussion groups . . .

V-4. through the printed page . . .

V-5. become familiar with the areas of tension in the world, racial, social, and economic . . .

V-6. and lend a ministry of reconciliation in a broken world.

V-1. Too long we have been pulling *weeds*. It's time we started planting *seeds*. You can't empty a man unless you fill him with good. Then nurture him until he comes to full bloom.

MM. That is an interesting idea. What kind of seeds are you talking about?

V-1. Seeds of repentance

V-2. seeds of equality

V-3. seeds of freedom

V-4. seeds of peace.

ALL. Yes, we'll fill their minds with good.

W-V-1. [*Shaking heads in disapproval*] It won't work. It's too idealistic. Let's be realistic. The answer is to increase the police force, build up more armament. It's the only language people understand.

G-V-3,4,5. Without a vision people perish.

V-1. We do not form our own ethics. God has spoken. We need to be obedient. God will work things out for us.

MM. I see another group forming. What do you have to say?

GROUPE V. [*Rise with their sign LOVE IN WORK CLOTHES*] Our bodies like to work.

V-1. Christians have always responded in time of crisis and we are no exceptions to the rule.

V-2. After World War I our people started relief work in India. A missionary project was under way.

V-6. In the 1920's the MCC led a famine relief in Russia.

V-3. After World War II the Voluntary Service for young people was started. This became the forerunner of the Peace Corps. They also saw the plight of the mental hospitals and did something to reform the conditions.

V-4. So today if we don't agree with what our government is doing we have to come up with an alternate way.

G-ALL. Oh! Tell us more.

V-1. As a minority group we can readily identify with other minority groups.

V-2. We can work in the field on how to stay healthy, discover cures for disease, and find food substitutes.

V-3. We'll deal with primary problems — not so much bringing food to the hungry but help them build their own dams, go and show them agricultural practices.

V-4. We could study oceanography and find a fresh water supply.

V-5. You hear so much about pollution. Why couldn't we be the ones who find the solution to save our plants and animals?

V-6. And do something about the noise pollution in big cities.
[*They begin marching around ready to tackle anything and singing, "They Will Know We are Christians By Our Love."*]

W. [*Scratching heads in unbelief*] Perhaps these people do have answers.

V-8. I wonder why they are so hesitant to share them?

V-1. Wonder why there are so few letters to our congressmen?

V-2. I wonder if they know that protest marches do not go by unnoticed?

V-3. What I've seen so far seems like an honest effort.

V-4. Do you suppose there is anything to it?

GROUP VI. [*Hold up YEAR OF JUBILEE. The Piano is playing "Hark the Song of Jubilee," or a group could sing it.*]

MM. Hey! Who are you?

V-1. We've come to celebrate the year of jubilee.

G-ALL. Year of Jubilee?

V-1. We'll plant a tree as a symbol of life. It will grow and blossom.

V-2,3,4. We've got these symbols: a crown, flame, cross, dove, plant, Bible. We're going to develop an artistic design to make people aware of our selfless love, spiritual fullness, and servanthood.

MM. What will it look like?

V-2. We haven't designed it yet, but it will be good.

G-[*All clap their hands. Everyone sings with gusto "The Work is Thine," "Come, Come, Ye Saints" or similar songs to show this is God's work.*]

MM. It doesn't look like we're going to solve all the problems but we'll have to draw it to a close.

G-V-1. [*Announces to the audience*] Let's pray. Please stand, and join us in the prayer of St. Francis of Assisi. [*Or he may ask the audience to turn to page 741 in THE MENNONITE HYMNAL to pray this prayer in unison.*]

G-V-1. Lord, make me an instrument of Thy peace; Where there is hatred,

G. Let me sow love;

V-1. Where there is injury,

G. Pardon.

V-1. Where there is despair,

G. Hope.

V-1. Where there is darkness,

G. Light.

V-1. And where there is sadness,

G. Joy.

V-1. Divine Master, Grant that I may not so much seek to be consoled

G. As to console;

V-1. To be understood
G. As to understand;
V-1. To be loved
G. As to love;
ALL. For it is in giving that we receive; It is in pardoning that we are pardoned; And it is in dying that we are born to eternal life. Amen.

[*The audience may participate in a closing hymn.*]

Suggestions for Discussion

1. Divide a chalkboard into two halves by drawing a vertical line; on the left, write down convictions and goals expressed by national leaders of the past and present that you deeply appreciate and that do not conflict with your beliefs. On the **right, list convictions and goals which trouble you as a Christian.**

2. Civil religion, in the play, is defined as "a cloak of righteousness to cover evil deeds." Do you agree? Can you illustrate this? What are some examples you remember from the play?

3. In the section entitled "Conflicts," the church is shown as having become self-righteous and apathetic about the world's problems. Have you seen the church or people in the church display this attitude? Can you explain why it is time for confession and repentance?

4. The last section of the play shows the people of God taking actions to live out their faith. They call for sharing food, living simply, identifying with the enslaved, and doing voluntary service. Break down each of these actions into manageable steps we can take a) in our community, b) in our nation, and c) on an international level.

KING MIDAS III

by Ingrid Rogers

CHARACTERS

KING MIDAS
REPRESENTATIVE
PRIESTESS
SHEPHERD

SCENE 1

At the palace, the king receives the representative of the people.

KING. Well, what news do you bring? Are the citizens of our country satisfied with their lives and with me, their ruler?

REPRESENTATIVE. Your Majesty King Midas, the people love and honor you because you always aim to do what is best for them. However, all is not well in our country. The people are dissatisfied.

KING. Dissatisfied? Why? What do they need? Don't they have food and shelter? Aren't we at peace with neighboring countries and don't we have the law to maintain justice?

REPRESENTATIVE. The people have all that, great King, but their dreams go further. They want big cars, colored TV's, indoor swimming pools, beautiful houses with plush carpets, a wide variety of luxury goods, and plenty of money to buy all that.

KING. [*Disappointed*] I am afraid I know of no way to help my people. Remember what happened to my grandfather? According to his wish, all that he touched turned to gold — even his daughter. In his greed he destroyed himself and his family. I don't want to repeat his mistake.

REPRESENTATIVE. There is another solution to our problem, King Midas. The wise men held counsel last night and suggested that you turn to our great god, Mulloch, who has the power to grant us wealth. Do not ask for the golden touch. Ask that he give us *oil*. If we have oil, we can fulfill all our dreams. Go to his temple and ask for the favor, for the sake of your people's happiness!

KING. I have always put the interest of my subjects first. Therefore, I shall go to Mulloch and do as you said.

SCENE 2

At the temple, the priestess performs ceremonial tasks before the altar of Mulloch. The altar might be set with items such as a rifle and a poster of a starving child. The King enters.

PRIESTESS. I know what brings you here, King Midas. The god has decided to grant your wish. Starting tomorrow, all your subjects will have access to an abundance of oil.

KING. How grateful I am to Mulloch for his generosity! Now my people will be happy and willing to worship him! [*He bows and turns to leave.*]

PRIESTESS. Wait, Midas. The god demands a sacrifice for his favor.

KING. Of course we will sacrifice. Now let me go and tell the citizens the good new. [*He leaves.*]

PRIESTESS. Midas! Midas! Don't you want to hear about the details of the sacrifice? [*King is gone.*] Oh, miserable, wretched humans!

SCENE 3

Back at the palace.

KING. How proud I am of my achievements. My reign has been ten years of bliss. Never has a country seen such wealth, never have people enjoyed such a high standard of living. The oil has given us all we needed, all we wanted and will ever want. [*Representative has come in.*]

REPRESENTATIVE. Your Majesty!

KING. Speak, friend. What news do you bring from the people?

REPRESENTATIVE. Not good news, King Midas. There seems to be less oil all of a sudden. And the citizens' dreams have grown bigger! We need more oil, much more.

KING. Why do you suppose the generosity of Mulloch is suddenly ceasing?

REPRESENTATIVE. I do not know for sure. But yesterday at the counsel meeting the wise men recalled that the sacrifice for Mulloch was never performed. Maybe he has turned his wrath against us!

KING. You are right. We completely forgot about the sacrifice. I shall go to the temple at once and inquire the details for the ceremony.

SCENE 4

At the temple of Mulloch.

PRIESTESS. It has been a long time since I saw you here, King Midas. Why did you forget your promise? The god is angry. It is

126

high time that you satisfy him.

KING. We are ready to give whatever he asks to show our indebtedness and gratitude.

PRIESTESS. Hear then, Mortal, the words of the god. Within the next year, each family must sacrifice the first born son.

KING. *What*? Is it possible? What an atrocious crime! You cannot ask that of us!

PRIESTESS. The god Mulloch has spoken. He will not settle for less.

KING. But the people will never comply! They love their children! How can they murder them?

PRIESTESS. You have not heard all. Mulloch also demands the first born sons of each family in your neighboring countries. [*The King sits down and buries his face in his hands.*] But here is a consolation. You do not have to kill within the family. Let the sons of each country go and kill the others. You are committed, Midas. The worship of Mulloch means sacrifice in human blood. [*Priestess leaves. King remains in position of woe.*]

SCENE 5

Open field. The King is still brooding. Shepherd enters and sees the King.

SHEPHERD. You look distressed. Can I help you?

KING. I am the most wretched ruler. The god Mulloch, in whom we trusted, has asked us to sacrifice our first born sons in return for the oil we want from him. It is too late for help. I have brought ruin over my people!

SHEPHERD. I think I know an alternative.

KING. You? Who are you?

SHEPHERD. Just an unimportant Hebrew shepherd. But I trust in a God more powerful than Mulloch.

KING. You mean, if we turned to *your* God, Mulloch could not harm us and would not destroy our children?

SHEPHERD. Your children will be saved.

KING. What a wonderful bit of news! All will be well!

SHEPHERD. But wait. Service of my God will also mean a sacrifice.

KING. You frighten me!

SHEPHERD. You have nothing to fear. But no one can serve two masters. If you want to rely on the help of God, and save your children, you must learn no longer to rely on Mulloch's favors. Give up your wild dreams which put luxury above human lives! Request no more oil!

KING. But the people . . .

SHEPHERD. The people will have to make up their mind, one way or the other. [*Shepherd leaves.*]

SCENE 6

King addresses audience.

KING. Dear subjects, I come before you with a choice we have to make and make soon. Do you want oil and the luxuries it brings, or do you want to save the lives of your children? I turn to you, trembling, hoping that your choice will be a wise one. Tomorrow, your representative will let me know your decision.

Suggestions for Discussion

1. The play, of course, has a fairy tale setting. But in one sense the message is realistic. Can you formulate the "grain of truth" in it?

2. Name some modern gods we worship with enough dedication that human lives are not too great a sacrifice.

3. Do we also face the choice King Midas III places before his people at the end?

HAGWINE AND GENEVA

by Kate Maloy

CHARACTERS

KING RONEGAN. *King of Amberwavia.*
SIR HAGWINE (later known as CASANDER). *Chief Knight and Advisor to the King.*
LADY GENEVA. *Lady-in-Waiting to Queen Lenox of Haviland.*
CARPENTER. *An impertinent artisan who appears to Sir Hagwine in dreams.*
SPIRITS. *Five shadowy figures called brothers and sisters by the carpenter.*
QUEEN LENOX OF HAVILAND. *Wife of King Ronegan. Queen of Amberwavia.*
KING BREADNYET. *King of Rushland.*
A nameless Rushland footsoldier.

PROLOGUE

This entertainment begins with a medieval monarch and his chief knight — King Ronegan and Sir Hagwine — meeting to discuss the battle in which they are currently engaged. Ronegan and Hagwine are leaders of the thriving and enlightened Amberwavians, a God-fearing people by their own description who in fact have no particular reason to fear a God who has blessed them with abundance. This blessing they see as evidence of their inherent goodness. Their foes are the inhabitants of Rushland, a boggy and benighted country to the east, led by the beetle-browed King Breadnyet. The Rushlanders are not so fortunate as the Amberwavians; their history has been a perpetual struggle, in a harsh climate, to glean a living from their ungenerous bogs and tangled forests.

The battle that rages is, in terms of ideology, between the Godly and the godless (according to the Amerwavians) or the greedy and the just (according to the Rushlanders). In practical terms it is a contest between the hungry from Rushland and the well-fed from Amberwavia. The Amberwavians have enough grain to feed both themselves and the Rushlanders, but they fear that a well-nourished Rushland, like an overindulged peasantry, would become willful. They prefer to deal with a needy country to whom — in exchange for tithes and timber — they can trade just enough grain to keep them cooperative. King Ronegan does not seem to consider the current attack by Rushland a refutation of this theory. He and his loyal followers see the Amberwavian policy as the only way to handle a race of people who, by the evidence of their misfortune and deprivation, are out of grace with God and must therefore be inherently evil.

The Rushlanders, for their part, resent being characterized in this way, and in their determination to prove their worth and righteousness would seize the Amberwavians' grain by force and distribute it, according to their definition of equity, among all people — including, they say, the Amberwavians, who just can't seem to embrace the idea. This just distribution of grain would exact a price from all the recipients, of course. They would have to pledge fealty to King Breadnyet and support his plan to raise the masses and lower the nobility (leaving royalty in place) until all in his care are equal and have no cause for unrest. King Breadnyet does not appear to see any inconsistency with this plan in the fact that the Amberwavians — who are to the Rushlanders as the nobility is to the masses — do not wish to give up a large portion of their grain and hence their power.

Nevertheless, theoretical loopholes aside, this is what the battle is about. The Rushlanders are after the Amberwavians' fields of grain, which the Amberwavians believe are theirs because God is on their side. Unfortunately, the course of battle begins to favor the Rushlanders, heralding an unprecedented and unthinkable outcome.

ACT ONE

SCENE 1

King Ronegan's counsel chamber, at dusk after a day of heavy losses in battle. Hagwine and the King confer.

HAG. The forces of evil are strong, Your Majesty. We must pray for strength from the first Christian soldier, who came to earth with a sword. We must purge our hearts of fear and our minds of unclean thoughts unworthy of Him. We must temper our own swords with righteousness!

RON. Soon we will have something better than a sword . . .

HAG. That isn't hard, damn clumsy things!

RON. . . . better than a lance or halberd. Better even than a crossbow! Our artisans have prayed, at our command, for inspiration. They have conceived a weapon the likes of which the world has never known. It will hurl missiles of unimaginable power! No armor known will protect the godless against its devastation! The puny arrows of our enemy will be weak as straws!

HAG. [*Amazed.*] But, Your Majesty, how can this be? How can any weapon improve on the crossbow? By its very shape it is a holy instrument of holy war! Surely nothing can match it. My mind is staggered!

RON. Ah, Hagwine, wait until you see! They call this weapon a longbow. It has the simplicity of true genius. It is taller than a man, made of wych-elm or yew, and its length imparts a power that sends arrows through mail like needles through silk. It has tremendous range and keeps its user clear of harm. It can kill a horse at 200 yards, it can penetrate oak four inches thick. It is lighter than a crossbow, shoots deadlier, sharper arrows, and best of all it loads six times as fast!

HAG. [*Awestruck.*] Oh, truly inspired! Only divine light could show our humble artisans such a weapon — and just in time to save our lives and fields! [*Excitedly.*] How many longbows have we? Can we use them at dawn, when battle resumes?

RON. [*Holds up a hand to hush Hagwine.*] Look, here comes the Lady Geneva. Not a word, you know how she is.
[*Enter the Lady Geneva, serene and stately, a lady-in-waiting to the Queen. She bows to King Ronegan, nods to Sir Hagwine.*]

RON and HAG. Good evening, Lady.

HAG. [*Smirking a bit.*] You're looking fair, my Lady, as always.

GEN. [*Politely.*] Thank you, Sir Hagwine. [*Turns to King Ronegan.*] Your Majesty, I bring a request from your Lady, Queen Lenox of Haviland. She is preparing for the evening feast and begs to know which robe you plan to wear, that she might choose her gown, the banners, and the table linens accordingly.

RON. Then I must go, of course. Visual harmony before our people in time of war is no small matter. [*Whispers to Sir Hagwine.*] Till dawn, Sir Hagwine, and mind those unclean thoughts! [*Exits with a wink.*]

SCENE 2

Same scene as before.

GEN. [*Formally.*] The battle turns for Rushland?

HAG. Oh, my Lady, you must never say so! Tomorrow will be a rout. Amberwavia rests on the eve of glorious victory! Here true and holy supremacy is soon to be restored!

GEN. I will never understand, Sir Hagwine, how rout can be holy and the shedding of blood glorious. Do you not kill God's image when you kill a man?

HAG. [*With a wise smile.*] My Lady, you are too gentle for the real world's grim and unrelenting realities. That is why knights and footsoldiers must keep the infidel far from our gates, that you and your sisters, and the children whom in spirit you resemble, can be spared that sight.

GEN. [*Ruefully shaking her head.*] I see it always in my mind. You cannot spare me, for my imagination follows every arrow and feels its sharpness. In that I am different from a child, who only sees its flight and does not understand that human targets leak blood instead of straw. Even so, some of the little ones dream of mayhem at night — those who do not dream of glory.

HAG. Then, my Lady, you must wish with all your heart to see the battle over. [*Pauses.*] I beg you, give me your colors to wear to war, that war might sooner end.

GEN. How would that speed the longed-for peace, Sir Hagwine?

HAG. Your scarf on my sword-hilt would remind me of our holy cause. A token from one so kind, whom I would lovingly protect, would urge me to greater courage and, through me, spark my men to bolder acts.

GEN. For which they could be maimed or killed, and I would be the cause.

HAG. [*Passionately.*] No, my Lady, you would honor them! And me!

GEN. [*Considering.*] What color should I give you, then? What would you say to red? [*Draws a red scarf from her belt and tentatively holds it out to him.*]

HAG. Yes! Red for heart's courage. A fine and noble choice! [*Reaches out for the scarf.*]

GEN. [*Looking doubtful, putting the red scarf back.*] Or red for blood, spilled ceaselessly from the limbs and breasts of the world's best youth. No, red I cannot give. White, perhaps. [*Takes a white scarf from her belt.*]

HAG. Very well, white then. For purity of heart and spirit, which strengthens us against the hated enemy. [*Holds out his hand for it.*]

GEN. [*Sighing.*] I think not white, after all. White turns red too quickly, as purity is stained by hatred. [*Puts the white scarf back.*]

HAG. [*Growing impatient, touching the end of a blue scarf tucked in her belt.*] Then blue, perhaps, my Lady? This simple, vibrant blue for loyalty? Surely you cannot object to blue. Or loyalty.

GEN. [*Puzzling.*] But I myself am loyal to only one monarch, Hagwine, and He is the Prince of Peace. How then could I tie blue to your weapon of war?

HAG. Your Prince of Peace came with a sword, my Lady. Or did you forget?

GEN. No, Hagwine, I am not permitted to forget. I see swords drawn endlessly in anger and in fear of His example. He forged those swords in sorrow; they are fashioned out of His own refusal to wield one Himself. He was powerless to force peace on men who did not want it. They love their glory more, which He foresaw, and wield their swords more fiercely in resistance of His ways. Oh, surely, Hagwine, you never thought He wanted men to hate and fight? Not in the name, or honoring the word, of One who only loved, even those who murdered him?

HAG. For which we must avenge his blood with blood of the faithless!

GEN. Pay for blood with blood? Oh, Hagwine!

HAG. Lady, you fail to see! And clearly you mean to refuse my request. Why could you not say so?

GEN. [*Sadly.*] You mistake me, Sir Hagwine. I mean to honor your request, and meant to all along. I had only to choose a color, which I have done at last.

HAG. Then you did not tease, my Lady, and I beg your pardon. [*Begins to strut a bit.*] What color have you chosen, then?

GEN. [*Gravely.*] Black, Sir Hagwine, to wear on your left arm. [*Draws out a black scarf, ties it on his arm.*] I can in conscience send the color of death and mourning into battle with you.

HAG. [*Tightlipped, jerking away from her.*] You dishonor me, Lady.

GEN. You do that yourself, Sir, killing your brothers.

HAG. [*Furious, tearing the scarf off.*] Women should not judge what they do not know! The Rushland warriors know nothing of honor and do not observe the laws of chivalry! Their cunning and savagery cannot be imagined by a naive mind like yours! Would you have all Rushland at your chamber door? They are godless and half-wild!

GEN. [*Mildly.*] I do not think all Rushland wants to enter my chamber door. I believe they would prefer to enter the kitchens. And as for godlessness, what good does it do *you* to have a God if you fail to obey His word? "Love your enemies. Do good to them that hate you."

HAG. I love them, Lady, I assure you. I have in mind the state of their darkened souls when I beat the fear of God into them, and I do them good when I bloody their hard heads.

GEN. [*Musing.*] I see, Hagwine. You love a thing by beating and killing it. How do you hate, then? You must hate tenderly. With prayers for the object of your feeling. Then you are not so far from God as I thought! Merely give up love, and strive for perfect hate! You will cause great joy in Heaven!

HAG. You utter what is dangerous, Lady Geneva. A lady who looks so fair should not speak foul.

GEN. Does it follow, then, that a lady who looks foul should not speak fair?

HAG. Take heed, Lady! Your words sound treasonous. Are you a lady at all? You cannot be; no lady would make me forget chivalry.

GEN. Oh, knights know all about *ladies*, Sir Hagwine, and nothing at all about *women*! It is our great loss, and yours. I wish you knew us as we are. [*Shrugs.*] But then you wouldn't be knights. And chivalry would die! [*Exits.*]

HAG. By God, her tongue is faster than a snake's! But black is her true color, I swear, blackhearted witch! She'll burn if she's not wiser. No woman thinks like that. She must have help from hell. Imagine a world of thinking women, quick and clever but not wise. For all her words she cannot comprehend war, and what could be clearer than the need for war?

SCENE 3

Later that night. Hagwine's bedchamber, where he is asleep. Enter the Carpenter.

CAR. Hagwine. Hagwine, listen to me.

HAG. What? What's that? Who calls me Hagwine? Who is there?

CAR. It is I, Hagwine, the carpenter.

HAG. A carpenter? An artisan? How dare you! It is *Sir* Hagwine, and I sent for no carpenter!

CAR. [*Laughing.*] Perhaps I should call you Casander. You will soon be a prophet!

HAG. Casander! My childhood name! Only my mother calls me Casander. You risk your life, carpenter!

CAR. [*Amused.*] Impossible, Casander. I did that once, forever. It is you who are at risk.

HAG. [*Peering into the darkness.*] Who are you? I see you and yet I don't. Are you there? What do you want?

CAR. I am always here. I want you to open your heart to the Lady Geneva. She counsels you well.

HAG. Open my heart to her! So that she can pierce it again with her unkind words and confound it with her devilish cleverness? Impossible, carpenter, I did that today, forever. Never again.

CAR. [*Sternly.*] You never opened your heart, Casander; you sought to impose it. I warn you, there is more danger before you tomorrow than arrows can threaten. Your new weapon imperils you. You cannot see where you are going. Follow the Lady, for she has eyes.

HAG. [*Grumpily sitting up.*] Oh, for sweet Christ's sake . . .! [*A flash of sudden light, immediately gone.*] What was that? Lightning? [*In a panic he runs to the window to look at the sky.*] Oh, we cannot have rain tomorrow! The crossbow strings go limp in rain, and even with the new longbows we'll need our crossbows firing! The Rushlanders outnumber us in every other weapon. Dear God, let it not rain tomorrow!

CAR. [*Sighing.*] It will not rain, Casander.

HAG. Oh, how would *you* know, carpenter! And who *are* you?

134

CAR. As I said, the carpenter.

HAG. Go away, carpenter. [*Gets back into bed.*] You are a dream. *I* know that, if you don't. You are the boar's tonque and mead I consumed at midnight. [*Sinks back down into his pillows.*]

CAR. You will sicken tomorrow and grow faint at the sight of blood, and when you do, remember me. I will return tomorrow night, with my brothers and sisters. [*Exits.*]

ACT TWO

SCENE 1

A hill overlooking the battlefield.

RON. [*Exulting.*] Sir Hagwine, this exceeds my expectations! See how the Rushlanders panic? The war cannot last; it will be over within a week, though they outnumber us.

HAG. The longbow is our salvation, Your Majesty! Its arrows darken the air! No sooner is one loosed than another follows from the same bow, and then another. [*Laughs.*] Its only drawback is the strength required to draw it back. If all our men were tall and strong enough we could train an army of longbowmen!

RON. [*Clapping him on the back.*] Well said, Sir Hagwine! Praise God, we'll have the time before another war to choose our best and sturdiest youths and school them well. Rushland will not attack again so soon! [*Points excitedly.*] Oh, Hagwine, look below!

HAG. [*Looks where Ronegan points.*] Oh God, my God, Oh Majesty! [*He clutches his stomach.*] My eyes deceive me!

RON. [*Gleefully.*] No, Sir Hagwine, they show you a miracle! A man pinned to his horse, through both legs, with a single arrow! Oh, the terror on his face! Look! His horse falls, he cannot free himself from the weight of the beast. Oh beautiful, oh timely invention! It has saved us!

HAG. [*Weakly, under his breath.*] A single arrow . . . through his leg . .. . through his horse . . . through his other leg. Oh, God! [*He doubles over with faintness and nausea.*]

RON. [*Catching him.*] Sir Hagwine! Sir Hagwine, are you ill? Come, come, my brave one . . . [*starts to laugh*] . . . it isn't you that's wounded! Shall I tell the Lady Geneva? Shall I send you to rest and recover with the ladies? Would tea and a lute refresh you?

HAG. [*Shakily recovering his dignity.*] I am fine, my Lord. I drank too deeply of mead and wine last night . . . [*his voice fades*] . . . and had the strangest dream. [*They exit, toward the castle.*]

SCENE 2

Inside the castle gates. King Ronegan and Sir Hagwine, returning, encounter the Lady Geneva.

GEN. [*Curtseying.*] Your Majesty. Sir Hagwine.

RON. [*Expansively.*] Lady, see to jugglers and musicians for the evening feast. Call the jesters and acrobats. We have much to celebrate! Where is my Queen?

GEN. She is at the falconry, Your Majesty, dressing her peregrine in a jeweled hood to match her hunting gown.

RON. I must give her the good news. [*With a broad wink.*] How battle rouses me! [*To Lady Geneva.*] You owe much to this good knight, Lady. See that you treat him well. [*Exits.*]

HAG. [*Sits down heavily on a low stone stair.*] I never saw such a battle, Lady.

GEN. Sir Hagwine, do you not rejoice? You are ghastly pale, your brow is beaded, and you tremble. What has happened? [*He stares into space.*] Sir Hagwine?

HAG. [*Almost inaudibly.*] I sickened and grew faint . . . .

GEN. What? You? But why, Sir Hagwine?

HAG. [*Runs his hand across his eyes.*] So young. Oh God, so young.

GEN. Who, Sir Hagwine? Oh, you are ill, shall I fetch some herbs?

HAG. [*Feverishly seizes her wrists and clamps one to each side of his thigh.*] Like this! [*Stares intently but unseeingly at her.*] Like this! With a single arrow!

GEN. [*Struggles briefly, but seeing his pain stops resisting and kneels to look into his face.*] What, Hagwine? What was like this?

HAG. The Rushlander! Pinned to his horse with . . . just . . . one . . . arrow! [*Releases her.*]

GEN. [*Softly.*] Dear God. What tortures men devise.

HAG. [*Striking his breast with a fist.*] It was as if I felt it! The pain, the fear! As if they were my own! And he was so young!

GEN. [*Touching his shoulder.*] Like a young brother, Hagwine? One whose pain you would expect to feel?

HAG. [*Leaps distractedly to his feet.*] No! Not my brother, my *enemy!* I have betrayed my trust! These feelings are not worthy of a knight! You would make me a woman! Away from me! [*Brushes violently past her and exits.*]

GEN. Praise God, he wakens from his dream of war. The line drawn with his sword grows faint, and he begins to see what joins us all. I pity him in his dread, for all that has been and done will yield to his becoming something new, a thing he can't yet see.

SCENE 3

Hagwine's bedchamber again, that same night.

CAR. Which holds the dream, Casander? The battlefield or the bedchamber?

HAG. You again, carpenter. You are impudent. [*Strains his eyes into the darkness behind the carpenter.*] Is someone with you? I see shadows moving.

CAR. To those shadows you are a shadow. Yet they see each other perfectly.

HAG. [*Long-sufferingly.*] Carpenter, I am weary. My bones ache from battle. Why do you not leave me in peace?

CAR. [*Smiles radiantly, mischievously.*] Peace, is it? How can you want peace? Are you not fond of telling how the One you call Lord came not to bring peace to the earth but a sword? Is it not blasphemy to long for peace? Stay, Casander, do battle with me. It is good for your soul!

HAG. [*Groans.*] For God's sake, be quick then. What *is* it?

CAR. [*Sweetly.*] For God's sake, it will take as long as it takes. I want you to meet my brothers and sisters. I said I would bring them.

HAG. [*Folds his arms across his chest with weary resignation.*] Well, then?

CAR. Let me introduce them to you. As you meet each one, though not a word will pass between you, your eyes will see farther and more clearly than they have ever seen. Indeed, when you have met them all, it will be as if you see for the first time. Only then will you begin to understand the nature of war — that simple thing — as well as the Lady Geneva.

HAG. [*Muttering.*] Witch!

CAR. [*He jestures and the shadows begin to move forward. As he says the name of each, that shadow stands before Sir Hagwine's bed and gazes steadily at its occupant.*] First, my sister Kuan Yin, beloved bodhisattva, giver of mercy, an enlightened one who postponed her own reward to help others in their search for the truth. How well she embodied the spirit of love for her fellow beings.

HAG. [*Shrinking back into his pillow before her gaze, then tearing his eyes from her to look at the carpenter.*] What kind of person is this, carpenter? What do you mean, calling her your sister? I have never seen a human creature with skin the color of mead and black slant eyes! This is a devil you have brought! Worse than the infidel! Get her out! Get out, all of you, I am dreaming. Let me awake!

CAR. You will surely awake, Casander, though you sleep so deeply you are nearly dead. Calm yourself. Be civil when you meet my brother Martin. On earth he was — or on another plane will be—like you, a leader of his people in a struggle. He had a dream, and saw a promised land to which he pointed out the way. But in his eyes you'll see he never did or caused a violent act—except his death. He died by violence, as peacemakers tend to do.

HAG. Oh, worse and worse! This man—if he is a man—is *black*, carpenter! Can you not see? He is soot-colored everywhere, skin, eyes, hair! Oh, Heaven save me, another devil! His evil is so profound it extrudes through his very skin, it won't be hidden! And this, *this* is your brother? [*Gestures wildly at the spirit of Martin Luther King.*] Get thee *behind* me! [*Spirit stays before him, regarding him with compassion.*]

CAR. Oh, Casander, that was not kind. Here is one who is less black, but not less pure of heart. [*Spirit of King retreats, that of Gandhi moves forward.*] This is my brother Mohandas, called Mahatma. He championed the despised and taught his people to resist oppression, yet he never sanctioned war. Like Martin, he died violently. [*Sorrowfully.*] I ask you, Casander, why do those who would love and unite die violently?

HAG. [*Impatient.*] Oh, carpenter, is it not obvious? Look at him, how puny he is, that *he* should champion anyone. He is frail, and half naked. Who can wonder that if such a one puts himself forward he will be squashed? As if a bug challenged a hawk! And what are those disks before his eyes? They look like ice. Who but a madman would view the world through ice? You waste my time. Bring me someone to respect, or go away!

CAR. [*Angrily.*] Oh, Casander, why do you persist, you child! You cling to hell from petulance, when heaven is yours! Look, then! Look into the eyes of my brother Albert and see the horror to which your persistence will lead! Look at his grief if you can stand it! [*Spirit of Albert Einstein steps forward.*]

HAG. [*Closes his eyes stubbornly.*] No, carpenter, enough. I am going to sleep.

CAR. [*Claps his hands loudly.*] Casander!

HAG. [*Starts violently, his eyes fly open, and he stares directly into the spirit's eyes. A pause. Horror grows on his face.*] Oh! Oh, no! No! [*He struggles but cannot look away from the spirit.*]

CAR. Oh, yes, Casander. You see what war becomes—you who look for salvation in new weapons. Do you think Rushland will long be without longbows? And then come firearms. See what they do! With each new engine of obliteration war reveals itself more fully until it is stripped of chivalry, honor, pageantry and law. It moves with each advance farther from civilization and decency. Look, Casander. Sicken and grow faint at the war of Albert's time. At the slaughter of innocents, at bitter struggles, years long. At war among millions. At bright-haired children steeped in a madman's evil. **At their leader's** deathgrip on his people's souls and sanity. And look at what my brother Albert, to his endless sorrow, released in the effort to end such a war. Look at the sword *he* brought to earth!

HAG. [*In a cold sweat.*] No! These generations have corrupted war! Honorable wars are fought to *protect* innocents! To *save* them from oppression!

CAR. Of what was that young Rushland warrior guilty that he deserved a skewering? Why should he suffer lifelong hunger — a terrible oppression — at the hands of honorable men like you?

HAG. [*Beside himself.*] The Rushlanders are *evil*! Would you have us stand defenseless before them? Do you know what they would do to our fields, our women, our halls and stables?

CAR. Do you?

HAG. Oh, *carpenter*! They would plunder and destroy! I tell you, they have no honor, are not like other men!

CAR. Are they not made by God and born of women? Does the sun not shine on them as well as you?

HAG. [*Stubbornly.*] Not as often, carpenter. Their country is a gloomy, gray-skyed place, damp and densely wooded.

CAR. Oh, Casander, you fool. Will you quibble after what you have seen? Can you still not see that war makes use of every evil it would obliterate? Uses murder, oppression, and hatred to overcome murder, oppression, and hatred? Fends off the imposition of another's will be imposing an unwelcome will on him?

HAG. [*Half apologetic.*] But that is so far hence, another world, another race. I can do nothing now, in my world and age, to strike from the future's record the atrocities I have seen.

CAR. How do you know, Casander? You see so far for one without eyes. Tell me how you know your Rushland brothers are evil — know what they would do if you stopped fighting — know you have no power for future good. Does God speak to you in your dreaming? [*Stares at him in wonder.*] Are you more than human? Oh, Casander, grant me pardon! I fall at your feet! [*Kneels and puts his forehead to the floor.*]

HAG. [*Horrified.*] Stop that! Get up! [*Pleading.*] Oh, please stop, you mock and confuse me. [*Whining just a little.*] I feel unwell.

CAR. [*Dusting off his knees.*] You should not make divine pronouncements, Casander, without divine knowledge. [*Beckons to the last spirit.*] But here is one thing you *must* know, for it will surely happen if you remain a slave to the fear of your brothers. Meet my sister Molly and see in her eyes the ultimate outcome of mistrust. Look at the magnitude of the peril that a mere woman, a mother and grandmother, contemplated daily. See what she fought against with all her heart out of love for children, humankind, and God. She broke man's law for a higher law. She served in jail and grew in freedom there. She lost her life — her

daily rounds of family and chores — and gained her life in greater
measure. What she faced — not strewn and streamy fields or
knights pinned to their horses — will undo your mind and heart,
but you must look. [*Spirit of Molly Rush steps forward and
looks long at Hagwine.*]

HAG. This is . . . this . . . is . . . OH! . . . horrible . . . [*faints.*]
[*The spirits gather around the foot of his bed, joining hands with
the carpenter. Hagwine stirs, opens his eyes, moans softly.*] I
surrender, carpenter. Have it your way. [*Passes out again.*]

ACT THREE

SCENE 1

*The castle gates. Ronegan, in full regalia, waits for Hagwine to join
him on the way to battle. He glances often and impatiently at the
sundial. The Lady Geneva appears.*

GEN. Good morning, Your Majesty. I did not expect to see you
here at this late hour. I had thought by now you would be at
battle with Sir Hagwine.

RON. [*Testily.*] And so I should be, Lady. What keeps him, and
why he keeps me, I cannot say.

GEN. Has he not appeared this morning? Perhaps he is ill, Your
Majesty. He acted strangely yesterday.

RON. [*Roughly dismissive.*] Not Sir Hagwine, Lady. I have never
known him to be ill. He is strong, his endurance is limitless.
[*Hesitates.*] But then, he has never been late before . . . . [*Enter
Sir Hagwine with an air of unreality and absorption. He is wearing only a tunic and leggings, no armor or helmet. He carries no
weapon.*]

RON. [*Relieved.*] Ah, *there* you are, my brave one! Where have
you been? And what's this, what's this? No armor? What means
this, Hagwine? Are you ill?

HAG. [*Looks unseeingly at Ronegan.*] Ill? Ill? [*Shakes his head and
murmurs softly.*] I am undone. My heart and mind . . . dis-
mantled and re-formed. [*Begins to recognize Ronegan and
Geneva.*] How can you know me? I am not who I was.

RON. [*Dismayed.*] Oh, Sir Hagwine, what can ail you, knight-
at-arms? Your are pale. You loiter aimlessly. Hagwine,
Hagwine, what is it?

HAG. [*A slow smile lighting his face as if from within.*] Hagwine?
Who can Hagwine be? A dream I had . . . a long and tedious

dream. [*His lassitude is suddenly gone, his face and body come alive, he almost hums.*] No! I tell you, king, whatever kind of king you are, you have seen the last of Hagwine! Casander! Ha ha! That's me! [*Grins and strikes his breast.*] Casander is awake! And has a tale to tell!

GEN. [*To herself.*] Can I believe my eyes and ears? Awake? Is he? Am I?

RON. [*Baffled, trying to act as usual.*] Sir Hagwine, we are late to battle. Why are you not armed and armored?

HAG. Why should I ever have been? [*Affecting boredom.*] I have grown stale, king. I have not fought in weeks. A hilltop job is all I have had, standing at your side, advising, watching others fall, sprout gouts of blood, cry piercingly for pity. I have missed all the fun!

RON. [*Seizing his arm joyfully.*] Is that it! Oh, Hagwine why did you not say so? You old warhorse, you! We'll both go into battle, join the fray, lop some heads, revive our fierce and feverish purpose!

HAG. [*Gently disengaging himself.*] Too late for that. Too late, old king, I'll go to war no more.

RON. Not go to war? Not go to war! My ears deceive me!

HAG. [*Smiling.*] No, old Ronegan, they tell you a miracle.

RON. [*Blustering.*] You're mad! You're ill, you're drunk, you've been possessed! You disgrace your standing and your brotherhood. To bed with you! Recover from this . . . this . . . *fit* . . . of yours. And then consult with me.

HAG. [*Bowing graciously.*] I thank you, king, with all my heart, but I feel no need of counsel.

RON. You are in need of leeches! Bloodletting!

HAG. Oh, no, I've had enough of that. I tell you, no more blood. No more war.

RON. [*Trying emotion and sweet reason.*] Hagwine, listen to me, I implore you. We are engaged in a strenuous battle against the godless. We fight for our freedom, our bread, our faith. Ours is a just and holy cause, Sir Hagwine. Do not abandon righteousness; do not let us down!

HAG. [*Roused to anger.*] These just and holy causes make me sick! [*Pokes a finger at Ronegan's mail-clad chest.*] I tell you a madman will come full of *his* just cause and *his* hated infidels. He will sway whole cities with just his voice, which will deafen them to their own inner words. He will kill millions and burn them like loaves in great ovens! He will rise out of a whole history of holy wars and bleat a cry of righteousness and no one will stop him but with more holy wars! It all begins again! [*Stops short.*] But not with me. I'll stop him, starting now. I will not kill, I have no enemies. [*Grins fiercely at Ronegan.*] Do you know, king, what you get when you make room for . . . just . . .

141

one . . . just war? [*Waits a moment and then laughs bitterly.*]
Just war! That is all! Just war! Nothing else! No other way stays
open! No other path gets cleared! *All wars become just!*

RON. [*Nearly dancing with frustration and distress.*] You babble,
Hagwine! Stop it! You make no sense! You pervert the truth!
Our enemies! Evil! Evil!

HAG. Oh, enemies and evil are excuses. We come to love them,
for they let us fight. We strap on righteousness with our swords,
but it is the *swords* we love!

RON. You speak in riddles! You mock our purpose! I'll throw you
in the dungeon, Hagwine, I'll have you in chains!

HAG. [*Pacidly.*] Yet I'll be free, like my sister Molly. What a pity
you could not meet her.

RON. [*Apoplectic.*] Sister! You have no sister! Oh, you madden
me! You goad me! Fiend! Devil!

HAG. [*To Lady Geneva, who has watched the scene unfold with
amazement, silently.*] Look at him my Lady. He rages and turns
blue. What is he like?

GEN. A child, Casander, in a tantrum. [*They watch Ronegan
pace and tear his hair.*]

HAG. Exactly, my Lady. Is it not odd? God says Love. All He says
is Love. Love me, love yourself, love your neighbor as yourself.
Love your enemy.

GEN. And man, like an angry child, says, I don't *want* to. I don't
have to. I *can't*. It is *his* fault I can't. If I loved him, he would rob
me blind, steal my wife, murder me in my bed.

HAG. And the other says, no, it is *his* fault, *he* is evil!

GEN. [*Pointing at Hagwine.*] Your fault!

HAG. [*Pointing back.*] No, *your* fault!

GEN. No, *yours*, you foul demon!

HAG. No, *yours*, you butcher of babies!

GEN. No, *yours*, you spitter on crosses!

HAG. No, *yours*, you eater of pork!

GEN. Bather on Sundays!

HAG. Cracker of the broad end of the egg!

GEN. Saver of toenail parings! [*By now Hagwine and Geneva are
doubled over with laughter, clutching their sides.*]

GEN and HAG. [*Pointing at the speechless Ronegan.*] You see
how wars begin!

RON. [*Utterly aghast.*] You have both gone mad! I am made mad
by you! You mockers of righteousness and honor! [*Hagwine and
Geneva in an agony of laughter.*] I'll pray your reason is
restored. You are weary, take time off. It will go hard with you
if you persist in disrespect! [*Exits with much dignity.*]

HAG. Poor king, poor king. But what to do, my Lady? I need an
act, a task, a gesture. What to do?

GEN. I have an idea, Casander . . . [*whispers to him.*]

SCENE 2

Queen Lenox of Haviland's dressing chamber.

LEN. I still say, off with his head!

RON. Not yet, not yet, I dare not be too hasty. Perhaps he'll come around.

LEN. From what you say he just gets worse and worse. The nerve of him! The madness! Just the foremost things you say—his cowardly withdrawal from war, his mockery of you, his wild predictions of future wars, death camps, world-killing weapons—in these are manifest treason, mutiny, designs upon your throne!

RON. [*Arrested in his pacing.*] Designs upon my throne? How so? That cannot be!

LEN. [*As if to a child.*] My dear, if he can make your men believe that he is chosen by God to see what comes, then he can claim a divine right to rule!

RON. [*Taken aback.*] Oh no, my love, you do him wrong. Sir Hagwine is my friend, my counsel, my dearest companion next to you. He honors me in his heart, I know. His curious behavior is a fit, a passing thing. He'll be himself again.

LEN. And give up being Casander, prophet of doom? He likes his role too well. I am sure a tunic weighs less than plate and mail! And is a safer costume if it keeps him far from risk!

RON. But he was always brave! He fought without regard for risk, he never gave a finger's width of ground without his all.

LEN. [*Shrugs.*] He is broken. His heart is gone and all he has is cunning. The longbow did him in and now his safety lies in your undoing. My simple-hearted Lord, you trust too much. Lop his head or see your crown on it!

RON. But he is my friend and brother!

LEN. Off with his head!

SCENE 3

The battlefield. Casander and Lady Geneva enter the throng unarmed, carrying great lumpy sacks slung over their shoulders.

CAS. [*Nervously.*] We'll never have enough, my Lady! What if they riot for more than we can give? We'll have betrayed our purpose!

GEN. Oh, ye of little faith, Casander! Trust! Follow me. [*Reaches into her sack and draws out a loaf of bread. Holds it aloft.*] Free bread! Fresh bread! Hot bread, my brothers! A better thing to slice than limbs and briskets!

CAS. [*Joining her cry.*] Baguettes! Bagles! Black bread and brown! Come, brothers, use˚ your swords to carve a crusty loaf!

143

[*Soldiers and knights in combat-locked pairs are distracted, dumbfounded. The fighting slows and diminishes. Curiosity and hunger prevail. Astonishment gives way to laughter. A Rushlander footsoldier speaks up in halting Amberwavian.*]

RUS. Oy hovv herring! Nize piggled herring! Will share, yes? Herring sangwidge, wery nize! [*Draws a pouch of herring from under his leather jerkin. More and more soldiers come running from distant parts of the field. The Carpenter skirts the scene unnoticed, distributing bread and herring from sacks labeled "loaves" and "fishes."*]

CAS. [*In a panicky whisper.*] We're running out, my Lady! Oh, this is terrible! What will we do?

GEN. Look again, Casander. You've left a full sack of bread lying on the ground. Do you want it trampled?

CAS. But . . . I didn't put . . . where did that *come* from?

RUS. More herring! Ho! Loog, loog, w'ere did I ged zo mudge fishes? Come! Ged herring! [*Enter King Ronegan, looking about him in astonishment.*]

RON. Hagwine! Lady Geneva! How dare you! What do you mean by this! What are you *doing*? [*Draws his sword and a passing soldier sticks a loaf of bread on its point. He shakes it furiously to get if off.*]

CAS. Doing? Doing, old Ronegan? Why, we're ending the battle! Giving them what they fight for so they need not fight! A neater thing than skewering them like meat on spits that fly from bows! [*Continues joyfully tossing loaves to the crowd of intermingled men from Rushland and Amberwavia. A grand picnic is in progress. Forgotten swords litter the ground; wineskins are passed in a holiday spirit.*]

RON. [*Raises his sword, minus breadloaf.*] OFF WITH . . . ! [*Bumps into King Breadnyet, who has entered the scene and grabbed his arm before it can fall.*]

BRE. Not here, old enemy. You would be killed. Come with me.

RON. What? Breadnyet! [*Swallows his initial protest.*] You are right. Yes. I am in your debt. Let us have a word together. [*They move away from the picnicking crowd.*]

BRE. Your man forgets his place. Does he not know that peace is yours, and mine, and ours alone to make? That it is not the simple mockery he makes of it, forgetting all that honor asks of us?

RON. Honor? You speak of honor? [*Shakes the confusion from his mind.*] He must be stopped. I will not suffer insult from a subject!

BRE. Ah, we understand each other, King Ronegan. You are an honorable enemy.

RON. And you an adversary worthy of my finest men and strategies. [*Gesturing with disgust at the joyful gathering.*] And yet you see what they have made of all our struggle, yours and mine. We are disgraced, dishonored.

BRE. Indeed, King Ronegan, we are taunted. By one impudent knight and his unladylike friend. See the damage two can do! The loss of discipline! It sickens me!

RON. King Breadnyet, you are right. He must be stopped. The Lady, too. She has corrupted him, I should have seen. He was honorable once.

BRE. You'll do him justice to save him from his present dishonor. Kill him and you'll kill the foolish peace of foolish men. What can all these crude unsubtle subjects know of what our roles demand? They need the strength and cunning of our long years and lineage to bear for them the burden of reality. Poor simple souls!

RON. It is a pity we were meant to fight, King Breadnyet, for the loss of my most trusted knight has left me lonely. Only such a one as you can understand my lot. [*Sighs heavily.*] It is the way of the world! I'll see to his demise, that battle can resume. And may the best man win!

BRE. And may the best man win! [*They seize each other's hands in a paroxysm of brotherhood and exit side by side.*]

CAS. [*Back at the picnic.*] Did you see, Lady Geneva? Did you see our two fierce leaders side by side? Surely they rejoice together! Surely war is ended!

GEN. [*With a look of doubt and sadness not noticed by Casander.*] I saw, Casander, I saw. I wonder what it means . . . . [*Turns to him and takes his hand.*] We must stay together, and gather others close.

Suggestions for Discussion

1. After the performance, have the actors maintain their roles as they respond to questions from the audience. Each actor could join a small group for a more conversational atmosphere.

2. In groups of four to six, talk about the scene you found most impressive and convincing. Give your reasons.

3. Characterize the five spirits. What do they have in common? Why does the carpenter call them brothers and sisters?

4. Do you find the conflict between the USA and the USSR appropriately described? In what respects?

5. Discuss the ending. Explain the "look of doubt" on Lady Geneva's face. Do you share her hope for peace? Do you think it is possible for people to rally together gainst the wishes of government leaders?

The Threat of Nuclear War

Waging nuclear war means the ultimate negation of God. It negates the Creator God in that it aims to destroy all of creation. It negates the God of love and justice because it entails murder on a massive scale, murder of those whom God created and for whom Jesus died on the cross, murder of Christ himself, for "what you have done to the least of my brothers, that you have done unto me." These words should remain in the minds of all Christians as we help assemble the bombs: actively, passively through our tax money, or merely through refusal to speak out against this most premeditated of murders. Every weapon directed against a fellow human being is directed also against Christ in whom God became incarnate.

Two opinions have been voiced among Christians which could mislead us into tolerating the intolerable. One idea has it that the nuclear disaster is part of God's plan to punish the wicked. Jesus allegedly will descend on a mushroom cloud for the Second Coming and usher in the Judgement Day. "Good Christians" need not fear for they will be saved. In this context, a leader of the Moral Majority asserted that if the bomb would fall, he would jump on it and ride it to glory. Another idea, less obscene but also dangerous, holds that nuclear holocaust is evil but that accordingly God will not allow it to happen. Ever since Noah and the rainbow, we have had the promise that God will not destroy His people. These two opinions complement each other in that they both deny the need to cry out against the folly of the arms race. One claims that war may happen and is good (i.e. God-willed); the other, that it will not happen because it is evil.

The first approach we can dismiss without further discussion. What human being can see documentaries of Hiroshima after the bomb and not be stirred by the incredible devastation, by the agonies of the wounded, by the helplessness of the children whose parents were incinerated? How can a human mind conceive of the miseries caused by one hundred thousand Hiroshimas and then praise it as the will of God?

The latter idea however deserves serious attention because it is based on trust and hope, two essential ingredients in the faith of a peacemaker. But to sit back and rely on supernatural interference to rid us of nuclear arms will not do. God in history has used human agents to carry out His will. It is true that He promised not to terminate human existence; but in His infinite mercy and love He left us the power to choose good or evil and thus ultimately the

146

power of terminating human history ourselves. God, to be sure, calls us, invites us, urges us to live at peace with one another, to be obedient to Him by following the example of Jesus Christ. Surely God did not condone the virtual extermination of native Americans after Europeans landed on this continent, nor the mass executions in Indonesia in 1965, nor the cruelties of South African Apartheid, nor the gas chambers of Auschwitz, nor any other of the many attrocities dreamt up by the human mind. Yet these things happened. Therefore we must not fool ourselves into believing that the threat of nuclear war will subside on its own. God deplores evil. God suffers along with the tortured human community. And with unending love, God still calls us back and will accept our pleas to be forgiven if we promise to sin no more by violating Him in our brothers and sisters.

Many plays in this book are related to the nuclear issue. What the following three short skits have in common is their satirical, half-bitter, half-humorous approach to the horrifying end toward which we are racing. Humor is an effective device to combat psychic numbing. These skits reveal how the lives of millions of people are irresponsibly toyed with. They intend to wake people up, to energize them, to move them to action. "The Last Inquest" has a similar goal, although its tone is deeply serious. It documents how easily our ideological conflict with the Russians and the double standard we apply when comparing our policies to theirs could result in global catastrophe. When staging any of these plays, it is important to follow the presentation with suggestions on how we can stop the move toward omnicide. Any witness for peace, no matter how insignificant it may seem, is one further step toward the prevention of nuclear war.

SAM AND IVAN

by The Fisherfolk

CHARACTERS

NARRATOR
SAM
IVAN
4 FOLLOWERS

PRODUCTION NOTES

The properties needed for the performance are a red, white and blue hat, a Russian hat with USSR symbol, 8 small bombs, 2 medium-sized bombs, and 2 large bombs, all made out of black poster board.

NARRATOR. Once there was a *nation* with a very powerful image. His name was Sam. [*On "nation" Sam and his followers turn to face front. The followers are so proud and show gestures which indicate this.*]
The people were very proud and close to their image and thought he was the *best* in all the *world*. [*On "best they step in and look at Sam admiringly. On "world" they step back again, still very proud.*]
They awarded him prizes; they showered him with honors. [*Follower 1 mimes pinning a great prize on Sam's chest and hanging a great medallion around his neck.*]
They even gave him a hat that said "Our Nation" on it. [*Follower 1 gives Sam the hat that Sam had placed on the ground. Sam puts it on with great ceremony and pride.*]
They made him feel special. "My," thought Sam, "being a powerful nation and a strong leader is the most important thing in the world." [*Sam puffs himself up, and his followers do the same.*]
One day as Sam was *leading*, a doubt nibbled at his mind. [*On "leading," Sam and his followers begin mime walk with great pride; on "doubt" Sam shrinks down and for a moment is overcome by doubt. His followers are oblivious to this and walk on with pride.*]
"What if I am no longer the most powerful nation in the world?" He thought. And then, "What if my people overheard these doubts?

148

They might stop giving me awards. They might even take away my hat! I'll just *gather a few more defenses* so nobody can take away my image." [*On "gather a few more defenses" Sam puffs himself up and goes on.*]

As Sam became even more powerful, the people cheered. [*The followers mime great clapping and cheering.*]

They liked to see Sam so powerful. "Such a good nation will have to have a special place," they said.

So they made a *rule*: "No one may have more defenses than Sam." [*On "rule" follower 1 stops Sam and follower 2, and then mimes making a rule. 2 agrees with 1.*]

And to *insure* his new position, they gave him a feather for his hat . . . large and impressive. Sam felt important and he walked in front of everyone with his bigger and better hat. [*On "insure" follower 1 picks up one of the small bombs. With great care she gives it to Sam who puts it in the elastic band of his hat. The followers love it.*]

One day there came another *nation*. [*On "nation" Ivan and followers turn and at that exact moment Sam and his followers stop and look aghast. The competition begins and is mimed out as the narration describes.*]

They also had a very powerful image. His name was Ivan. He had a hat like Sam, but no feather. Ivan wanted a feather just like Sam's. He saw how tall and powerful Sam's feather made him look. So Ivan decided to get a feather for *his* hat. He wanted to look just like Sam. [*Follower 4 gives Ivan his "feather" and now Ivan and his followers begin the race.*]

Sam didn't like that. "I shouldn't feel afraid," he thought. "I'm a strong nation. I can make it. I just need a few more feathers to make me a little more powerful." [*Sam gathers one more bomb to put in his hat. His followers feel better, and then Ivan does the same.*]

From then on Sam and Ivan competed to keep up with each other. [*Sam and Ivan and all followers begin to walk again.*]

If Sam moved up one step . . . Ivan moved up one step. When Sam got a more impressive feather . . . Ivan got one, too. [*Sam and Ivan take large steps and both get one more bomb to put in hats.*]

This went on and on and on for a very long time. [*One more bomb is added to both hats and the followers begin to look a bit tired and puzzled.*]

Some of the people wanted them to slow down. Others wanted them to speed up. [*Follower 1 tries to pull Sam back; follower 4 tries to slow Ivan down. Follower 3 urges Ivan on; follower 2 urges Sam on.*]

So Sam and Ivan decided to *talk*. They agreed they were in a race. They decided they would run together. *But*, they both knew they would have to run faster than they ever had before, just to keep up with each other . . . so the race *went on*. [*On "talk" everyone stops. Sam and Ivan turn towards each other pointing. On "but" Sam and Ivan pick up the medium-sized bombs. They are hard to carry and are heavy. On "on" everyone starts walking again, faster and more desperately.*]

Before long, some of Sam's people thought Ivan was going too fast and that Ivan's feathers were bigger than Sam's. [*Follower 2 points at Ivan accusingly.*]

And some of Ivan's people thought Sam was going to fast, and getting too many feathers. [*Follower 3 points accusingly at Sam.*]

And some of the people thought Sam and Ivan had better things to do than run the race at all. [*Follower 1 pulls on Sam to slow him down. Follower 4 pulls on Ivan to make him slow down. Both followers 1 and 4 hold up their hands and shrug their shoulders. No one notices.*]

So, Sam and Ivan kept talking to each other. One day, they came up with a new *agreement*. [*On "agreement" Sam and Ivan and their followers all stop. Sam and Ivan turn to point to each other again.*]

It took them a long time to make it and there were many details. They both agreed this time to run even faster *together*. [*After "together" they pick up the large bombs. The narration stops while the bombs are looked at and checked by all to make sure they are the same.*]

After all, they couldn't stop now. Racing to get more feathers was what Sam and Ivan did best. They had trained long and hard and were in good shape. [*Sam and Ivan flex their muscles and lift their bombs like weights.*]

As they *raced* onward, Sam and Ivan began to realize they were coming to the very edge. They raced on, not daring to admit they had made a mistake, hoping that the other would be the first to retreat. [*On "raced" everyone begins again. It's very desperate now. Sam and Ivan are loaded down by the bombs. The followers are worried.*]

But one day there it was: They were on the edge! They tried to stop, but the weight of their great feathers carried them over. [*On "edge" the followers mime looking a great distance away. As their "feathers" carry them over, Sam and Ivan fall dead. The followers stop.*]

By the time their lone survivors arrived at the edge, they saw Sam and Ivan at the bottom . . . crushed by the weight of their great hats. And the people thought to themselves: "Why didn't they just *stop*? Why didn't *we* stop them? [*The followers slowly mime walking to the edge and look very far down. While thinking they look up. On the last line, "Why didn't we stop them?" they look at each other shocked.*]

Suggestions for Discussion

1. What, according to the play, is the reason the arms race began? Who started it? Show that this is historically accurate.

2. The motives and actions of one side end up being identical to those of the other side. Do you agree this is true in reality?

3. Some of the "followers" begin to hold Sam and Ivan back. Explain why they may want to do this. Which groups and individuals do you know who are presently active this way?

4. Invent a different, more positive ending for the skit. Roleplay it. Then think about ways we can more toward this ending in reality.

5. Become informed about attempts to freeze the development, testing, and deployment of nuclear weapons.

6. In the light of your faith, consider unilateral disarmament initiatives.

ELFIE

by Peter Dougherty

CHARACTERS

GENERAL
ELF
SUBMARINE I
SUBMARINE II

A benevolent general introduces his "friend" ELF to the audience. Throughout, two other characters portray Trident submarines on patrol. The submarines carry helium-filled balloons which they release as missiles during the play.

GENERAL. Hello, everybody. I'm General Dominion, here to introduce to you a friend I hope you'll all get to know and love as I do: Project ELF. Say hello to the people, ELF.

ELF. [*Mischieviously*] Hello! [*ELF bows and giggles.*]

GENERAL. Our friend ELF here is an underground communication grid to be put in the upper peninsula of Michigan to communicate with the Trident submarine fleet: Thirty submarines, two of which we have placed in the river to help demonstrate the security of our defense posture with ELF and Trident.

SUBMARINE I. [*Steps forward*] I am the U.S.Michigan Trident Submarine. I have 2040 times the explosive power of the Hiroshima bomb. Look out! [*Starts patrolling again.*]

SUBMARINE II. [*Steps forward*] I can destroy Soviet Russia all be myself. Our whole family of 30 will be able to destroy all life on earth.

SUBMARINES I, II. Whoopieeee! [*They continue patrolling.*]

GENERAL. ELF, right here, is the communication link to Trident. [*ELF bows and giggles again.*]

ELF. [*Excitedly*] Can we show them? Can we show them? I want to show my stuff!

GENERAL. Just a minute, Elfie. The ELF communication is one way, though. The Trident cannot communicate back. So, if Elfie were to, say, communicate the message to destroy El Salvador . . .

ELF. Did you say "Destroy El Salvador?" Destroy El Salvador! Destroy El Salvador! [*The Trident submarine releases a balloon "bomb."*]

GENERAL. . . . then the submarine would have no way to communicate back. [*With much apology*] Son of a gun. Naughty, naughty Elfie, you shouldn't have done that. That was not the signal we gave you. Oh, well. Now that the people are destroyed, we may just have to go in there after a while and manage their coffee plantations until they get back on their feet. [*To audience*] As you can see, this is an important weapon to have for our *defense*. What if, for example, some Arabian country tried to cut off the oil supply.

ELF. Which one, General? Which one? I'll get it for ya, General.

GENERAL. No, no, no, Elfie, it didn't happen yet. But what would happen if Iran . . .

ELF. Did he say Iran? Iran?

GENERAL. . . . under their new Islamic government decided to cut us off the oil supply, what other response would we have but to defend our *God-given right* to their oil . . . er . . . our oil.

ELF. Destroy Iran! Destroy Iran! [*The Trident sub-marine releases another bomb.*]

GENERAL. Naughty, naughty Elfie! Now look what you have done! Well, at least the machinery is still working. We may just have to send American military advisors in to operate that machinery until we can see that a new government is elected. Okay, Elfie, not bad. Not bad at all. We've made El Salvador and Iran safe for democracy, and we still have time for a late evening snack. So, Americans, I ask you: don't you feel more safe with our friend Elfie around? In fact, Elfie and Trident are our most important defenses during a full-scale world war.

ELF. Did he say World War? Destroy the world! Destroy the world! [*Submarines release all their balloons at once.*]

GENERAL. Naughty, naughty Elfie! That's it. Don't you realize that in an all-out nuclear war, *we* die too?

ELF. Gee, General, I'm really sorry. I mean, after all, there were all those subs out there, ready and everything.

GENERAL. [*Puts his arm around ELF and begins to walk off the stage*] I know, I know, Elfie, but you should have learned to restrain yourself.

ELF. I'm sorry, General, I really am. I'll make it up to you.

GENERAL. [*As they exit*] Oh, well, Elfie, there's still the moon.

Suggestions for Discussion

1. In groups of four to six, share your immediate reaction to "Elfie." Let each person have a turn.

2. Roleplay a discussion with the General in the play.

3. Gather and share information about past incidents that brought us to the brink of nuclear war: the Cuban missile crisis, computor malfunctions, a flock of geese over Canada disturbing the radar.

4. Rent the film "The Last Epidemic" from AFSC, 915 Salem Avenue, Dayton, Ohio 45406; phone (513) 278-4225. Show it to your local physicians and see whether they might like to buy a copy for public education about the medical consequences of nuclear war. Also show it to any other group or individual that invites you to do so.

5. Write a letter concerning disarmament to the editor of your local newspaper. Also write to your Senators and Representatives.

CIVIL DEFENSE SATIRE

by the State of the Union Players

CHARACTERS

MOM
DAD
JOANIE, *their child*
WILLIE, *their child*
TV ANNOUNCER
TV STAR
SECRETARY OF STATE
PRESIDENT OF THE UNITED STATES

The properties needed for this play are a sofa, two armchairs, and a large TV frame, constructed of cardboard, through which the television speakers address the audience.

Joanie, Willie, and their parents are watching TV. Suddenly, a test button sounds. Beeeeeeeeeep.

ANNOUNCER. This is a test, only a test. For the next sixty seconds this station and other stations will be tuned to the emergency broadcasting system. This is only a test. [*Test button sounds again. Beeeeeeeeeep. Then the regular program returns with an advertisement for Piggy Rich Telephone Company.*]

TV STAR. Have you ever been caught in an uncomfortable situation that could have been avoided with a little planning? Such would be the case with a nuclear attack. Piggy Rich Telephone Company now offers the *Holocaust Effective Alert System*. How does it work? Well, it's very simple. When your phone starts to *glow*, you'll know that you have to *go!* So avoid being caught in the evacuation rush hour traffic with the *Holocaust Effective Alert System!* [*The family members start speaking to each other.*]

MOM. You children are living in a very important historical time. Just think of it, no one has ever lived on the edge of nuclear holocaust.

JOANIE. Gee, Mom, I don't know.

MOM. Don't know? What do you mean, you don't know?

DAD. Yes, Joanie, your mom's right, we have enough nuclear weapons to kill every man, woman, and child on the planet four times over and the Soviets can only do it three times. We really live in a great country!

WILLIE. How do you kill people after they are already dead?

DAD. Willie, don't they teach you anything in school? [*Emergency broadcasting beep comes on.*]

ANNOUNCER. Attention, attention, this is not a test, I repeat this is not a test. We are now in direct communication with our emergency broadcasting spokesperson at the Pentagon. Please tell us about the latest developments. Did we really drop those bombs on the Russians? [*Proud and pleased with being in control.*]

SECRETARY OF STATE. Here is what happened. A flock of communist mercenary Canada geese deliberately violated our Nora Early Warning Safety Radar Alert Network which automatically activated tactical counter-force measures; three Russian cities have already been vaporized. Realizing our mistake when only goose droppings and feathers scored a direct hit on Boisie, Idaho, we were forced to close our window of vulnerability by immediately launching 2000 additional missiles.

ANNOUNCER. What! Do you mean we started a nuclear war by accident?

SECRETARY OF STATE. Actually, we only fired a nuclear warning shot. We expect the entire Soviet Union to be totally incinerated, I mean, functionally incapacitated, in the next twenty minutes. We estimate Soviet offensive capability to be reduced by 50 percent. This means their overkill ratio has been brought down to 1.5. Therefore, we can expect only moderate retalliation and acceptable casualties with every American being killed only 1.5 times rather than 3 times, which was the ratio before "equalization."

This is a great victory. The best defense is a good offense. What good are nuclear weapons and the first stike capability if you don't use them. We have been stockpiling thousands of warheads since Hiroshima and have not gotten to use any!

The American public has nothing to worry about, we have a game plan, but it is so secret we can't tell you what it is. Who says we can't win a nuclear war? There has already been too much negative talk and communist propaganda about the non-survivability of nuclear war. It is time to say something good about total destruction! There are, after all, more important things than peace. Sacrifice is what made this country great. What good is democracy if you don't destroy it. I mean, defend it! Don't look at this as suicide but as a cure for inflation and unemployment . . . .

[*At this time two people come in and cart the Secretary away. The announcer comes back.*]

ANNOUNCER. Thanks for your clarification. You heard it folks! You heard it folks, we have just entered a nuclear war. And now all Americans should proceed with evacuation plans. Get out your phone books folks and follow the instructions. [*Mother gets phone book out and starts to read it aloud to her family.*]

MOM. George, look, it says here that this is just like going on vacation. [*She reads the list of items from the phone book.*] Let's see, shovel, flashlight, . . . maybe suntan lotion.

DAD. I wonder if Ed Jones brought my shovel back. He borrowed it three weeks ago. That shovel is mighty important! Why, Deputy Secretary of War T.K. Jones says, "Everybody will make it if there are enough shovels to go around."

MOM. What do we need shovels for, to dig our own graves?

DAD. No, we need them to dig shelters. The dirt makes the difference!

MOM. Dirt! We'll need to stop by Sears and buy a family pack of detergent. I hope there is enough toilet paper.

DAD. We better go by Skaggs and pick up an air-wick. Those fall-out shelters can get mighty stinky. I wonder where those kids put my flashlight! Last time they killed the batteries playing Space Face.

MOM. We should have our sleeping bags dry cleaned. You know how filthy the kids get!

DAD. I hope that I am not going to have to loan my tools out. People always forget. What with the holocaust and all, I'll probably never see them.

MOM. What about Fifi and Fufu? Who is going to feed them? We can't just leave them!

DAD. Someone has to water the lawn, after all those years of fertilizing, de-weeding, and buying Ronco garden tools! I'm not about to have it ruined.

WILLIE. Dad, do they have PAC-MAN at the fall-out shelter? I'm not going if they don't have video games!

JOANIE. Mom, can Susy spend the night at our fall-out shelter, please?

MOM. George, I don't think we can get all these things together in time.

DAD. Don't worry honey, we have 17 minutes till the bombs hit.

[*Announcer comes back on the television screen.*]

ANNOUNCER. The President is now going to deliver a message of faith to the Nation.

PRESIDENT. This is a time of crisis, and it is very important for all of us Americans to keep a cool head and make the necessary adjustments. We are all called upon to make heavy sacrifice, and we will proudly carry them out.

ANNOUNCER. Mr. President, a last minute report. L.A. has just been hit. We have an initial estimate of six million dead.

PRESIDENT. The situation is not as bad as it seems. Do not listen to the doomsayers and panicmongers who are predicting the end of the world.

ANNOUNCER. Mr. President, New York has just been hit. Twelve million people are believed to have died in this latest attack.

PRESIDENT. We have incurred many losses, but remember our enemies have had more losses than we have. Already, almost all of the Russian population has been exterminated, as well as a large part of the population of Eastern Europe and Northern China.

ANNOUNCE. Mr. President, the Detroit areas has been hit. We do not have an estimate of the number of casualties.

PRESIDENT. This is a tremendous victory for us. It is premature and precipitous to predict that when their missiles hit us, we will be wiped out. I have made it a point during my term as president of the U.S. to get the American people top dollar for defense spending. Now the time has come for you to appreciate the results of my efforts. You will be housed in shelters which have been designed for maximum comfort and security under the present circumstances. We have built enough shelters to protect one half of the American population from nuclear fall-out with provisions that can last from 2 weeks to 6 months, depending upon your appetite.

Have faith that there is life after the bomb. The losses and sacrifices we are going to suffer are not for nothing, because the world is now free of Communism. America can be a great country again. We will pull out of this terrible ordeal as the unchallenged world leaders. Now that the Soviet threat has been eliminated, have faith that my program will work.

[*Aide in mask pulls President away as they hurry out. Announcer comes back on the air.*]

ANNOUNCER. The President, his family, and his aides have now boarded the doomsday shuttle which is ready to take off at any minute taking them to outer space. The shuttle has been loaded with food, water, jellybeans, medicine, and fuel to last up to 2 years. The President believes that he will not have to stay in space that long, in fact he has given orders for the next cabinet meeting to be held in 2 weeks, intending to set out immediately to the task of reconstruction. Good bye, and good luck America.

[*Test button sounds. The family collapses to the floor.*]

Suggestions for Discussion

1. Invite a person from the Civil Defense Agency to present the evacuation plan that would apply to your family and town. Ask any questions you wish. If you do not feel safe enough, write to your congressmen and the President. Consider writing a report for your local newspaper about the discussion and the responses to your letters.

2. As you work for peace, prevent possible isolation by joining or forming a local group that shares your convictions.

3. Keep educating yourself. *Fellowship Magazine*, *Sojourners*, and *The Other Side* are three publications among many others that will keep you updated and will lead you to further resources. Also, invite friends to study with you *A Matter of Faith: A Study Guide for Churches on the Nuclear Arms Race*, available from Sojourners Book Service, 1309 L Street N. W., Washington, DC 2000.

THE LAST INQUEST

by John Somerville

PROLOGUE

The nuclear war that everyone was talking about took place and was over very quickly, like a combined tornado and forest fire on a planetary scale. The big cities, the nerve centers of what is called civilization, were the first to go; along with them went their massed populations and the main networks of industry and social services, including the health services. People in the countryside and the relatively undeveloped regions of the planet held on longer, but they could not escape the radiation-saturated atmosphere which poisoned them and burned them away. Not a bite of food nor a drink of water was uncontaminated, and within a year there were four billion corpses of unburied dead. For a time the stench was so great that it might have been imagined that if there had been people on the moon they would have been sickened by it. But radiation is a wonderful sterilizer, so that it was not long before all life processes on earth came to a halt, even the biochemical processes of decaying corpses. Thus, life and its silent partner death were both banished from the earth. The very last groups of people to go were the top leaders of government in the most highly industrialized countries, where dwelling and meeting places had been constructed far underground. These were to enable government and military leaders to carry out their executive functions in safety even when nuclear missile exchanges were incinerating people and melting buildings up above. These retreats were well stocked with provisions, commnication systems and oxygen. But of course such supplies were of limited duration, and there was no way of replenishing them once they were exhausted. The United Nations headquarters in New York also had a complex of this kind which it utilized to hold its last session. This was given over to a Commission of Inquiry created to determine how and why the uniquely final catastrophe had come about. The Commission was empowered to summon any witnesses it needed to fulfill its task. However, its communication system could get replies only from the subterranean headquarters of the American government leaders. Whether this was because the other headquarters had already been destroyed, or their inhabitants had already perished, was not known. In any case the Commission invited the President of the United States to testify; and he accepted the invitation.

The underground Council Chamber of the U.N. Center stage, on a raised dais, three Commissioners are seated, the Chairperson in the center, flanked by his two deputies. The Chairperson is male, a rather young-looking Black. The two other Commissioners are middle-aged — a European man and an Asian woman. In front of them, at floor level, are a stenographer and a clerk. On this level, farther to the right, is a table with seats for witnesses. Along the left side of the stage are rows of seats for U.N. officials. As the curtain rises, the Chair is rapping a gavel.

CHAIR. The Commission will come to order. Let the record show we are all aware of the fact that this is the last proceeding of the United Nations, convened in accordance with the provision added to the Charter at the outbreak of the present nuclear war. This provision, as you know, is to be carried out only when there has been unanimous agreement in the Security Council that the human race and the planet Earth are irreparably and irreversibly damaged, with no possibility of recovery or survival of the few remaining people — in short, when the human world, to all intents and purposes, has already come to an end. Since the Security Council is in agreement that this point has now been reached, it is our duty to try to determine how and why the human world has come to such an end. The record of any testimony given before us is to be placed in a specially constructed vault conspicuously marked so that it will be discovered in the future by other beings if there are any other living beings in the universe who might find their way here. If they do, let us hope that our record will help them to avoid the fate that we have brought upon ourselves. Since this is the whole aim of our Commission, let the record show that we have deliberately agreed not to burden our testimony or report with the sufferings, agony and grief we have all undergone — those who have already died and those few survivors who, like ourselves, have but a few weeks left. Having lived with the knowledge of the untimely death — not only untimely, but more horrible than anything ever imagined — of our nearest and dearest and the rest of the human family, all we can say now is that we will not be sorry to join them. Our one remaining wish is not that others who may read this record should weep for us, but that they should take thought for themselves. To give us the benefit of his testimony in this regard we call to the witness table the President of the United States. [*President enters from side, accompanied by the Secretary of State and the head of the U.S. Security Council, and they seat themselves at the witness table. After they are seated, the Chair continues.*] Mr. President, will you please give us, or, to speak more realistically, will you please give to future beings who might possilby follow us, the benefit of your viewpoint on the present ending of the human world.

Why did the nuclear war take place?

PRESIDENT. Thank you, Mr. Chairman, for this opportunity to testify. I am glad to respond to your request. This honorable Commission will recall that at the regular session of the General Assembly, on October 4, 1977, the President of the United States made the policy speech for our delegation. In that speech he plainly said, quote: "I hereby solemnly declare on behalf of the United States, that we will not use nuclear weapons except in self-defense; that is, in circumstances of an actual nuclear or conventional attack on the United States, our territories or armed forces, or such an attack on our allies."[1] End quote. Let me repeat, "in circumstances of an actual nuclear *or conventional* attack."

CHAIR. Why did he say that?

PRESIDENT. Why, that was a plain warning to the Soviets and their allies, of what would happen if they made any armed attack against us or our allies. It is therefore clear that the blame for the present situation rests entirely upon them. When our intelligence sources fully agreed with the reports we received from the South Korean government that the new fighting which broke out between North and South Korea was caused by North Korean forces attacking South Korean border units, I was duty bound, as Commander-in-Chief, to order nuclear retaliation when the conflict began to widen. I had to carry out the policy commitment that had been solemnly declared. But the communists refused to recognize our signals. The North Koreans replied to our nuclear weapons with nuclear weapons which they could have obtained only from the Soviets, so we had no choice but to use nuclear weapons against the Soviets' military installations. The Soviets retaliated in kind, and the nuclear conflict became world wide. That is what brought the world to its present end. The responsibility for what happened is entirely theirs.

WOMAN COMMISSIONER. Mr. President, were you aware that the North Korean government denied that its forces had made any attack?

PRESIDENT. Of course I knew that. But I also know that they can't be trusted. They always say they didn't attack.

WOMAN. Could you not have called for an impartial investigation by the United Nations before using nuclear weapons?

PRESIDENT. A *United Nations* investigation? Forgive me, Madame Commissioner, if I remind you that these very Communist states are members of the United Nations with the power to veto and block any effective military measure that is not to their liking.

WOMAN. Don't you have the same veto power as the Soviet Union?

PRESIDENT. Yes, but we don't use it as they do. We have never hesitated to approve military measures against the enemies of the free world.

WOMAN. Didn't your country at one time have a policy of not using nuclear weapons unless they were first used against you? [*President has a whispered consultation with the Secretary of State and the head of the U.S. Security Council, who hands him a document, pointing his finger at a certain passage.*]

PRESIDENT. That situation was cleared up before I took office. In 1975 the American Secretary of Defense, James Schlesinger, called a press conference in Washington in order to set the public record straight, so there would no longer be any doubt in anyone's mind. In that conference, which was correctly reported by *The New York Times* of July 2, 1975, Secretary Schlesinger said, quote: "Under no circumstances could we disavow the first use of nuclear weapons." End quote. He further pointed out, as the *Times* reported: "Under the new doctrine of selective strikes against Soviet military installations, Mr. Schlesinger did not foreclose the possibility of first use of strategic weapons." End quote. That meant of course the most powerful nuclear weapons. That press conference was a public signal to the Soviets and their allies, a signal they could not fail to notice.

WOMAN. Was this the reason the President refused the offer the Soviet Union made four times — in 1976, 1979, 1980 and again in 1981 — to sign a joint treaty of no-first-use of nuclear weapons?[2]

PRESIDENT. Of course it was. We had to retain the option of first-use of nuclear weapons in order to counter their superiority in tanks. Forgive me again if I remind you that our long experience with the Communists in general and the Soviet Union in particular has taught us a number of things, and we have to form our policy in the light of these realities. First, the only argument they really understand is force, deadly force. And the reason for this is that they just don't put the same value on human life that we do. And they don't believe in God, so they're not bound by the Commandments the way we are. If we signed a no-first-use agreement with them, how could we trust them to keep it?

WOMAN. Didn't you feel they wanted to live as much as you did?

PRESIDENT. Not at all. How could they? They're atheists, and they don't believe in human rights — the right to life, liberty, and the pursuit of happiness — the way we do. They didn't care about life so long as they could destroy us.

WOMAN. But how would you have lost anything by signing a treaty of no-first-use? They still might have wanted to go on living, for their own ungodly reasons, and they might have kept their word not to be the first to use nuclear weapons. After all, under such a treaty you still would have had your own nuclear weapons, and could still have used them in case the other side broke its word. What would you have lost?

PRESIDENT. Why, we would have lost the advantage of making the first nuclear strike. Don't you see, *our* policy allowed us to make the first nuclear strike with a clear conscience.

WOMAN. Is your conscience clear now, Mr. President?

PRESIDENT. Of course it is.

WOMAN. Even though your action resulted in ending the world?

PRESIDENT. It was our duty to follow the commitment we had made.

WOMAN. No matter where it led? Does anyone have a right to make war in a way that ends the world?

PRESIDENT. [*After conferring in whispers with the Secretary of State*]: Madame Commissioner, there are things more important than peace.

WOMAN. You mean it is sometimes necessary for a nation to go to war in order to protect its national interests and its people's lives?

PRESIDENT. Exactly. That is why every nation has a right to go to war.

WOMAN. Let me ask you, Mr. President, can national interests ever be protected by destroying all national interests?

PRESIDENT. Of course not.

WOMAN. Can human lives ever be protected by destroying all human lives?

PRESIDENT. Of course not.

WOMAN. Then no nation has a right to wage war with weapons that destroy all national interests and all human lives.

PRESIDENT. But it's still war, and all nations have the right to go to war.

WOMAN. Mr. President, are you familiar with the form of athletics called boxing?

PRESIDENT. Yes, of course.

WOMAN. Would it still be boxing if we put a hand grenade in each glove, so that when one boxer hits the other, they would both be dead?

PRESIDENT. No. That would hardly be boxing. You would need a new word for that.

WOMAN. And the fact that people still had a right to box, and to promote boxing matches, would not give them the right to do the new thing?

PRESIDENT. Certainly not.

WOMAN. Is it the purpose of war to annihilate all national interests and all human lives?

PRESIDENT. Not at all.

WOMAN. Then if you are engaged in armed conflict and you begin to use weapons that can annihilate all national interests

163

and all human lives, it could hardly be called war, could it?

PRESIDENT. But we don't have any other word.

WOMAN. But surely we can make one. When we have a new thing, we can make a new word to go with it, can we not?

PRESIDENT. Yes, that has been done.

WOMAN. In this case, would it be apropriate to call the new kind of armed conflict omnicide rather than war?

PRESIDENT. Omnicide?

WOMAN. Yes, because it is the annihilation of all human beings. Suicide is killing oneself; genocide is killing a whole nation; omnicide is killing everybody including oneself. This word was actually proposed by an American philosopher.

PRESIDENT. It seems logical.

WOMAN. Then would nations have the same right to commit omnicide that they have to wage war?

PRESIDENT. No. Omnicide would be a different thing.

WOMAN. Your conscience wasn't clear about omnicide, only about war?

PRESIDENT. That's right. I was faced with a war, and I made my decisions on that basis.

WOMAN. Would you have done the same thing if you had thought of it as omnicide?

PRESIDENT. Probably not.

CHAIR. Let me go back, Mr. President, to your earlier statement that you felt the Soviets and their allies, because of their communist ideology, didn't place as high a value on human life as you and your allies did. If that were true, how could we account for the behavior of the Soviets in the Cuban missile crisis of 1962?

PRESIDENT. What behavior are you referring to, Mr. Chairman?

CHAIR. I'm referring to their behavior as reported by President Kennedy's brother, Robert, in his memoir about that crisis in which he had played a leading part as the President's adviser and personal negotiator with the Soviet Ambassador. I believe Robert Kennedy was at that time Attorney General of the United States.

PRESIDENT. That is correct, Mr. Chairman.

CHAIR. It appears from Robert Kennedy's report, which I have before me — I mean his memoir that was published under the title, *Thirteen Days*, with the subtitles, "Memoir of the Cuban Missile Crisis" and "The Story about How the World Almost Ended" — it appears that the American government already had nuclear missile bases in Turkey, closer to the Soviet Union than Cuba is to the United States, before the Soviets placed their missiles in Cuba. That is true?

PRESIDENT. Of course. Everyone knew that.

CHAIR. And the year before, in 1961, the unsuccessful Bay of Pigs invasion of Cuba by forces trained, equipped and financed by the U.S. government had taken place?

PRESIDENT. Yes, but President Kennedy later admitted that was a mistake.

CHAIR. I see. But it must have had something to do with the Soviet missiles being placed in Cuba at the time. Isn't that so?

PRESIDENT. There was no need for them to do that; and they knew we considered those missiles an intolerable threat.

CHAIR. Didn't your missiles in Turkey equally threaten them?

PRESIDENT. Certainly not. Our missiles in Turkey were purely defensive. Furthermore, they lied to us. They said they would never put offensive missiles in Cuba.

CHAIR. Didn't the American government lie to them when it said it had no spy planes flying over their territory from the American bases in Turkey until one of them, piloted by a man named Powers, was shot down? Didn't the American government lie to them about not training, equipping and financing an invasion force to overthrow the government of Cuba until the truth came out at the Bay of Pigs, and it had to be acknowledged?

PRESIDENT. Those things were different. They were military secrets. Everyone tells lies about military secrets; everyone expects it.

CHAIR. Then why were you so surprised when you discovered they were placing missiles in Cuba?

PRESIDENT. Because they themselves had told us they wouldn't do that.

CHAIR. Well, wasn't that a military secret, like the American plans for the invasion of Cuba, or the American spy planes flying over the Soviet Union?

PRESIDENT. They didn't lie because those were military secrets. They lied because their Communist ideology teaches them they have a right to lie and cheat, and because they don't believe in human rights.

CHAIR. Did you say human rights?

PRESIDENT. Yes.

CHAIR. Under human rights, do you include equal rights for all nations?

PRESIDENT. Certainly we do.

CHAIR. Then if you had a right to have your missiles in Turkey, why didn't they have an equal right to have their missiles in Cuba?

PRESIDENT. Mr. Chairman, we always had to remember that when we were dealing with them we were dealing with international outlaws who believe in force and violence. They were trying to blackmail us, and we had to keep the upper hand. They were nothing but terrorists.

CHAIR. And that is why President Kennedy rejected the Soviet offer to settle the crisis peacefully by a simultaneous removal of the missiles both from Cuba and from Turkey?[3]

PRESIDENT. Yes. They were blackmailers and terrorists. We wouldn't make deals with them.

CHAIR. And that is why the President sent an ultimatum to the Soviets that they must undertake to remove their missiles from Cuba unilaterally and unconditionally within twenty-four hours, or they would be destroyed by American bombing?

PRESIDENT. Certainly. If we had let them threaten us and get away with it, what kind of a future could we have looked forward to? We had to teach them a lesson.

CHAIR. And now we are trying to find out why your lesson deprived all of us of any future at all. On page 108 and 109 of the American Library edition of *Thirteen Days* Robert Kennedy describes how he delivered the ultimatum to the Soviet Ambassador in Washington, and what followed. Let me read that passage and ask you a question about it. "I returned to the White House. The President was not optimistic, nor was I. He ordered twenty-four troop-carrier squadrons of the Air Force Reserve to active duty. They would be necessary for an invasion. He had not abandoned hope, but what hope there was now rested with Khrushchev's revising his course within the next few hours. It was a hope, not an expectation. The expectation was a military confrontation by Tuesday, and possibly tomorrow . . ." End quote. It is evident from this that the American President actually did not expect the Soviets to obey his ultimatum; Soviet obedience was only a hope, but not an expectation. Yet he sent the ultimatum which he expected to result in nuclear war. Did you agree with that kind of policy?

PRESIDENT. I certainly did, Mr. Chairman. That became a model not only for me, but for every President that followed John Kennedy. It is courage and patriotism of the highest kind to sticl· to your principles even when you expect the worst.

CHAIR. But in this case Robert Kennedy himself tells us on page 106 exactly what the President and the other leaders expected to result from nuclear war between the United Staes and the Soviet Union, each with its overkill nuclear arsenal. Referring to the President, Robert Kennedy wrote, quote: "The thought that disturbed him the most, and that made the prospect of war much more fearful than it would otherwise have been, was the specter of the death of the children of this country and all the world—the young people who had no role, who had no say, who knew nothing even of the confrontation, but whose lives would be snuffed out like everyone else's." End quote. In other words, all the children and everyone else would be killed off. Were you familiar with this memoir, Mr. President?

PRESIDENT. Of course. It's well known. It was first published in a popular magazine.

CHAIR. A *popular* magazine?

PRESIDENT. Yes, a family magazine. *McCall's* magazine.

CHAIR. I see. In fact, on the very first page of his memoir, Robert Kennedy spoke of the Cuban missile crisis as, quote, "a confrontation between the two giant atomic nations, the U.S. and the U.S.S.R., which brought the world to the abyss of nuclear destruction and the end of mankind."

PRESIDENT. Exactly. But you see, it didn't happen. They would have destroyed the world, but we prevented them from doing so because we made them back down.

CHAIR. But why did they back down?

PRESIDENT. They backed down because they didn't have courage enough to face the war that would destroy the world. Only we had that courage.

CHAIR. I see. But after that, they didn't back down again, did they?

PRESIDENT. No, they didn't. It only goes to show we were right from the beginning.

CHAIR. What do you mean by that?

PRESIDENT. I mean, they can't be trusted.

CHAIR. I see. Now I believe I understand your policy as a whole. I have no further questions. [*Looks inquiringly at the two other Commissioners.*]

MAN COMMISSIONER. I would like to ask the President about certain aspects of American policy in the period preceding the outbreak of the war that put an end to the world of which we are the last survivors. I am thinking particularly of what took place in Iran and Afghanistan at the end of 1979 and the beginning of 1980. I remember reading President Carter's address to the American people explaining his policy. I believe the press at the time called it the Carter Doctrine, and in it he used the concept of "containment" in the sense that the Soviet Union must be contained within its own borders. Do you recall that, Mr. President?

PRESIDENT. Yes, I do. That word and concept, as you call it, dates back to the period following World War II, during the early stages of the U.N., when we were faced with Communist expansionism. Afghanistan was another instance of that. It's the Communist tactics of infiltration and external domination. We had to put a stop to that.

MAN. And by what method did you intend to restrain Soviet expansionism and put an end to the external domination that you felt it involved?

PRESIDENT. Obviously, there's only one method of doing that. You've got to expand; you've got to go into those countries the

167

Soviets would like to influence, and gain control there by giving them aid and support, especially military aid and support. Give them all kinds of inducements to oppose the Soviets and to follow our policy. Take food as an example. They're usually short of food, and food is a weapon that can make them dependent on us, and keep their policy in line with ours. They won't want to bite the hand that feeds them.⁴ But the best way the governments of those countries can resist their own Communists and remain independent of the Soviets is to supply them with modern weapons of whatever kind they can use, and keep them well supplied as time goes on.

MAN. In other words, the containment policy is to prevent Soviet Communist expansion by means of a world-wide American capitalist expansion.

PRESIDENT. Yes, that's the point. After all, we represent the free world, so when they become dependent on us, that is not external domination because we're making them part of the free world, bringing them freedom.

MAN. Is that why, in the Carter Doctrine address, the President said that his warships were going to control the Persian Gulf, and if the Soviets tried to move in there, he would keep them out, by force if necessary?

PRESIDENT. Of course. We wanted their oil to come to us, that is, to the free world, and we had to protect Iran against Soviet invasion.

MAN. You are aware that the government of Iran repeatedly declared that the United States was its greatest enemy, and any American blockade of the Persian Gulf would be an act of war against Iran?

PRESIDENT. Of course I am aware of that, but we have to be aware also that people don't always know what's good for them. Didn't Iran have to be protected from the kind of Soviet invasion that took place in Afghanistan? Didn't the U.N. itself, by majority vote of the General Assembly, condemn the Soviet invasion of Afghanistan?

MAN. Mr. President, I have to correct you on that point. I took part in the General Assembly debate to which you refer. The U.S. delegation argued for the word "invasion" and the word "condemn,' but the majority of the General Assembly did not accept either word.

PRESIDENT. But the Resolution was passed by majority vote. What did it say?

MAN. It said that the General Assembly *deplores* the *intervention*.

PRESIDENT. Well, isn't that the same thing?

MAN. No, it is not.

PRESIDENT. Why not? What is the difference?

MAN. The difference is this: Invasion is by definition something that could not have been requested, and must be illegal. Intervention, whether wise or unwise, can be requested, and is legal when requested.

PRESIDENT. Do you think Afghanistan requested the Soviet troops?

MAN. I do. That was the testimony of the delegate from Afghanistan during the debate. That delegate was appointed by the Afghanistan government.

PRESIDENT. Of course he was. After the Soviet troops came in, they took over, and put their own people in power.

MAN. You didn't understand me, Mr. President. This was the delegate who had been appointed by the previous Afghanistan administration, that of President Amin.[5] We had to take account of the fact that, ever since the Marxist-oriented revolution of 1978 in Afghanistan, there had been a treaty of friendship and cooperation, including military cooperation, between Afghanistan and the U.S.S.R. As you know, a civil war had been going on in Afghanistan, and the rebels were being increasingly aided and supported from across the border, by Pakistan and its friends. It did not surprise us that Afghanistan should request Soviet troops to come to its aid, in accordance with the treaty; but we thought it unwise of Afghanistan to request such troops, and unwise of the U.S.S.R. to undertake such military intervention. Thus we deplored it, but we had to recognize the difference between a requested military intervention in accordance with a treaty, which is legal, and an invasion, which is illegal. What worried us was the degree to which calling it an "invasion," and claiming that the U.N. had "condemned" it, contributed to the atmosphere of are hysteria in the United States.

PRESIDENT. Why do you think it contributed to an atmosphere of war hysteria. Why do you call it that?

MAN. I will answer that question, Mr. President, by asking another if I may. Do you think the American public would have accepted draft registration in peace time, the shelving of Salt II, the return to the cold war, and the threats to use nuclear weapons, unless the public had first accepted the term "invasion" of Afghanistan, and imagined it to be similar to Hitler's invasion of Poland? [*President has whispered consultation with Secretary of State.*]

PRESIDENT. Mr. Commissioner, the American public is justifiably suspicious of anything the Communists in general and the Soviet Union in particular may do. We have some good reasons for comparing Soviet behavior with that of Hitler.

MAN. I should hope, in view of the Soviet role in the alliance *against* Hitler in World War II and in the founding of the United Nations, that you also have some good reasons for *contrasting* the behavior of the Soviets to that of Nazi Germany. Most of us in the U.N. shudder to think what might have happened if we and the U.S.S.R. had not been allies fighting on the same side in World War II.

PRESIDENT. You mean you have nothing against the Soviet Union?

MAN. No, I don't mean that. Most of us differ profoundly with the Soviet Union in regard to the question of freedom — the freedom of the individual and individual conscience — but we differ with them as we differ with those who follow a different religion. We do not regard them as criminals outside the law, but as competitors who have equal rights with ourselves. As equal founding members of the United Nations, they have as much right to their Communism, and to their views on freedom and atheism as we have to our capitalism, and our views on freedom and religion. They have as much right to expand as we have, as much right to make treaties and alliances as we have, as much right to be atheists and to convert others to atheism as we have to be religious and convert others to our religion. Within the United Nations the game is often power politics, but it can never be cops and robbers. There had to be a single standard that applied to all members if we all wanted to survive in a nuclear world.

PRESIDENT. We had nothing against a single standard, Mr. Commissioner. We didn't demand a double standard for ourselves.

MAN. If you didn't demand a double standard, why did you maintain your naval forces inside Cuba, even though the Cuban government had for years protested against your presence and repeatedly asked you to withdraw those forces, at the same time that you condemned the Soviet forces in Afghanistan repeatedly declared they had requested the troops in accordance with their treaty? This is only one instance of your double standard; others have emerged in earlier testimony. [*President confers in whispers with Secretary of State.*]

PRESIDENT. Mr. Commissioner, we do not recognize the present government of Cuba, nor do we regard the present government of Afghanistan as legal. We feel that Communists or friends of Communists can never be trusted.

MAN. Unfortunately, that is exactly what created your double standard. I have no further questions.

CHAIR. Do you wish to add anything to your testimony, Mr. President, before we retire to deliberate on our conclusion?

PRESIDENT. I have nothing to add, Mr. Chairman.

CHAIR. Thank you, Mr. President. The session will adjourn until we have arrived at our conclusion. [*The three Commissioners retire.*]

Two days later. Same persons present, in same places.

CHAIR. The Commission will come to order. I will read our conclusion, to which all members of the Commission have agreed.
[*Reads from paper.*] The physical cause of the ending of the
human world was the use of nuclear weapons. If the war had
been fought with conventional weapons the human world would
have survived and continued. But of course nuclear weapons as
such cannot be charged with the blame. They do not make
themselves nor do they use themselves. They are made only by
governments, and are used in war only by the decision of
governments. Therefore, the ending of the human world could
have been prevented by human beings in several ways: 1) By
not producing the nuclear weapons. 2) By destroying the
nuclear stockpiles before they were used, and prohibiting further
production of such weapons. 3) By mutual agreement not to be
first to use them even though they existed. 4) By refusal of those
attacked with nuclear weapons to fight back with nuclear
weapons.

Thus the direct and primary human cause of the end of the
world was the decision of the American government to be the
first to use nuclear weapons after World War II. The main moral
responsibility therefore lies with those who made that decision.
Secondary causes were the failure of the American people to put
pressure on their government to adopt the Soviet proposal to
conclude a mutual treaty of no-first-use of nuclear weapons, and
the fact that the Soviet government responded with nuclear
weapons to the American government's first-use of those
weapons. In one sense the Soviet government had a legal right to
reply to the American nuclear weapons with its own nuclear
weapons. However, at a deeper moral level, the U.S.S.R. could
still have chosen not to use its nuclear weapons, but to resist by
non-nuclear means. Though this choice would have led to initial
or temporary defeat and occupation, the other choice led to
results even worse.

In any case, in terms of the direct and primary cause, there was
an inexcusable failure of common sense on the part of the
American government — first, a failure to realize that no one
could win a world nuclear war, that its only result could be the
destruction of everyone and everything; and second, the failure
to realize that the persistent attempt to deny equal rights to the
Soviet Union and it allies, that is, to use a double standard
against them, could not be continued with success. This fatal
failure was aided and abetted by the failure of the American
educational system to fulfill its educational duty, its duty to
teach the documented truth about these matters, and the failure
of organized religion in America to condemn sufficiently, in the

strongest moral and religious terms, the policies that admittedly could end the human world.

Our final words to any other beings of any other world who wish to avoid the tragic fate that we failed to avoid ourselves, and that turned our once green earth into a dead planet, are these: Call things by their right names, and put first things first.

CURTAIN

FOOTNOTES

¹None of the quotations or citations is imaginary. President Carter's speech was reported in the world media on October 4 and 5, 1977.

²These offers, made publicly from Bucharest, Budapest, and the U.N., at Warsaw Pact meetings and from Moscow, are of course not imaginary. They were so scantily reported in American media that our public is scarcely aware of them.

³Everything said about the Cuban missile crisis is explicitly documented in Robert Kennedy's *Thirteen Days.*

⁴John Block, President Reagan's Secretary of Agriculture, in a radio interview on December 24, 1980, emphasized that the U.S. has the most productive agriculture in the world, and said that "food is a weapon" which can make other countries "dependent on us," thus keeping their policy "in line with ours because no one wants to bite the hand that feeds them."

⁵All this was reported in the media. Everything said by the Commissioner about the U.N. debate and the General Assembly Resolution is documented fact.

Suggestions for Discussion

1. What information revealed in the play was new to you about the following: a) the Cuban missile crisis, b) the statements made by Robert Kennedy, c) the first strike policy of the U.S., d) the Russian intervention in Afghanistan?

2. Repeatedly the play refers to a "double standard" in evaluating of U.S.S.R. and U.S. foreign policy. Define in your own words what this double standard is and what examples in the play show that it exists.

3. The final document passed by the UN Commission outlines how the disaster could have been avoided. Compare this with the recommendations made by the UN during the Second Special Session on Disarmament in June/July 1982. Develop your own scenario outlining steps that should be taken to create a completely nuclear-free world ten years from now. Suggest activities for each of the ten years. When you are done, share your scenarios in groups of five.

4. Explain how the "fatal failure was aided and abetted by the American education system to fulfill its educational duty." What is taught in schools regarding peace and the survival of the human race? What should be taught? How can you help make this change in the educational system? Think about possibilities for your local schools.

5. The play also points to the failure of the religious community to speak out strongly against policies which could end the human world. What is our responsibility in this area? What has already been done by leaders of your denomination and members of your congregation? What other steps could you see taking on a national and local level? Brainstorm about possibilities.

Prejudice

The New Testament records many instances in which Jesus acted without prejudice against women, gentiles, and Samaritans, none of whom an orthodox Jew at that time would have considered his equal. The Pharisees would never have stooped to address a woman on the street, ask a woman at the well for water, or approve of female disciples the way Jesus did of Mary, Martha, and Mary Magdalene.

Jesus also showed no professional prejudice. Learned and respected though he was, he did not look down on common people. The disciples he chose were fishermen and other simple folk. Where most would have worried about their reputation, he did not hesitate to eat with a despised tax collector or to heal the daughter of an officer of the occupying Roman army. His sermons were not for the highly educated Scribes and Pharisees but for people who, like children, could receive the news of the kingdom with an open heart.

And what about racial or national prejudice? When Jesus cleansed the temple, it was in part to allow Gentiles to worship there. When he sent out his disciples, he wanted the word of God told to *all* people, including gentiles, a mission that Paul later proceeded to carry out. A most striking effort to counteract national and religious prejudice is the New Testament's portrayal of the Samaritans; for although the Jews despised them, they are repeatedly shown as fulfilling the will of the Lord. The woman at the well was from Samaria. Of the ten lepers that Jesus healed, only the Samaritan returned to give thanks. The most outstanding example, of course, is the story of the Good Samaritan, who is held up by Christ as one who acted upon God's highest commandment: Love your neighbor as yourself.

Jesus' actions showed that men and women of all professions, races, and nationalities are deserving of God's love. Since we are to follow Christ's example, we also need to overcome our biasis and reach out to all people. Yet our history is one long record of our blind refusal to recognize our fellow human beings as brothers and sisters. The notion that "I am better than you" has made possible the institution of slavery, the imposition of Western civilization on cultures we thought inferior, the denial of rights to women, the continued racial discrimination against blacks, and the attempts to force other countries into economic dependence. Propaganda and ideology has encouraged prejudices. In Nazi Germany, a society permeated by violence, aggressive behavior was systematically channeled against Jews. Jews were presented as the root of all evil, and their extermination as the solution to all problems. During the Second World War, Pearl Harbor set off a wave of resentment against the Japanese which ultimately made the dropping of two atomic bombs on civilian populations seem acceptable. Today, prejudice is rampant in the cold war between East and West. We know little of the Russians, and they know little of us. Yet prejudice allows us to proclaim that "the Russians can't be trusted" and to target nuclear warheads against cities in the Soviet Union. Today as in the past, we feel justified in killing if the other side is presented as all evil while we are totally good.

What can be done? First of all, it helps to be informed. Prejudice implies not knowing one another; and this can be corrected. As long as Russians think all Americans are out to kill for profit and Americans believe that Russians cannot wait to come over and destroy democracy, we will keep building bombs. Why not show films on television that value the Russian culture and show people who laugh, cry, celebrate, mourn, love, and die like people anywhere else in the world? They in turn should portray American individuals with the same respect. Recently, a group from California asked US families to participate in a Soviet-American photo exchange. The idea was to put the portrait of the other family in one's living room to remember that they, too, had parents and children and pets as we do; they, too, have human faces and feelings and a desire to live.

Another way to overcome prejudice is to participate in exchange programs and actually live with families in another country. Neither the visitor not the host family will ever again think of members of the other nations as abstractions. Rather than draft young people into armies, governments could draft every sixteen to eighteen year old in this global village to spend one year doing voluntary service in another country, preferably the country his or her nation is most ready to harm. This would soon end the desire to wage war against one another. It would also create the sense of world community we so desperately need.

The three plays in this section deal with the problem of prejudice at different levels. "The Stone Wall" shows how suspicions and mistrust can escalate into hatred. "Don't Cry, Chiisai" recounts how two young people, a Japanese American and a Quaker, battle against racial and national prejudices that threaten their relationship. A positive outcome in both plays depends upon people's willingness to set aside their biases and learn to relate to each other as human beings rather then "enemies." The last play, "The Trial," reveals how we tend to place blame on individuals but ignore the systemic evil of which we are a part. In the play, a judge is invited

175

to preside over the trial of a woman who has broken all the commandments of God. In his condemnation of her, he forgets that he, too, has sinned against humanity by tolerating corporate evil. In the end he realizes that the way of redemption is not self-righteous aloofness, but self-identification with the fallen.

THE STONE WALL

by Ingrid Rogers

(Dedicated to my friend Heidrun on the other side of the Iron Curtain and to people like her on either side.)

CHARACTERS

GROUP I: *Betty and Bob and their daughter Barbara, Bob's sister Brenda, and their friend Bill, and his brother Ben.*

GROUP II: *Dick and Dora and their son Don, Dora's sister Darlene, and their friends David and Dwight.*

STAGING

No costuming or stage sets or furniture are needed. Imagine the stones and the wall. An open area for the stage and at least two aisles through the audience are all that are necessary, except for a sign that says "TEN YEARS LATER" to be held up at the beginning of Scene 2.

SCENE 1

Bob and Dick start collecting imaginary stones on opposite sides of the stage area. They pile the stones higher and higher. The dialogue runs parallel, switching from one group to the other. Bill enters and walks up to Bob.

BILL. Hey, what are you doing, Bob?

BOB. Time to start protecting myself. I don't trust those people over there. [*David comes and approaches Dick.*]

DAVID. Hey, Dick, what are all the stones for?

DICK. See that fellow over there? He's been piling them up for a while. Makes me nervous. I know he's getting ready to throw them at me. So I'm getting ready to defend myself, if need be.

BOB. Don't just stand there, Bill, Get busy. When they start throwing stones, you'll get it, too, you know.

BILL. Yeah, I guess you're right. [*Bill bends over and starts helping.*]

BILL. Maybe I should get my brother Ben to help me, too. [*Bill goes off and returns with Ben.*]

DICK. Go get Dwight, will you? Looks like they are increasing their work force there. We'd better be prepared when it all breaks loose.

DAVID. I hate those folks! Why can't they leave us alone? [*David leaves to get Dwight. Betty appears next to Bob.*]

BETTY. Now what's gotten into you? Are you crazy? Wasting all day with those dumb stones. Who's going to get the farmwork done?

BOB. Oh, Betty, you need to get your priorities straight. What good will the farmwork do us when they have killed us all? Look at that pile of stones they have gathered. Can't you tell what's up?

[*The men continue piling up stones. Dora comes up to Dick.*]

DICK. It's about time you got here, Dora. We are going to run out of stones soon. They have better resources over there. I need our household money to buy some more stones.

DORA. You've got to be kidding! How can I give you the household money for stones? What are we supposed to use for food, pray tell?

DICK. Better to tighten our belts a little than be destroyed by those people over there. If they can do it, we can, too. [*The men continue to pile up stones.*]

SCENE 2

Someone walks across the stage with the sign "Ten Years Later." Barbara and her aunt Brenda come onto the "B" area of the stage, and Don and his aunt Darlene come onto the other.

BARBARA. Hey, Aunt Brenda, what's behind that big wall?

BRENDA. Bad people, little one. Very bad, ungodly people.

BARBARA. Why, Aunt Brenda?

BRENDA. They want to kill us, baby. Some people are just mean, you know. You don't understand that yet.

DON. Why do Dad and Dwight keep working on that wall, Aunt Darlene?

DARLENE. To protect you, Don.

DON. Protect me from what?

DARLENE. From the bad people that live on the other side of the wall.

DON. But the wall is so high already! Aren't we protected enough?

DARLENE. So long as they keep working on the wall, we have to, also.

DON. What do you think the people are really like over there?

DARLENE. Hush, Don. They are bad people. Don't ask any more questions.

178

SCENE 3

As Bill, Bob, and Ben go up one aisle, they talk to the people and shout out the slogans below. Dick, David, and Dwight do the same in the other aisle. Each repeats the slogans over and over while moving around. Both groups use the same sentences but don't say them at the same time.

BILL/DICK. Give to the great cause. Help protect our families from the enemy.

BOB/DAVID. Don't worry about unemployment or education. Help us pile up the stones. Do this for democracy and freedom! Only $200 billion a year!

SCENE 4

Betty and Dora are asleep on the floor, each on her own side of the wall. Betty wakes up.

BETTY. Only 5 a.m. I wish I could sleep some more. There is so much on my mind. All anyone seems to care about is that cursed wall! Sometimes I want to go and see what they are really like on the other side of the wall. [*Betty lies down again. Dora sits up and yawns.*]

DORA. Morning already! I wish I didn't have to face it. All this worry and always feeling so afraid. Sometimes I wonder why we couldn't just tear that wall down. Would they really throw stones at us if we did that? [*Betty sits up again.*]

BETTY. I wonder if there are women over there who are just as upset about this stone wall as I am.

DORA. If only I could let someone over there know how I feel. [*Both stand up and begin to move toward the wall. Each climbs up on the wall. Suddenly they notice each other. As they do, they look terrified. Then they slowly nod their heads for a greeting.*]

BETTY. [*Slowly, hesitatingly*]: Hi!

DORA. Hi!

BETTY. [*Still looking scared*]: Are you . . . are you from over there?

DORA. Yes . . . and you? [*Betty nods her head.*]

DORA. Do you . . . have children?

BETTY. Yeah, we have two—Barbara and Belinda.

DORA. We have three—two boys and a girl. Don, the oldest, just started school.

BETTY. Funny that we can talk to each other, isn't it?

DORA. They say over here that you're going to kill us.

BETTY. Oh, that's what they tell us about you, too.

DORA. But . . . you look friendly!

179

BETTY. I guess we just haven't had a chance to look at each other, face to face . . . . [*They reach out and join their hands.*]

BETTY. What if we went back . . .

DORA. and told them . . .

BETTY. that it all isn't true . . .

DORA. and that we both have children . . .

BETTY. children who need food . . .

DORA. and jobs . . .

BETTY. and life.

DORA. Yes! Life! A future in peace without fear! [*They embrace and say together as they walk away from each other:*]

BETTY/DORA. Let us tell them quickly!

Suggestions for Discussion

1. Do you think the hostility toward people of other nations is a matter of "not looking at each other, face to face?" Explain.

2. Does Bob's and Dick's desire to protect themselves seem reasonable to you? What kind of activities by others make *you* feel threatened? What "defensive measures" do you take?

3. How could the activity have been stopped when it was still in the initial stages? Why does it become harder and harder to control as the building continues?

4. Think of situations at school, at home, or at work when you have a) built walls or prepared to throw stones, and b) removed walls or climbed over them.

DON'T CRY, CHIISAI, DON'T CRY

by Jonathan Lindley

(An adaptation of the book "Don't Cry, Chiisai, Don't Cry"
by Ruth Farlow Uyesugi)

CHARACTERS

RUTH ANNA FARLOW, *a student at Earlham College*
LOTTE, *her roommate*
EDDIE UYESUGI

*There are also a large number of students, professors, friends and
enemies. These should by played by an ensemble with a great deal
of doubling and possibly tripling. Five additional men and five additional women can comprise an ensemble to handle all other parts.*

LOCALE

*December 7, 1941 and the years that followed in Richmond, Ind.
and Portland, Oregon.*

PRONUNCIATIONS

*Three basic rules to follow when pronouncing Japanese words and
names are: 1) Sound each syllable. 2) Give each syllable equal emphasis. 3) All vowels take the short sound. For example, Hiroshima
would be pronounced Hih-roh-shih-mah.*

*The name Uyesugi has two pronunciations within the context of the
play depending upon who is speaking. Anyone who speaks proper
Japanese in the play should pronounce it Wuh-soo-gi. American
characters who are not Japanese should pronounce it Yuh-soo-gi.*

*The space should be flexible enough to accomodate a representa-
tion of the various scenes necessary. Each scene can be created by
the placement of various pieces of furniture and properties. The
only fixed scenery should be a raised area approximately 4½ ft.
above floor level, and a larger area about 6½ ft. high.*

Dominating center stage is a large rear-projection screen on which images can be projected during transitions. This device, like the entire set, should be as flexible as possible. It should also be able to blend into the rest of the set during scenes to represent a wall or a map. To help facilitate the flow of action, the screen should be able to be flown out during some scene changes so that furniture and props can be transferred through this portal.

SCENE 1

Out of the darkness comes a gradually intensifying image of a Japanese flag. Music also swells up and under all of the following. This fully realized image slowly dissolves into an image of the American flag. This bursts into a sequence of World War II photos including the Pearl Harbor attack, the Japanese-American relocation process, Hiroshima, and a Library of Congress photo of a Japanese boy sitting on a suitcase. As this last image is seen, it slowly gives way to the date, December 7, 1941, on a blood red background.

This fades as lights rise on a dorm room at Earlham College. By now, the music is coming from a portable radio sitting on a nightstand. Ruth is at her desk working on Spanish. Lotte is asleep on her bed with a sheet pulled over her head.

RUTH. Duermo, duermes, duerme, dorminos, duermen. I sleep, [*She moves to Lotte but continues to look at her book.*] You sleep, he sleeps, Lotte sleeps, [*She uncovers Lotte.*] Wake up Lotte, we sleep, they sleep . . . [*She continues. Lotte's alarm clock goes off.*]

LOTTE. Good morning! [*She goes about gathering things together for her shower.*]

RUTH. [*Looking at clock*] It's nearly three in the afternoon. Why were you out so late last night?

LOTTE. Farlow! You can't be that naive. You know very well what I was doing.

RUTH. I know what you were doing, I was just asking "Why were you out so late" meaning: Why should I have to help you sneak in the window at four in the morning?

LOTTE. 'Cause that's what pals are for. [*She flings a towel over her shoulder then exits for showers.*]

RUTH. [*To herself, still trying to study*] Pals! . . . She never helped me sneak in the window . . . [*She flips a page over angrily.*] . . . Course I've never needed to . . . [*Cindy comes to door and waves down hallway to Lotte.*]

CINDY. Hi, Lotte. Merry Christmas!

LOTTE. [*From down the hall*] Happy Hanukah.

CINDY. [*Entering*] Hi!

RUTH. Oh, hi, Cindy.

CINDY. I brought you and Lotte your Christmas presents.

RUTH. Well, thanks . . . but isn't it a little early for Christmas? It's only the 7th.

CINDY. Not too early for me. As soon as it turns December 1st I can't get Christmas off my mind. It reminds me of bein' a kid . . . I get awful homesick sometimes.

RUTH. Yeah, me too.

CINDY. Watcha doin'?

RUTH. [*She shows her the cover of the book.*] Spanish test tomorrow.

CINDY. Oh, I love Spanish. Even if it's in English. [*Ruth looks up, puzzled.*] It's the accent mostly. I'm a fool for accents. Ya know what else is great. Listen to someone from Hawaii sometime. I heard it when I went to visit my brother. It's such a tropical sound.

RUTH. Figuratively speaking?

CINDY. [*Nodding agreement*] Mmm.

RUTH. What's your brother doing in Hawaii?

CINDY. Navy, He's stationed there . . . Say something in Spanish for me.

RUTH. Oh . . . Well, let's see . . . Tu es una senorita muy simpatica.

CINDY. [*With delight*] That's wonderful! What did you say?

RUTH. I think I said 'You are a very nice senorita,' uh . . . girl.

CINDY. [*Unsure*] Gra-ci-as?

RUTH. De nada. [*Cindy looks overwhelmed. They laugh.*]

CINDY. Can I help you study?

RUTH. Sure. [*She hands Cindy the book, indicating a spot on the page.*] Right here.

CINDY. O.K. . . 'to eat.'

RUTH. To eat: Como, comas, coma, comamos, coman. I eat, you eat, he eats, we eat, they eat . . .

CINDY. Good! . . . I think. 'To run.'

RUTH. To run: corro, corras, cor . . . [*The music on the radio suddenly skids to a halt. There is some commotion, shuffling of papers, and a frantic radio announcer.*]

ANNOUNCER'S VOICE. Ladies and gentlemen . . . [*More confusion*] Ladies and gentlemen . . . Pearl Harbor is being bombed by the Japanese . . . I repeat . . . [*More confusion. Ruth moves to the radio and turns up the volume.*] I repeat, ladies and gentlemen, the Japanese are attacking Pearl Harbor . . . This is not a test or a maneuver . . . Japanese war planes are attacking Oahu at this moment! We will bring you more details, ladies and gentlemen, as they come in . . . [*Music returns.*]

RUTH. Where on earth is Pearl Harbor? I've heard of it but . . .
[*She turns to see Cindy sitting motionless, staring straight
ahead, a frightened look on her face.*] Cindy? . . . What's
wrong? What is it?

CINDY. [*Quietly*] Joey . . . [*She suddenly bolts wildly for the
door. As she reaches it she runs into Lotte who is returning from
the showers.*]

LOTTE. Hey! [*She sees that Cindy is crying.*] Hold it! Cindy,
what's wrong?

CINDY. Let go! [*Cindy tears away and runs out the door.*]

LOTTE. Farlow, what happened?

RUTH. The radio just said something about Japanese bombing
Pearl Harbor.

LOTTE. God, no wonder! [*She starts back out the door after
Cindy.*]

RUTH. Lotte, what is it? What's Pearl Harbor?

LOTTE. Farlow, that's gonna be a real stupid question someday.
[*She exits. Dazed, Ruth goes back to her books. At first, she has
trouble concentrating. She looks off toward the door as her
mind returns to Cindy and Lotte. Finally, she resigns herself to
studying — bombing or no bombing. She opens her book and
recites as before.*] . . . mato, matas, mata, matamos, matan. I
kill, you kill, he kills, we kill, they all kill . . . [*A spot tightens on
her and she continues to repeat this softly under the following.
At another part of the stage, another spot picks up Mrs. Lamb.
In the pool of light we can just make out a metal coffin next to
her. She is reading a letter but we hear a man speaking the
words.*]

MAN'S VOICE. Please, Mrs. Lamb, don't look inside. The army
doesn't recommend it. Bombs aren't kind to country boys with
wind-kissed cheeks. You'll only cry. Besides, we've brought back
his dog tags and the colonel sends his deep regrets and assures
you that Private James Lamb died in the line of duty. So why do
you cry, Mrs. Lamb . . . why cry . . . why cry . . . [*The voice
fades out slowly as we see Mrs. Lamb crying uncontrollably into
the letter using it almost as a handkerchief. The spots on Mrs.
Lamb and Ruth both begin to fade slowly as we watch Mrs.
Lamb continue to cry, clutching the letter to her, and we hear
Ruth continue but also fading as she repeats her Spanish: "I kill,
you kill, he kills, etc."*]

SCENE 2

ON SCREEN: Willamette College, Portland Oregon.

Willamette College, that night. Outside Eddie's apartment we see

Kichi, a Hawaiian born Japanese boy playing in the snow in pan-
tomime building snowmen, fortresses, castles, etc. Eddie is inside
studying. After a few moments, Kichi scoops up a handful of snow,
burying his face in it. He then collapses in the snow on his back,
laughing.

KICHI. I love you, snow! [*He begins making snow angels with his*
arms.] I love you, snow! [*He rises and runs excitedly to Eddie's*
door and knocks. Eddie turns the volume down on his radio just
a bit, but doesn't look up from his book.]

EDDIE. [*Mumbling*] Who's there?

KICHI. It's Kichi.

EDDIE. Yeah, Kichi, what do you want?

KICHI. [*Entering*] I got to show you something. Look, look out
there! See? You see it?

EDDIE. [*Coming to doorway*] Where? See what?

KICHI. The snow! The snow! While I was asleep.

EDDIE. Oh, I'm sorry, Kichi. I forgot you Buddha heads don't
have the finer things of life in Hawaii. [*Too excited to stand still,*
Kichi runs out to play in the snow, giggling with delight.]

KICHI. I love you, snow! [*Eddie goes back to his book, turning the*
radio up again as he sits. Kichi goes back to his pantomime. A
song finishes on the radio and an announcer's voice takes over.]

ANNOUNCER'S VOICE. Now, the news from WKAH Portland:
Hearings were held in San Fransisco today in connection with
plans to evacuate the thousands of Japanese and Japanese
Americans living on the West Coast. Although no known
sabotage has been perpetrated as of yet by the Japanese, officials
both in Washington and in the Western Defense Command feel
that evacuation is a necessary and vital step in sustaining and en-
suring national military defense. Lieutenant General John L.
Dewitt commented:

DEWITT'S VOICE. . . . along the vital Pacific Coast over 112,000
potential enemies, of Japanese extraction, are at large today.
There are disturbing indications that these are organized and
ready for concerted action at a favorable opportunity. The very
fact that no sabotage has taken place to date is disturbing and
confirming indication that such action will be taken . . .

ANNOUNCER'S VOICE. Local officials endorsed the action
wholeheartedly today, pointing out the alarming number of
Japanese and Japanese Americans living and operating
businesses in the Portland area, especially along the water front
section of the city . . . [*During the above, Kichi continues his*
"snow ballet." He throws armfuls into the air, dancing in it as it
falls. He finally sculptures a woman out of the snow, a "snow
goddess," which he ceremoniously kneels before. After a mo-
ment, he slowly and solemnly moves closer and kisses the statue
with the reverence he would give an object of worship. As he

bows before the snow lady, two policemen enter and see the prostrate Kichi. One nods to the other and they approach him. Kichi raises his head to find the two policemen hovering over him. Silent dialogue occurs ending with Kichi pointing toward Eddie's door. The policemen hoist Kichi up between them and go to the door and knock. Eddie is startled by the knock, having become thoroughly absorbed in the radio broadcast. He shuts off the radio and returns to his book.]

EDDIE. Go away, Kichi. I have to study. [They knock once more. Eddie goes to the door and opens it to see Kichi restrained between the two policemen.]

KICHI. I sorry, Eddo, but Kichi needs you. Please, Eddo.

EDDIE. What's wrong?

KICHI. I was playing in the snow, then they come and say I am Peking Tom.

EDDIE. You're what?

KICHI. Peking Tom. What is Peking Tom?

EDDIE. Oh, a peeping Tom? What do you mean, officers? This kid was just playing in the snow — his first snow.

FIRST POLICEMAN. Yeah? Playing in the snow? A woman in that house next door swears this little Jap was looking in her window making obscene gestures at her.

SECOND POLICEMAN. [Closely examining the eyes hidden behind Eddie's glasses] You a Jap, too?

EDDIE. No, I'm an American.

FIRST POLICEMAN. I'd like to ask you a few questions. First of all, I need both your names. [He has a note pad and pencil ready to write.]

EDDIE. Edward Uyesugi and Kichimatsu Kaihatsu. [The officer hesitates in his pencil track and in one sweep tears off a sheet and hands it to Eddie with a pencil.]

FIRST POLICEMAN. Put you names down on this sheet of paper. Print in large, clear, American letters.

EDDIE. I'll be sure to print horizontally.

SECOND POLICEMAN. Don't get smart, Yoyo. [Eddie finishes writing and hands the paper to the First Policeman.]

FIRST POLICEMAN. O.K., Mr. Ki-chi . . . let's hear you explain why you were spying on that lady.

EDDIE. He wasn't spying on anybody. He was just playing in the snow . . .

KICHI. [Overlapping with Eddie] I never see snow before. I play in the snow. I love snow . . . [First Policeman cuts them off.]

FIRST POLICEMAN. Hold it, one at a time. [To Kichi] I was talking to you, mister.

KICHI. Please, sir, I no Peking Tom. I never see snow before. I love snow. I make castle in snow and I make snow lady. Come, I show you to it. [He starts for door.]

186

FIRST POLICEMAN. Sit down! [To Eddie] You got any friends in Tokyo?

EDDIE. I've never been there.

FIRST POLICEMAN. But have you got any friends there?

EDDIE. No, Sir.

SECOND POLICEMAN. [To Kichi] You ever go around the docks?

KICHI. [Confused]. . . I have little puppy once . . .

SECOND POLICEMAN. Docks! Docks! No dogs!

FIRST POLICEMAN. All right, that's enough. You're too stupid to know what an obscene gesture is. [Sizing him up] That or else you're puttin' it over on us. [To Eddie] And you're a little too smart. [To both] So just to be safe, we're going to keep a close eye on you two from now on. You better watch what you do, Japs, or we'll be on your tails quicker than you can say sayonara. [To his partner] Let's go. [They exit giving an "and we aren't kidding" look to Eddie and Kichi as they go. Kichi sits, still confused, but now becoming angry. He runs outside and begins kicking over all the invisible creations he made from the snow. His choreographic "snow ballet" now becomes a violent "hate ballet."]

KICHI. I hate you, snow! I hate you, snow! I hate you . . . [Lights slowly fade to black.]

ON SCREEN: Earlham College, Richmond, Indiana.

SCENE 3

Outside the girls' dorm. Ruth and Lotte are sitting on a bench waiting for the bus. There is another bench a few feet away. Ruth is writing a composition, obviously having trouble. Lotte is doing her nails.

RUTH. [Counting words] . . . twenty-three, twenty-four, twenty-five.

LOTTE. What are you writing about?

RUTH. Well, I was trying to do a little preaching on the evils of college life.

LOTTE. And you could only come up with twenty-five words?

RUTH. You know me, Lotte. I don't have too much first hand experience. ·

LOTTE. Why don't you just consider me a resource.

RUTH. Thanks, I'll do that.

LOTTE. With my help, your sermonette will soon become the gospel according to Ruth.

RUTH. Let's work on it tonight. I've had enough for a while.

LOTTE. O.K. [Finishing nails] How do you like this color?

RUTH. Nice. What is it?

187

LOTTE. Passionate Pink.

RUTH. Goes well with your eyes.

LOTTE. Why, thank . . . [*She realizes she's been insulted.*] . . . you. [*Ruth smiles.*] Where's that bus at? We should be throwing our money away by now. [*Looks at watch.*]

RUTH. [*Grabs her purse and rummages through it.*] Oh, my God!

LOTTE. What's the matter?

RUTH. My coin purse. It had my ten dollars in it.

LOTTE. Where is it?

RUTH. It's still sitting on my bed, right where I left it.

LOTTE. Well, you can't go all the way back up to the room now. Sure as you do, the bus'll pull up.

RUTH. Guess I blew that shopping trip.

LOTTE. Cheer up. If we're lucky, I think I can persuade that guy at the drug store to cash a check for you. I think he kinda has a thing for me. He gave me extra syrup once.

RUTH. Well, just to be sure, you better put on another coat of Passionate Pink. [*Lotte starts to put the last coat on her nails when Eddie enters, passes Ruth and Lotte and sits on the other bench to wait for the bus.*]

LOTTE. [*Jumping when she sees Eddie*] Farlow, there goes one!

RUTH. One what? Will you be careful! You're getting that passion stuff all over me.

LOTTE. One of those Japanese fellas. It's Eddie, I think. I hear he came from Portland when they started the evacuations. Isn't he a doll? Hey, dare you to ask him to cash a check for you. [*Ruth can't refuse a dare. She stands but looks nervously at Eddie and then back to Lotte. Finally, she collects herself and marches up to Eddie.*]

RUTH. Could you cash a check for me? [*Lotte gives a sign of approval. Eddie forces back a smile.*]

EDDIE. Yes, if you can make do with ten dollars.

RUTH. Oh, that'll be fine. [*She sits down by him, gets out her checkbook, and starts to write.*] Pay to the order of Eddie . . . . [*They look at each other, Ruth a bit embarrassed.*]

EDDIE. How did you know my name was Eddie?

RUTH. [*Fighting for an answer*] You look like an Eddie.

EDDIE. Oh.

RUTH. And you last name?

EDDIE. You don't know it, too?

RUTH. I'm only good with first names.

EDDIE. It's Uyesugi.

RUTH. [*Thinking she's making a joke*] Oh! You look like a . . . [*Realizing she is about to put her foot in her mouth*] . . . uh . . . Uyesugi.

EDDIE. Thank you.

RUTH. How do you spell that?

EDDIE. Which? Uyesugi or . . .

RUTH. Uyesugi.

EDDIE. Oh. U, y, e, s, u, g, i. [*Too fast*]

RUTH. O, u, y . . . I'm sorry . . .

EDDIE. [*Slower*] U . . . Y . . . E . . . S . . . U . . . G . . . I.

RUTH. Got it. Thanks. [*Finishes check, tears it off and hands it to him.*] There you are.

EDDIE. And there's your ten dollars.

RUTH. Thanks. I really appreciate it.

EDDIE. Glad I could help. [*She starts to go.*] Hey, believe it or not, I didn't get your name. [*He holds up check and she realizes she didn't sign it. She rushes back.*] Oh! I'm sorry. It's Farlow. Ruthanna Farlow.

EDDIE. You look like a Farlow.

RUTH. [*Chuckles*] Thanks.

EDDIE. Nice to meet you, Ruthanna.

RUTH. Nice to meet you, too. [*She goes triumphantly back to Lotte. They rather covertly shake hands as lights fade to black.*]

SCENE 4

The George Fox Reading Room of the Earlham campus library. Eddie and Ruth are lying on their stomachs studying, Ruth on a small rug. Both are silent for a moment. Ruth makes a few attempts to speak but reconsiders each time. Eddie, on the other hand, is quite comfortable without conversation and merely looks preoccupied with his studying. After some time he begins humming "I want a paper doll that I can call my own . . ." Finally Ruth speaks.

RUTH. You really don't like me, do you?

EDDIE. I like you very much, Furlow.

RUTH. Well, why are you so . . . so detached? It's like you're afraid to give any of yourself.

EDDIE. You're right. I'm afraid because when the war's over, your boyfriend in CO camp and the captain in the big picture on your dresser will come back.

RUTH. Oh, someone told you.

EDDIE. They enjoyed telling me. They also liked telling me when your old boyfriends come home, your experiment in interracial relations will terminate very quickly.

RUTH. Oh, no, Eddie. I'll always want you. [*Eddie yanks on the rug, catapulting Ruth into his arms. They kiss.*]

RUTH. What if the librarian comes up?

EDDIE. I never did like librarians.

RUTH. Me neither.

EDDIE. This isn't biologically intelligent, you know.

RUTH. I never liked biology either. [*They continue to embrace as offstage we hear the librarian call "lights out." They don't seem to hear. A few seconds later, the lights go out leaving the two in a pool of moonlights which slants in from a window. They look around, then at each other, then kiss again.*] I'm starting to like librarians a little better.

EDDIE. Biology's not so bad, either.

RUTH. [*Giggling*] Eddie, we've got to get out of here. It must be near curfew.

EDDIE. O K. Let's go. [*They rise and start to move. One of them trips on something, giggles.*] Hey, wait a minute. I bet the doors are locked. . .

RUTH. What'll we do?

EDDIE. Let's try the window. [*He goes to the window and opens it.*] Here we go. [*Eddie climbs out.*]

RUTH. Eddie, I can't jump that far.

EDDIE. Come on. I'll catch you.

RUTH. O.K. Here I come. [*She goes, squealing all the way. They are out of sight for a moment.*] Eddie? I have a very important question to ask you.

EDDIE. Yeah, what is it?

RUTH. Am I heavy?

EDDIE. Heavy? No, not a bit.

RUTH. Then why are your knees buckling? [*They come around the corner into view. Eddie strains, obviously overdoing it to play along with joke.*]

EDDIE. Why, what do you mean? You're light as a feather . . . Now hop down, fatty. [*They laugh. She gives him a playful swat and they embrace affectionately.*] Oh-oh!

RUTH. What?

EDDIE. Curfew lights are flashing. Come on. [*Lights fade as they run, laughing as they go.*]

SCENE 5

Richmond Town Hall. A town meeting is in progress. It is silent except for the footsteps of the chairman who is walking to a platform.

CHAIRMAN. You all know why we're here. Nobody hates this kind of thing more than I do. But you all know as well as I that something has to be done. If they didn't want these yellow-bellies in Portland, Oregon, God knows we don't want them in Richmond, Indiana.

FIRST MAN. Amen!

CHAIRMAN. Now I figure there are about 150 of us, and that ought to be enough to . . .

SECOND MAN. [*Abruptly but apologetically*] Mr. Chairman. . . [*Everyone turns but looks away quickly.*] Could I read you a letter from my son David? I received it today, but it was written just the night before he was killed in Guadalcanal. [*The other men nod triumphantly.*] I'll just read you part of the letter because I think this part he meant for you. The rest is just for his mother and me. [*His voice catches for a moment, he clears his throat and continues in a loud, clear voice.*] "Dad, I have a favor to ask you. Remember my two Japanese-American friends at Earlham? I understand some of the people of Richmond aren't making them too welcome. Well, Dad, Earlham College is still my college, too, even though I had to leave before graduation, I learned a few things there I haven't learned in the Navy. And I know the war is not Eddie and Newton's fault. They didn't start Pearl Harbor. They aren't bombing our planes. They're just a couple of ordinary guys like me and the other kids at Earlham. No, it's not their fault. So will you tell the people of Richmond that, Dad?" [*There is silence except for the thud of his footsteps as he walks out of the room.*]

SCENE 6

Ruth's dorm room, later that evening. Lights rise dimly on Ruth tossing and turning in bed. Above her head, we see the following characters flashing in and out of Ruth's dream. Lotte is also in bed, asleep.

DEAN OF WOMEN. What will your parents say?

HEAD OF ENGLISH DEPT. Your children . . . Have you thought of them?

PAT. But your backgrounds are so different . . .

PRESIDENT DENNIS. Eddie, you have a governor on you as long as you are at Earlham. What you do will affect the chances of all other Japanese-Americans getting accepted to college. We have no objections to your dating our girls, but don't date a particular one. Date all of them. And when you get back to this one, be conspicuously inconspicuous.

COLLEGE BUSINESS MANAGER. [*He has played detective for the administration.*] Where were you on the morning of April 16? Didn't you go to the biology lab during Quaker meeting and listen to Beethoven's Fifth Symphony? And in the afternoon, did you collect leaves for your botony project in the woods on back campus?

PRESIDENT DENNIS. We at Earlham are not prejudiced. As President, I say that Eddie can go to school here. He can date our white girls, but he cannot fall in love. I have lived with Orientals. I have worked with Orientals. I respect them. But I would rather die than have my daughter marry one.

191

SCHOOL LIBRARIAN. . . . and they checked out every book we have on genetics! I nearly died . . .

BETTY. God knows you've tried everything . . . Letting other guys dance you past the chaperone line at dances, hiding in the shadows of the gym bleachers at ball games. Even climbing up behind the football scoreboard. But you might as well face it, Farlow, you can't hide two people in love. There's just no place . . .

PRESIDENT DENNIS. Ruth, I've written to your father. No self-respecting, intelligent man would allow his daughter to do this thing. [*This last face fades out. Ruth, at a boiling point, screams out in anger.*]

RUTH. Stop it! . . . Leave us alone! [*She wakes up.*]

LOTTE. [*Waking up, too*] Wha . . . Whatsa matter? Oh, nightmares again, kid?

RUTH. Yeah.

LOTTE. Farlow, this is the third night in a row. I'm gettin' kinda worried. Maybe you should see someone about this.

RUTH. Oh, no, Lotte. I'm O.K.

LOTTE. What was it this time?

RUTH. Nothing.

LOTTE. Come on, you can tell me. What were you dreaming about?

RUTH. Well, at first, it was kinda neat . . . I was flying. I was some kinda bird, I guess . . . an eagle or somethin' . . . I felt like an eagle. There were other eagles flyin' around with me. Then I looked and flyin' next to me was the most beautiful bird I'd ever seen. I didn't know what kind it was, I hadn't seen one like it before. Well, we flew around awhile, then I noticed the other bird gettin' tired. Next thing I knew, all those other birds were just all over the place, crowdin' in on us, we couldn't fly through them. The other birds kept cackling all through this, more like chickens than eagles. And this big ugly bird kept ploughin' into my bird, my friend, I mean. It was like he was tryin' to knock him right out of the sky. That bird had the most hateful look in his eyes, it was awful. But is wasn't just him, they were all like that . . . he just seemed to have more guts . . . more something. Anyway, my friend couldn't take it. He crashed to the ground . . . [*She hesitates.*]

LOTTE. What is it?

RUTH. He looked so sad . . . He wanted to cry, I could tell, he looked so sad, I know he wanted to cry . . .

LOTTE. . . . but he couldn't, could he?

RUTH. No.

LOTTE. Then what happened?

RUTH. Things started changin'. Nightmare Part Two was comin' on . . . The birds started changin' into people. Ears were growin' out of the feathers, their beaks became mouths. The cackling

192

was still there, but now it was human cackling . . . a cacophony of all the gossip, malice, and insensitivity we've been confronted with . . . tormented with . . . It made me so mad.

LOTTE. Yeah, I heard you. Well, I guess it's little wonder with all the hassle you two have been getting. [*Ruth has risen and made her way to the desk by now.*]

RUTH. I know. Now I can't even get away from it when I'm asleep.

LOTTE. How does all this affect Eddie?

RUTH. Oh, you know Eddie. Nothing ever seems to really bother him. At least he doesn't let it show. Not even to me.

[*Mardy barges in making herself at home on Ruth's bed.*]

MARDY. Hi, guys. Still up?

LOTTE. Yeah, Mardy, come on in.

MARDY. Farlow, I'm glad your up. There's something I'd like to ask you.

RUTH. If you want to know where babies come from, I'd rather not discuss it.

MARDY. No, seriously, Farlow. I was in anthropology class, to-day, and Dr. Meredith told us that people of different races have a distinct odor. And I was just wondering . . . [*Ruth sits down, obviously disturbed and fed up.*] Now don't get sensitive. I was doing this for your benefit. I even held up my hand and asked Prof. Meredith if this same theory applied to Orientals, and he said 'Yes, Miss Warfel, it applies to all races, and it is not a theory. It's a fact.' Now, what I want to know is, does Eddie smell any different?

RUTH. Yes, Mardy. He smells different. He smells like the air after a spring shower. He smells like a walk on back campus when the apple orchard is in bloom. He smells like . . . [*She finally breaks down. She drops her head to the table, crying. Then she begins banging her head repeatedly on the table unable to stop.*]

LOTTE. . . . and Vitalis, too. Mardy, you've got the worst timing in the world. Get out of here! [*Trying to help Ruth*] Stop it, Farlow! [*She can't. Lotte scoops her up and drags her out and down the hall. They pass Betty and Pat coming the other way in their night robes.*]

BETTY. What's the matter with her?

LOTTE. She feels like screaming. Didn't you ever feel like scream-ing? [*Lights rise on the doorway of Dorothy Bond, the school nurse. Ruth and Lotte approach. Lotte knocks and Bond answers immediately. She doesn't seem at all surprised to see Ruth in this condition, but instantly ushers her into the room.*]

BOND. I wondered how much longer she'd take it. Put her in that bed there. I've had it ready for her for two weeks. [*Fade to black.*]

193

SCENE 7

Ruth, Lotte, Betty, and Pat are walking down a hallway as lights come up. They come to a door which reads, Eva Moore, Head Resident.

PAT. So what do you think she wants to see you for?

RUTH. What do you think?

PAT. Again? Why don't you tell 'em to leave you alone, Farlow?

RUTH. I wish it was that easy.

LOTTE. Well, you might as well brace yourself, kid. Moore's gonna give you the same as all the rest. She's a terror.

BETTY. I wonder why she never married. She still has her looks, don't you think?

LOTTE. She's always givin' me dirty looks. Does that count?

PAT. I think someone left her at the altar. Who'd want to get married to a woman who'd always be smelling in the keyhole to see if you're smoking?

LOTTE. I don't think she wanted to get married. She'd rather stay here and stage two o'clock fire drills to catch people out on all-nighters.

BETTY. I'm sure her husband died in World War I and she cries herself to sleep every night in her lonely room.

RUTH. Well, whatever her life story is, I think Eddie and I are about to become her latest chapter. Here I go . . . [*She goes in.*]

LOTTE. Poor Farlow. If she only knew the lady and the tiger were both behind that door.

PAT. I think she does, Lotte. [*The lights fade on them walking off as they come up on Ruth inside the office. Miss Moore is seated at her desk.*]

MOORE. Sit down, Ruthanna.

RUTH. I'd rather stand, please.

MOORE. I've been wanting to talk with you . . .

RUTH. [*Cutting her off*] Yes, I know what you want to talk to me about.

MOORE. Really?

RUTH. You want to tell me that it's unfair to my parents who love me, to my children who will look like God knows what, to the world that expects white to stay white and yellow to stay yellow . . . The facts are so simple, Miss Moore. Two human beings love each other. I happen to think love is God's greatest creation. And I can't believe he frowns on any kind of love, whatever the circumstances are. Love is a wonderful gift. Why is everyone so hung up on what color the wrapping paper is? I'm sorry Miss Moore, I won't listen to you or any of the rest of them. [*She starts out of the room. Moore stops her.*]

MOORE. Ruthanna! Sit down. [*Ruth a bit reluctantly comes back and sits.*] To say this is probably very unethical, but my Quaker conscience demands it. Although I'm sure there are many who would like to disbelieve it, I, too, am a human being. I used to hide in the shadows of the grandfather clock in Earlham Hall parlor to say goodnight to my love just as I've seen you and Eddie do. There wasn't anything exotic about my man. But he wasn't ordinary . . . because I loved him. The memories have been stored away for a long time now and aren't really important except for the fact that my parents said "no," and I closed the door. Ruthanna, don't let anyone do that to you. Listen to what your heart's telling you, not all these people. Keep remembering, their prejudice is born of ignorance. But your heart . . . now there's something that's a lot more clever. Listen to it. It knows you better. [*They embrace as lights fade.*]

ON SCREEN: Months later. Portland, Oregon.

SCENE 8

An office belonging to the Uyesugi's family attorney. He is surrounded by stacks of law books which he has been searching through. Ruth and Eddie are seated next to his desk.

LAWYER. This kind of marriage is legal only in three states in the union, New Mexico, West Virginia, and lucky for you two, Washington.

RUTH. Eddie . . . !

EDDIE. No, Furlow, you won't be living in sin if we ever go back to Indiana. There's such a thing as reciprocity, you know.

RUTH. [*To herself*] Reciprocity? [*She looks disturbed.*]

EDDIE. [*Rising and shaking hands with lawyer.*] Thanks, Mr. Benton. We'll try Washington, then, and let's hope they live up to their legalities.

RUTH. Thank you. [*Ruth follows Eddie as he exits.*] Eddie. What's reciprocity . . . ? [*The office fades as lights come up on a door. Ruth and Eddie approach out of the darkness and knock. Rev. James Miller answers.*]

MILLER. Yes?

EDDIE. Mr. Miller?

MILLER. Yes.

EDDIE. My name is Eddie Uyesugi. This is my fiancée, Ruthanna Farlow. We're wondering if you could help us.

MILLER. What can I do for you?

EDDIE. We'd like to get married.

MILLER. Just what nationality are you, Mr . . . Uh . . . what was it?

EDDIE. Uyesugi. I'm Japanese-American, but what dif . . .

MILLER. And you Miss Farlow? You look like a nice decent American girl.

195

RUTH. I am, Mr. Miller, and this is a nice decent American boy.

MILLER. I don't understand. Why have you come to me?

RUTH. I'm a Quaker and I was hoping to be married by a Quaker minister.

MILLER. Well, Miss Farlow, I must say, I'm a bit surprised. You call yourself a Quaker, but to tell the truth, I don't see how any good Quaker could ever do a thing like this.

RUTH. I'm a bit surprised, too, Mr. Miller. You call yourself a Christian.

MILLER. Now, look . . .

RUTH. And as for the Quakers, I've always taken pride in the fact that our ancestors were precursors to those of us today that still believe that all men are created equal. It makes me mad to see what you've brought that belief to.

MILLER. Miss Farlow . . .

RUTH. Not to change the subject or anything, Mr. Miller, but have you ever read Romeo and Juliet?

MILLER. What? . . . well, . . . yes, I have . . .

RUTH. Good, then you know how the story ends. How would you like that on your head?

MILLER. Why . . . I . . . I . . .

RUTH. Come on, Mr. Miller. You represent the United Capulates of America. What do you have to say for yourself?

MILLER. Please, Miss Farlow . . .

RUTH. Give us one good reason why you can't marry us.

MILLER. I told you. I don't see how any good Quaker . . . Speaking of that, what do your parents think about this?

RUTH. I have their approval. As a matter of fact, I have this state's approval. It's perfectly legal here . . .

MILLER. Look, I'm sure you're both fine young people, but I can't allow this. Why don't you kids just take your time and see if you don't change your minds? You've got a lifetime ahead of you. I suggest you try to find someone of your own . . . kind.

RUTH. You bigoted . . . bigot! You haven't heard the end of this. I'm making some phone calls. I'll call your Yearly Meeting if I have to. How dare you call yourself a minister? [*Miller is hiding behind his door now so that only his head is sticking out. Ruth, who backed him into that position, is now being restrained by Eddie. He drags her off. Miller watches them off, looks a little relieved, and then goes inside. Lights dim on his door and rise on another door where Ruth and Eddie approach, much calmer now.*]

EDDIE. Now I want you to promise me you'll control yourself. It's very likely we'll get the same routine.

RUTH. Oh, Eddie, don't say that. What if no one will marry us? What'll we do?

EDDIE. I don't know. Now do you promise me?

RUTH. Yes, I promise. I'm sorry, Eddie. I know getting upset didn't help any, but he made me so mad. Don't worry, I'll be good.

EDDIE. That's my girl. [*He gives her a quick kiss on the forehead. Then looking at the door, they cross their fingers and knock. A young Quaker minister answers this time.*] Mr. Davis?

DAVIS. Yes?

EDDIE. My name's Uyesugi, Eddie Uyesugi. And this is Ruth Farlow. We were hoping you could marry us.

DAVIS. Of course, I'll marry you. [*Ruth and Eddie look relieved.*]

EDDIE. Thank you.

RUTH. Yes, thank you very much. You can't imagine the troubles we've had. [*As she speaks, the phone rings inside.*]

DAVIS. Excuse me. [*He goes inside. Ruth and Eddie wait.*]

RUTH. Well, that's better.

EDDIE. Yeah. Seems like a nice guy.

RUTH. Yup. Looks like we're finally gettin' hitched, Soogi.

EDDIE. [*He looks at her a moment.*] Hitched?

RUTH. That's Paolian for getting married. I'll teach ya the language sometime.

EDDIE. No thanks. I'd rather speak English. [*David returns, rather sheepishly.*]

RUTH. Oh, Mr. Davis . . . listen, how soon could we get the church? We'd like to start making plans as soon as . . .

DAVIS. [*Cuts her off.*] Something's come up. I can't perform the ceremony. I'm very sorry.

RUTH. What!! You can't perf. . . [*Eddie has put his arm around her shoulder and she realizes the futility of her protests.*]

EDDIE. Thanks, anyway, Mr. Davis. [*They turn and walk away. Davis looks as though he might call them back, but reconsiders, looking back in the direction of the telephone. He goes inside. As they go, Ruth and Eddie stop a few feet away, look back at the door, then back to each other.*]

RUTH. Betrayed without a kiss. [*They exit arm in arm as lights crossfade to next door. Ruth and Eddie return.*]

RUTH. Eddie, why try? You know that guy's called every pastor in the state by now.

EDDIE. Well, maybe this one had sense enough not to listen to him.

RUTH. Eddie, we might as well give up on a church wedding.

EDDIE. No . . . we'll try one more time. [*He knocks. Rev. Goodman appears.*] Rev. Goodman?

REV. GOODMAN. Yes. What can I do for you . . . Oh! . . . Would your name happen to be Uyesugi?

EDDIE. Yes.

GOODMAN. And you must be Miss Farlow.

EDDIE. That's right, but . . .

197

GOODMAN. I received a phone call concerning you two.

RUTH. Oh?

GOODMAN. And I must say, Miss Farlow, I've heard a lot about you.

RUTH. I was afraid you might have.

GOODMAN. And on behalf of clergymen everywhere, please let me apologize for that man.

RUTH. [*Relieved*] Thank you, Mr. Goodman.

GOODMAN. Please, come in. [*They all start in.*] Did you really threaten to pull a Romeo and Juliet on him?

RUTH. uh-huh.

GOODMAN. [*Laughing*] I'd have loved to have seen that old blister's face . . . [*He trails off as they exit. As door clicks, we hear wedding music and on the screen, the Richmond Herald headline and wedding announcement appear.*]

ON SCREEN: Farlow-Uyesugi exchange vows. Miss Ruthanna Farlow, a recent graduate of Earlham College, became the bride of Edward T. Uyesugi, also an Earlham alumnus, in vows read in the Saint James Episcopal Church at Seattle, Washington, on January 27 . . . [*Black*] Days later. [*Black*]

SCENE 9

Ruth and Eddie's new home, Portland. It is two days after the wedding. Ruth is sorting through wedding presents. While putting some things away in a drawer, she finds a box which has been opened and resealed. She reopens it. Inside she finds a black queue. She puzzles over it. Eddie enters.

EDDIE. Hand me those towels, honey. I'll put 'em in the bathroom. [*She does.*]

RUTH. [*As he starts away.*] Eddie . . . ?

EDDIE. Yeah?

RUTH. Was this one of the wedding presents?

EDDIE. Uh . . . yeah.

RUTH. What on earth is it?

EDDIE. It's a queue. [*Ruth examines the pigtail.*] You know the guys I have breakfast with over at the Welcome Inn. They gave it to me. I didn't know how to tell 'em it's the Chinese who wear these things, not the Japanese.

RUTH. What did you say when you opened it?

EDDIE. What could I say? I forced a little chuckle and said it'd make a dandy golf cap. [*Becoming angry as he recalls it.*] Why do they keep doing things like this? I know they mean well and they're just having fun but . . . my God, I wish they could see how much I hate it.

RUTH. How can they see it if you make jokes and chuckle.

198

EDDIE. Well . . . I couldn't say anyth . . .

RUTH. Why not? You've got to make up your mind, Eddie. Learn to live with it or put a stop to it.

EDDIE. Those aren't necessarily the choices.

RUTH. What do you mean?

EDDIE. I know . . . I would've liked to have said something but when you've been taught all your life to hold it in . . .

RUTH. Your parents taught you that.

EDDIE. Well, sure . . . My entire culture taught me that. "Good little Japanese boys and girls don't cry."

RUTH. Yes, but this isn't a scraped knee, Eddie. [*He is momentarily beaten.*] What were you going to do with this? Hide it?

EDDIE. No. [*Giving in*] Yes. I'm sorry. I should've told you about it.

RUTH. You should've told them about it. Then and there. And shoved this in their faces. [*Waving the queue*]

EDDIE. But I'm not so sure that's the answer, Ruth. That's hasty recrimination and I don't think that's the way to change things. It's a great way to start fights but they seldom get anywhere. There's only one way people will change and lose these misconceptions . . . [*Holding up queue*] . . . and really understand and that's to let them figure it out for themselves. They'll believe it if they think of it but if someone else forces it on them, especially me, they'll only fight it.

RUTH. But would these guys do that? You just said they meant well.

EDDIE. Just as bad. They'd apologize, but as soon as I leave the room, they'd say I was being oversensitive . . . No, they have to find it themselves.

RUTH. But why should people want to figure it out on their own? They're happy the way they are.

EDDIE. That's why things take so long to change.

RUTH. So what can we do? [*Pause as they look at each other. Then Eddie weighs the queue in his hand and starts for the drawer where Ruth found it. He looks at it once more, then places it in the drawer and closes it. Ruth watches, then goes to him and embraces him.*]

EDDIE. The day they realize, I can take it out and throw it away.

Suggestions for Discussion

1. How would you define prejudice?

2. Do you consider racial intermarriage unwise or wrong? If so, why?

3. Have you ever had a close friend belonging to an ethnic group or nationality other than your own?

4. How strongly do you feel about your own social group?

5. Which character from the play did you more closely identify with: Rev. Miller, Rev. Davis, or Rev. Goodman? Why?

6. When the Japanese attacked Pearl Harbor, thousands of Japanese-Americans living on the west coast were evacuated to desert camps. Do you feel this action was warrented under the circumstances? If a similar situation were to arise today, would you condone such action?

7. Suppose you were told that people of your eye color were not to marry people of an eye color different than your own. How would this make you feel?

8. How much validity do you find in statements such as "Jews are basically stingy," or "Most Irishmen drink a lot," etc?

9. If you feel that someone is prejudiced toward you, stereotyping you, or treating you unfairly, how do you deal with this? Passively or aggressively?

10. If you had been present when the men gave Eddie the queue, would you have spoken up if you felt it was wrong?

THE TRIAL

by John Ferguson

CHARACTERS

THE JUDGE
THE RECORDING ANGEL
THE BARRISTER
THE POLICE ANGEL
JANE
ELIZABETH
SITA
MARINA

The scene is a court-room. In addition to the normal judge's dais there is a higher dais curtained off. The Recording Angel is sitting at the table underneath the lower dais, writing. Enter, from the other side, the Judge wigged and robed. He obviously does not know where he is. His face lights up at the sight of the court: he looks round with interest and some bewilderment. Then he notices the Recording Angel, and speaks. There is no preliminary cough to draw attention to himself. He speaks, and behaves, as one who has authority.

JUDGE. The halls outside are empty. I thought
    That no one was here. Who are you?
RECORDING ANGEL. The recording angel.
JUDGE. Your wit has a long grey beard, as if it were
    Borrowed from Methusaleh, and if it's not careful
    Will trip over itself. These are the words
    The Roman clerk bantered with Cicero. Judge Jeffreys
    Blanched the red face that dared to say it to him.
    And only yesterday my colleague Burrows
    Got it from a clerk named Snooks. What is this court?
RECORDING ANGEL. One of the courts of heaven.
JUDGE. Better, by God.
    'Laughter, in which his lordship joined.' [*He chuckles.*]
        And here I suppose
    We give them hell. [*He pauses.*] Like her late and gracious
        Majesty
    You are not amused.
RECORDING ANGEL. This morning
    There was launched upon you that most lethal weapon

In the armoury of man, that most devastating pestilence
Since the Black Death, the bridgehead of annihilation,
A motor car, and, not to put too fine a point on it,
It killed you.
JUDGE. Damn your insolence! I beg your pardon.
I forgot your Puritanical scruples. Am I not here,
Flesh and blood?
[*He makes to grasp his left hand with his right but finds that it
has passed through. He is left gasping.*]
RECORDING ANGEL. It seems not.
JUDGE. I dimly remember
A shout, a screeching scream of brakes, then deep
And drifting blackness, then my boat, unroared and sailless,
Silently moving swifter ever swifter, foaming through the
floodgates
Of time and space. As the Greek philosopher
Held that we gropingly recollect the perfections of heaven
Among the grasping imperfections of earth, so now comes
back to me
The flash of the moment. Is this then death? —
The dying almost forgotten; the state of being dead
Whimsically like life, and yet unlike. What is this place?
RECORDING ANGEL. A court where souls are tried.
JUDGE. Is it so?
And am I then to stand in the dock of conscience,
And face the accusations of my own adolescent emotion-
alism,
My undergraduate cynicism, the age of manhood
When life is living and abstract problems cease
To trouble, and my whitening years when change
Is the greatest sin? I am not afraid.
RECORDING ANGEL. We need your help.
JUDGE. My help in the courts of heaven! Where is the
wisdom
Of the angelic doctors?
RECORDING ANGEL. The angelic doctors find that life
In the twentieth century moves too fast for them.
They apprehend it, but do not comprehend it. As a gramo-
phone record
When quickened up gives a shrill blurred sound, so is life
today
To them. They learn less quickly than they were used,
And were still talking about 'spiffing' when everything was
'wizard'.
We have a case we want you to try. Your coming
Is a godsend. We don't get many of her Majesty's judges
here.

JUDGE. A case to try! But shall I know the rules of the
court?
RECORDING ANGEL. Experience and wisdom will serve. There
are also
Some bound volumes on the bench. Lord Halsbury's eternal
life
Looks like being everlastingly occupied.
JUDGE. When
Does the case come up?
RECORDING ANGEL. As soon as your lordship
Is ready. Will you take your seat on the bench?
[*He escorts the Judge to the bench with dignified deference,
then goes to the door and calls.*]
Summon Jane Williams.
VOICE. [*Offstage*]: Summon Jane Williams.
[*The Judge is examining the furnishings of the bench and dipping
into the books. Jane Williams comes in under angelic escort. She
is a frowsy female in the middle thirties. She takes her place in
the witness-box. The Recording Angel picks up a New Testa-
ment from his table and takes it over to her. Meantime the Bar-
rister slips in and sits silently at the front.*]
RECORDING ANGEL. You haven't been sworn in this court
before. Raise
Your right hand, place your left on the Book, and repeat
After me: 'I swear to tell the truth, the whole truth
And nothing but the truth, so help me God.'
JANE WILLIAMS. I swear to tell the truth, the whole truth
and nothing
But the truth swelp me Gawd. Is that orright?
RECORDING ANGEL. It will pass. [*To Police Angel*]: Yours
we may I think take for granted.
JANE WILLIAMS. 'Ere, I want to 'ear 'im to it.
JUDGE. Swear in the witness.
RECORDING ANGEL. The rules of procedure in this court are
not quite
The same as those in earthly courts. But it shall be
As your lordship wishes. Take the Book.
POLICE ANGEL. I swear
To tell the truth, the whole truth, and nothing but the
truth.
So help me God.
RECORDING ANGEL. Now give your evidence.
POLICE ANGEL. [*With notebook*]: Acting on information re-
ceived, I took up my post
By the golden gates, and awaited the prisoner's arrival.
After what seemed an eternity in eternity she appeared —
JUDGE. What time was that?

POLICE ANGEL. Your lordship will forgive me —
 There is not time in heaven. She stood and looked at the
   gates
 And then she said [*turning the pages*] —
JUDGE. What did she say?
POLICE ANGEL. 'Cor, ain't it
 Just like glorious Tetchnicolor!' Then I approached her,
 Gave her the usual caution and apprehended her.
JUDGE. What are the charges?
RECORDING ANGEL. [*Rising and reading from his book*]:
 Transgressing all the Laws of God and man.
 We are happily not concerned with the latter; they are too
   numerous
 And too complex, and the British constables are more competent
 In the field than angelic superintendents. There are ten charges.
 First that God has meant nothing to her life.
 She has turned her back to Him.
JANE WILLIAMS. I know nothing about 'im —
RECORDING ANGEL. Except as a swear-word. Second, that
   she used
 That swear-word much too often and always meaninglessly.
JANE WILLIAMS. Ow! Wot-the-'ell! —
POLICE ANGEL. I shouldn't speak too lightly
 Of hell in this place, sister.
RECORDING ANGEL. Third, that never
 Did she join in worship with God's people on God's day
 Within God's church.
JANE WILLIAMS. Them stuck-up snobs. They 'ad
 No time for me.
RECORDING ANGEL. She was not even baptized nor married
 Within a church, nor buried.
JANE WILLIAMS. D'you mean to say
 They didn't give me a Christian burial. Well I'm damned!
POLICE ANGEL. Probably. Ssh!
RECORDING ANGEL. Fourth that she did bow down
 And worship photograven images of
 Humphrey Bogart and Gregory Peck, and prostrated herself
 Before the graven images of money. Fifth
 That she did covet others' goods, and sixth
 That coveting did steal, and seventh when put
 On trial for stealing bore false witness and tried
 To put the blame on others. Eighth that she
 Dishonoured her father and her mother.
JANE WILLIAMS. Fat lot
 They ever did for me.
RECORDING ANGEL. Ninth, that she dishonoured
 Her body in fornication and adultery

And prostitution, lying with men for money
And irresponsible pleasures, not thinking if this
Corrupted them, perhaps broke up their homes —
As more than once it did.
JANE WILLIAMS. If it 'adn't bin me
    It'd 'ave bin someone else — and I 'ad to live, 'adn't I?
RECORDING ANGEL. And at the last decided that she had not
    To live, and so with self and violent hands
    Took off her life, and with it too her child's,
    Transgressing the commandment 'Thou shalt not kill'.
    These things are written in the Book of Death
    Whose testimony is true. The case rests.
JUDGE. Will you call witnesses?
RECORDING ANGEL. No, my lord. The facts
    Are not in doubt. What is written within this book
    Is written. No blot can smirch its page,
    No india-rubber erase the ineradicable
    Truth.
JUDGE. Be it so. Jane Williams, what have you to say?
JANE WILLIAMS. I dunno what to say. I lived my life as it
      came.
    You talk of Gawd, but nobody ain't ever shown 'im to me,
    And the blokes what jaw about 'im ain't much advertisement.
    To tell the truth, we never see 'em; they're too respectable
    To come down the street where I live. They enjoy themselves
    In their churches in their way, singing 'ymns and praying.
    Why shouldn't I enjoy myself in mine? I ain't 'urt nobody.
    At least not much, and I 'ad a good time
    Till the money ran out, and no one'd look at me;
    So I thought 'It's curtains for you, my girl.'
    And I couldn't leave the kid — oo knows
    What'd become of 'im? So we took an excursion ticket
    To 'eaven; and it looks like we got in the wrong train.
JUDGE. Is that all you have to say?
JANE WILLIAMS. I think so, mister.
JUDGE. The facts are not in doubt. The prisoner
    Who has crossed the bar acknowledges the charges.
    The case would seem to me to merit the
    Most condign treatment. There are ten laws of God,
    Ten moderate laws, not arbitrary, tyrannical
    And oppressive, no Mogul's whim, no words of a fabulous
      Khan
    Tossed off in captiousness, but such as any decent person
    Would naturally follow; she has broken them all.
    Broken I say? Smashed them to smithereens.
    Not chipped them as one may in washing-up
    Catch a cup's lip against the tap; not cracked them

As when they fall from tired fingers, or slip
From hand well soaped to cleanse. But she has flung them
Against the wall for sport, snapped them
In jealous hate that others should possess them,
And trampled on the wreckage in furious petulance.
When a person has broken every law, and that deliberately,
Without excuse, he must receive the gravest penalty
This court commands, which is to spend out his soul
In the first division of Purgatory until such time
As there may be a full and sure repentance.

JANE WILLIAMS. What does 'e mean? I'm frightened.

RECORDING ANGEL. Has your lordship
Weighed her defence? Was it so light, as thristledown,
As child's balloons, as spiders' webs? Does it not move the scale
Of justice one millimetre?

JUDGE. Her defence was fiddlesticks.
She pleaded ignorance of God; but ignorance
Is no defence. For the rest, she gloried in
Her crimes, and sought only to throw some mud,
Making clean citizens appear as messy
As her unwashed self.

JANE WILLIAMS. 'Ere, lay off it.

RECORDING ANGEL. And what
Of her love?

JUDGE. Justice knows nothing of love;
It deals in facts — hard unsentimental massy blocks.
What love has she shown except self-love? She killed
Her child; she hated her parents; she took her lovers
To gratify her liking for pleasure and money.
The verdict is delivered.

RECORDING ANGEL. This is the punishment
Of Tantalus tormented by the grasp
Of not-to-be-grasped fruit till he shall learn to set
Greed aside, of Sisyphus sweating behind his stone
In dishonourable ambition, of Tityos gnawed at heart
Till the lusts of the flesh be lacerated. Shall she
Be among these?

JUDGE. I cannot help that. My verdict
Once given is unalterable.

RECORDING ANGEL. Unalterable?

JUDGE. And sure.

RECORDING ANGEL. Has your lordship looked at the first rule
of the court?

JUDGE. [*After a pause, reading*]: What's this? 'The President
of the Court shall undergo
In person any treatment he decrees.'

But this is monstrous. This is a hellish trap.
Is this your heavenly justice? What have I done
To merit such treatment?
RECORDING ANGEL. You yourself remarked
That ignorance was no defence.
JUDGE. In that case
I revoke my judgement.
RECORDING ANGEL. The verdict is unalterable
And sure; it may not be revoked. We have your words.
JUDGE. I won't stand it. I demand fair trial.
Show me to be guilty of these offences
And I accept your verdict — but you cannot do so.
My life has been respectable and honourable;
Peer in the inmost cupboards, sweep underneath
The carpets, reach for cobwebs in the corner.
Bring all your spiritual vacuum-cleaners — you will find
No murder, theft or adultery there.
RECORDING ANGEL. It shall be
As you desire. You shall be tried on those three counts.
JUDGE. Before whom, in the name of God? [*The curtains of the
upper dais are withdrawn and reveal a blazing light. The Judge
flinches for the first time*]: Yes, I see. The jury?
RECORDING ANGEL. Yourself.
JUDGE. Myself?
RECORDING ANGEL. Yes. You are a man of integrity;
If you are not convinced, the case falls.
JUDGE. And the prosecuting counsel?
BARRISTER. [*rising*]: I.
JUDGE. Who are you?
BARRISTER. One of God's servants. My name is Shaitan.
Allow me.
To introduce myself. [*He bows.*] They nickname me the
Accuser,
The Tester. Sometimes they get quite unpleasant;
But that's when they want to blame me for things,
When they know they're guilty themselves. I shall be
pleased to serve.
I have followed your career with the greatest interest.
[*To Jane*]: Step down, young lady, and sit in the corner.
Let me see.
Ah yes — adultery. Call Elizabeth Stone.
VOICE. [*Outside*]: Elizabeth Stone. [*She comes in, much
painted. Jane moves down from the box to make way for her,
and gives a squeal of recognition.*]
JANE WILLIAMS. Liz! Well! You 'ave done well for yourself!
ELIZABETH STONE. Glad you like it, darling.
JANE WILLIAMS. But look out;

They don't 'arf treat you rough 'ere.

POLICE ANGEL. Silence in court.

RECORDING ANGEL. In view of the Presence we shall dispense
  with the oath. [*The angels bow to the light. The Judge remains
  erect.*]

JUDGE. I never saw this female before.

BARRISTER. No? Elizabeth,
  What was your profession?

ELIZABETH STONE. I traded my skill in love
  For money.

BARRISTER. Have you ever seen this man?

ELIZABETH STONE. [*Looks intently*]: Yes. Yes — I recognize him.

JUDGE. It's a lie. I've never been with a woman except
  My wife.

ELIZABETH STONE. I've a good memory for faces. I was
    standing
  In a doorway near Piccadilly with the porch-light on me,
  Waiting for customers. He walked down the other side,
  Stopped under a street-lamp opposite and looked at me.
  He looked me up and down, mentally undressed me —
  He saw my body, but I saw his mind.
  I watched desire and fear, lust and conviction fight
  To win him, watched through the keyhole of his eyes.
  Then he muttered 'No, it's too risky; someone might find
    out', and walked on.

BARRISTER. [*To Judge*]: Is this true?

JUDGE. [*After a pause*]: Yes, it is true — but that is not adultery.
  My body is pure.

BARRISTER. We are not here to try your body
  But your soul. Did you lust for this woman, physically
  And mentally?

JUDGE. Yes, but I did not succumb.

BARRISTER. Why not? Through love of her, that you might
    hurt her
  and pull her deeper into corruption?

JUDGE. No.

BARRISTER. Through love of your wife, because she filled your
    loyalty?

JUDGE. No.

BARRISTER. Through the thought that you might be less fitted
  To serve your fellow-men?

JUDGE. No.

BARRISTER. Through devotion
  To the way of God and to the mind of Jesus?

JUDGE. No.

BARRISTER. Through what then?

JUDGE. [*In a low voice*]: Fear of being found out.

208

BARRISTER. And are you better
  Than those who, driven by the jeers of their fellows
  To 'be a man', go with a woman for the sake
  Of their reputation?
JUDGE. No. But I did not
  Commit adultery.
BARRISTER. Have you heard these words:
  'If a man look upon a woman to lust after her,
  He hath committed adultery with her already in his heart'?
JUDGE. Yes.
BARRISTER. Guilty or not guilty?
JUDGE. [*After a pause*]: Guilty.
BARRISTER. [*To Elizabeth Stone*]: You may stand down.
  [*Exit Elizabeth Stone.*]
  We advance, my friend; we advance. This will not be
  One of those examinations in which budding mathematicians
  Tackle one question only and fail to solve that,
  And yet become Wranglers. Our wrangling is not of that sort.
  Three questions for us, and we shall not be satisfied
  Till at the foot of each we've written the familiar letters
  Q.E.D. Thank you for your kind co-operation. Next,
  The charge of theft.
JUDGE. I have been scrupulously
  And particularly honest in regard to money — never
  Taken what was not mine to take, never defrauded
  A client, never deceived the Chancellor
  Of the Exchequer, never failed honourably to discharge
  My debts, never neglected responsibility
  Towards my family, never lacked in generosity
  Within my means to those in need.
BARRISTER. Yes, yes,
  We know — a Francis wedded to my lady Poverty,
  A Crates with but a scrip and staff, a Martin
  Tearing his cloak in half and shivering
  That another might go warm. This court is not
  A tube-station to be bedaubed with self-advertisements.
  Your virtues are written in the Book of Life — and that entry
  Is more durable than the one in Who's Who which they are
    already
  Expunging for the next edition. I hope it's as long.
  We are concerned with your sins. Call the next witness.
  [*Sita, the Indian woman, enters; she is thin and poorly clad.*]
  Come in, don't be afraid. What is your name?
SITA. They call me Sita.
BARRISTER. Ah yes, Sita. And your home?
SITA. Darnagore; it is a little village
  Within Madras, a tiny spot upon

The Indian leopard-skin, an almost unseen wrinkle
Upon the elephant of Asia.
BARRISTER. How old were you when you died?
SITA. Twenty-five years.
BARRISTER. And how did you come to die?
SITA. I had six children; there were more, but they
Didn't survive. There was not enough food to go round—
A handful of millet each day between us all.
I couldn't take it from the children, and so I died.
BARRISTER. What money had you to support the children?
SITA. Some twenty pounds a year, and of course the food
I grew with my own hands. It wasn't much,
But every little helped.
BARRISTER. Were you exceptional?
SITA. What do you mean? I do not understand.
BARRISTER. One single family may, by accident,
Even by fault, be poor. The better-privileged
May not know. Were there others?—other families like yours?
SITA. You ask strange questions. There were none within
our village
Whose children's ribs did not show through their drooping skin
Like a half-finished hut, none who did not scrape
The parched soil to add to their little store.
BARRISTER. One more question. Have you ever heard of the
Colombo Plan?
SITA. Yes. I remember. A few years ago a learned man
Came to our village and told us that the white man
Had taken pity on us; there would be food and comfort
And happiness for all. We shrugged our shoulders
And disbelieved, and nothing came of it.
BARRISTER. Thank you. [*To Judge.*] Now, sir, your income?
JUDGE. Eight thousand pounds
A year.
BARRISTER. Let me see. Was it not lately raised?
JUDGE. It was.
BARRISTER. Did you object?
JUDGE. Object? What do you mean?
Object to a rise in salary? Of course not.
I do not bite the hand the feeds me.
BARRISTER. Nor kill
The goose that lays the golden eggs nor spoil
The ship for a ha'porth of tar. I see you know
All the clichés. And would your ship have been less watertight
For a few thousand pounds' worth less gilt paint? [*Judge
says nothing.*] It would not.
Was it not about the same time as your salary was raised,
That the Government declared it was not able to give

210

A penny more to the Colombo Plan?

JUDGE. I really don't know.

It may have been.

BARRISTER. Some years ago you prosecuted

A man on the charge of receiving stolen goods.

They were furs — minks and siver fox, soft and luxuriant,

A peacock's tail appended to the neck of a human peahen.

You said to him 'And was it not two days before

These furs came into your hands that every newspaper

In London bore a description of them?' And he answered

'I really don't know. It may have been.' Do you remember?

JUDGE. Yes.

BARRISTER. And do you remember how you rent his answer

To shreds, not carelessly as a girl may ladder a stocking

Or rip a plastic mackintosh on some barbed wire,

Not for obvious constructive use, as a nurse may tear

A bandage to tie it the better, but wantonly, destructively,

Till the pieces got smaller and smaller, and with his answer

The man collapsed.

JUDGE. I do remember. But my increase

Was made to meet increasing responsibilities.

BARRISTER. How many houses

Did you have?

JUDGE. Two.

SITA. How can a man live in two houses?

I had one one-roomed hut.

BARRISTER. Dining alone at home,

How many courses did you eat?

JUDGE. Four, or five with coffee.

SITA. What does he mean — four courses? What else is there

to eat

Besides soup or a little grain?

BARRISTER. How many cars did you possess?

JUDGE. Three.

SITA. I had to walk wherever I went. But I have seen

Cars. How can anyone use more than one?

JUDGE. But my increase,

My whole salary, could not affect the problem of India.

Their inhabitants are as grasshoppers, and that small sum

Would have been but a drop in their empty bucket,

Incapable of cleansing their darkened windows

Which so pitifully shut out the light.

BARRISTER. It would not

Have seemed so to this woman and her children.

And theft is theft; it is no defence to say

You stole not a full-grown sheep, but a little lamb.

JUDGE. But to this woman and her children any of our

salaries

Would have seemed luxurious beyond dream.

BARRISTER. Does that make it better?

JUDGE. Oh God! [*At the divine name the Angelic Court rise and bow to the higher dais. The Judge remains impervious.*] I didn't see. But what could I have done?

BARRISTER. [*Inexorably*]: Guilty or not guilty?

JUDGE. Guilty.

BARRISTER. [*To Sita*]: You may stand down. [*Exit Sita.*]
We climb, my friend, we climb. Perhaps you know Tryfan?
A mountain in North Wales. Not far away is the place
They were gracious enough to call the Devil's Kitchen
If you climb Tryfan from the road, first you find
A short and steep ascent up the shoulder, then you pause
For breath, and start the long slow trek along
The Heather Terrace, till you reach the col
Which divides the summit from the main ridge. We have reached
That point; perhaps we eat an orange or a little chocolate,
Being careful not to litter the place with peel
Or paper. There is not much view from here.
And now we turn to the last scramble over
Gigantesque boulders which some primeval schoolboy
Among the ancient heroes has tossed about like marbles.
If we reach the top we shall see clearly — a grand panorama.
There will be a sense of achievement, of release.
The free winds of heaven will blow about us. The charge
Is murder. Call Marina Moriyama.

VOICE. [*Off*] Call Marina Moriyama.

JANE WILLIAMS. 'E gave 'im wot's wot orright. I feel a bit sorry for 'im.

POLICE ANGEL. Quiet, my girl: remember your own verdict is given. [*She relapses into silence. A Japanese woman enters and takes the stand.*]

JUDGE. You bring me yet another witness I do not know,
Yet murder is a crime deliberately
And consciously undertaken. How can I be quilty
Of killing a woman I never saw?

BARRISTER. Were you not on the Bench
When during the I.R.A. activities a man
Was condemned to death because he had placed a bomb
In a bus and killed people whom he had never seen?

JUDGE. That is indeed true. But what is its relevance to me?

BARRISTER. You will see. [*To Marina Moriyama: Tell us where you come from.*]

MARINA MORIYAMA. My home
Was Nagasaki in Japan.

BARRISTER. The name Marina

Is surely not Japanese?

MARINA MORIYAMA. No; it is my Christian name.
  I am a Christian, descended from a line
  Of Christians, who kept the love of our Lord alive
  Through persecution and death, fire and crucifixion.
  My town was the Bethlehem of Japan.
  Here the news of God's love was first made known to our
    people.
  Here it first set our love aflame. Here we have guarded
  Its warmth and light, and fanned it in the darkness.
  Here on August the ninth of nineteen forty-five
  Our Christian brothers let loose the fires of hell.

BARRISTER. Tell us what happened.

MARINA MORIYAMA. They had scattered leaflets
  Falling in white cascades, gentle as flakes of snow.
  'Back in April, Nagasaki was all flowers;
  August in Nagasaki, there'll be flame showers' —
  So they ran. We didn't know what they meant.
  Then the day came. I was over the hill,
  Away from the city. A single airplane passed over,
  A silver cross in the sky. Suddenly my eyes ached
  With a light more brilliant than the light of summer,
  With a glow more blinding than the sun's centre.
  The clap of thunder rang and the wind howled,
  Stripping the trees naked in lust. Then came cold
  And darkness. Day and night were at one. And the pillar
  Of fire and the pillar of cloud which once God sent
  To lead his people sprang into the sky, delivered
  By the devil. It was a pillar of death and doom.
  The colours of rainbow struggled for mastery
  Within it, for the devil had seized to himself
  The symbol of God's mercy. Then the cap
  Began to spread, to unroll is clammy fists,
  To reach those whom it had not grasped. I lay
  Flung to the ground, and smelt the smell of wild
    chrysanthemum,
  And saw a broken stalk beside me. My son
  Had been playing on the hilltop, a little innocent child.
  I rushed to where he had been. He was quite still.
  Soon came the procession, women and men, naked,
  No shirt, no trousers, sometimes with a leather belt
  Comically left around their waist. All were weeping.
  None laughed for tears. None even felt ashamed
  For tears on tears. And sometimes sheets of skin
  Hung down like clothing loose from the blood-smeared
    flesh.
  And in the days that came men pined and died;

213

They vomited and died. My child was already still.
Later in the city I saw where a man had stood;
There was no sign of him but a shadow impressed on the
    wall,
A silhouette sketched by the blast; the man had been
Whirled into nothingness. My child was at least still.
The Lord gave and the Lord took away; blessed be His
    holy name for ever. But I think
The devil ruled that day.
BARRISTER. I will say nothing
Upon your references to the devil, except that I think
You underestimate the power of human sin. But you—
You were alive. How did you come to die?
MARINA MORIYAMA. Our country was brought to peace, and
    in our sorrow
We women were glad. We thought the God of peace
Had come again. Our bodies were scarred. Our hearts
Were aching. But we lived on, in hope for the future.
But the devil was at work, and there were more explosions
Away in the sea; and the fish swam north, and I ate some,
And fell ill and died.
BARRISTER. I see. Thank you for what you have said. [*Exit
Marina.*] To Judge: On August the sixth, nineteen forty-five, a man
In an aeroplane pressed a button, and the city that had been
Hiroshima disappeared. Did you protest?
JUDGE. No.
BARRISTER. Are you a Christian?
JUDGE. I hope so.
BARRISTER. Are you aware that the Churches have declared
'The Churches must condemn the deliberate mass destruction
Of civilians in open cities by whatever means
And for whatever purpose'?
JUDGE. No, I was not aware of it.
BARRISTER. It is your business to be aware of these things
As a responsible citizen and churchman. Did you realize,
When the news of the first bomb came, that it was probable
That another might be dropped? Did you realize it?
JUDGE. I suppose I did.
BARRISTER. Then you are an accessory before the fact
To what was done at Nagasaki?
JUDGE. Yes, but—
BARRISTER. Have you heard
These words: 'Paul was consenting to his death'?
JUDGE. I have.
But this is different. This is war.
BARRISTER. Is the Christian conscience
Never to say 'No'? You destroy this simple Christian woman

214

In the name of experiment for defence, as you have destroyed
Her child in the name of war, and raise no voice in protest?
JUDGE. War is a hard master. All this is regrettable;
But it shortened the fighting and saved more lives in the end.
BARRISTER. Are you aware that at the time when the bombs
Were dropped Japan had already sued for peace?
JUDGE. Oh God! [*At the divine name the court again bow to the
higher dais. This time, after a moment, the Judge follows suit.*] It
isn't true! I didn't know.
BARRISTER. It is true, and you didn't even seek to know.
You raised not even a conditional protest. The blood
Of her child, your brother, cries from the ground at you.
JUDGE. But Her Majesty's judges must be above
The passing comments of politics. I couldn't protest.
BARRISTER. I have here a speech of yours given in nineteen forty.
'This war which we have not lightly begun,' you said,
'We shall inexorably finish. Our cause is just.'
If you may pronounce when a cause is just,
May you not protest if the means are unjust?
You did not protest, and the blood of Nagasaki
Is upon your head.
JUDGE. But who did protest?
BARRISTER. Precisely.
Who did protest? You cannot screen your failure
Behind the indifference of others. Guilty or not guilty?
JUDGE. Guilty. [*He pulls off his wig and gown and flings them
to the floor. The curtain is silently drawn across the higher dais.*]
I can't wear these any more. I am not
Worthy. [*To curtain*]: But remember one thing, mighty
    conjuror,
You who steal the truth from the unexpected places
Of a man's soul, like a playing-card from behind his ear:
Remember the first rule of this court is that the President
Shall undergo in person any treatment he decrees. [*The curtain
is withdrawn and in front of the blazing light stands a cross. The
Judge drops to his knees.*]
I understand. Haltingly, I begin to understand.
    [*He rises and addresses Jane Williams*]:
Jane, we have many things to learn, you and I.
It will be lonely for you and hard. Perhaps if I
Were with you it might help a little. And I think
That I shall need your help.
    [*He comes down and offers her his arm.*]
May I come with you?
    [*They go out together.*]

215

Suggestions for Discussion

1. The judge is found guilty on three counts: adultery, theft, and murder. Explain for each one of these a) why the judge thinks he is innocent and b) what evidence makes him change his mind.

2. On newsprint, jot down crimes that we easily perceive as such. Give examples of people who committed these crimes and of punishments they received. On another sheet next to this, write down crimes in which we share but that go unpunished.

3. Does the play suggest what we could do to avoid these crimes? What kind of defense, according to the play, would have been an acceptable argument in the heavenly court?

4. What does the Judge learn in the end? What actions show that he has taken the lesson seriously?

Militarism, the Draft, and War Taxes

From the beginning, Christians have had to decide what to do if demands of the government or another authority should conflict with the demands of God. The Bible consistently affirms that obedience to God must come first. But what is it God wants us to do? If we consider the example and teachings of Jesus as central for moral guidance, obedience of God excludes the use of violence and calls for love of neighbor, even love of enemies. Therefore a Christian cannot volunteer to participate in war in any form. But what if the law provides for a draft, requires some of us to fight or to execute prisoners, or forces us to pay so that others can kill? The question each Christian must answer is at what point, and in what form, to voice his or her conscientious objection.

As the draft is about to be reinstated, many eighteen year-olds must decide whether to register and whether to serve in the military. Older adults who encourage conscientious objection and support alternative service have to ask themselves whether these convictions should not logically lead to war tax resistance. Can we pray for peace, yet pay for war? Moreover, the change in warfare from armies on a battlefield to sophisticated, computor-guided weaponry may require more than just a refusal to fight physically. Many Christians feel called to acts of civil disobedience such as praying on forbidden ground near nuclear arsenals. What does it mean to be Christ's disciples today? And what consequences are we willing to bear for our witness: social rejection, financial penalties, jail, death?

Christianity as a movement was never as convincing and as rapidly spreading as during the time when Christians willingly let themselves be thrown to the lions. What would this world be like if Christians today chose to live out their faith in all its consequences, even to the point of self-sacrifice? Fortunately, penalties in our society today are not as drastic, but they can be severe. Another issue then, aside from our own willingness to be conscientious objectors or to commit acts of civil disobedience, is how we support those who witness in these ways.

The plays in this section question what the Christian response to war should be. "A Letter From Freddy" focuses on war tax resistance, while in "State of Siege" the pilgrims lay down their lives as they walk onto the battlefield to stop the fighting. "Oh Yes — I Guess" and "His Own Household" show young men who, having been brought up with both Christian and nationalistic ideals, suddenly face the draft and realize that killing and loving do not go together.

STATE OF SIEGE

by Charles Numrich

CHARACTERS

NARRATOR
KING
SOLDIER
PRIEST
PILGRIM

The scene is a large meadow in front of a castle; the narrator enters as a minstrel/story-teller.

NARRATOR. A distant kingdom, one you may never have heard of, once felt threatened by enemies. So the king gathered his finest knights; they stood before him in a large meadow, their weapons at the ready, their armor shining in the morning sun. [*Moves to the rear and off to one side. King enters and moves to center stage. Soldier enters from the audience, stands to one side of center-stage and bows his head to the king.*]

KING. My chosen ones; the bravest, the strongest, the best our nation has to offer; you will go into battle for me, for all of us; you will destroy the enemy, or be destroyed by them; but we will win. Their ways are not our ways; they cannot be trusted or ignored; they must be defeated. God will go with you and you will not fail. [*He turns to the priest who walks up to him.*] You must bless these knights before they go into battle.

PRIEST. But Your Majesty . . .

KING. It is your duty to give them hope and courage; they must fight bravely; they must win.

PRIEST. But I can't . . .

KING. Bless them! [*The priest hesitates; then he moves toward the soldier, who goes down on one knee. The priest puts his hand on the soldier's head.*]

PRIEST. You must be brave, my child; God is with you; and you must be with God; [*pause, leans close to the soldier*] and you must not go. [*The soldier looks up at the priest, puzzled. The priest stands up straight and moves back to the King's right side. When the battle trumpet sounds, the soldier rises.*]

KING. [*Moves to the soldier.*] There is the signal; the battle will begin soon. Go and fight bravely. [*The soldier bows until the king exits, then looks up at the priest.*]

PRIEST. [*Speaks quickly.*] You must not go. [*The battle trumpet*

sounds again. *Soldier exits toward the sound of the trumpet.*
The priest stands alone.]

NARRATOR. [*Moves again to center stage.*] At the same time, a
group of pilgrims were camped in the same meadow. They had
traveled together for years, from one holy place to another. One
of their leaders went to watch the military show, then waited
until the priest was alone. [*Moves again to the rear.*]

PILGRIM. [*A woman enters from the audience and approaches the
priest. She bows.*] May I speak with you?

PRIEST. [*Comes out of his reverie.*] What is it my child?

PILGRIM. My friends and I have traveled together over time and
distance, seeking holy places. Everywhere we stop, we ask to be
blessed by the local priest. If you will be so kind as to say a few
words for us now, we will continue our search.

PRIEST. [*Looks at her a moment.*] Receive my blessing.
[*Pilgrim bows her head.*]

PRIEST. Take my blessing, for strength. You [*to the audience*], all
of you go with God and you must follow wherever God leads,
however hard the way. [*The battle trumpet sounds in the
distance.*] Do you hear that? [*Pilgrim raises her head.*] That
sound will lead you where you must go. Two great armies are
about to join in battle, for no purpose but greed and ego. They
must be stopped, and you can stop them.

PILGRIM. We are simple pilgrims.

PRIEST. You are God's own children; you are peace-makers and
you can make them forget their madness.

PILGRIM. How?

PRIEST. [*Points offstage left*] Lead your group into that narrow
strip of land which still separates the two armies; stand silently
between them and pray; show them that war is not necessary.
Show them the way of peace and they will follow it. Go with
God.

PILGRIM. We must; there is no other way to go. [*Exits into the
audience. The priest watches the pilgrim leave. At the sound of
the battle trumpet, he looks off stage left and then exits slowly
upstage right.*]

NARRATOR. [*Returns to center stage.*] And so the peace-makers
marched, humble but determined, into the space between the
two armies; they bowed their heads and showed the way of
peace. [*The battle trumpet sounds.*] Then the battle began.
[*Silence for a moment.*] At first, soldiers on both sides were confused and did not know what to do. But their commanders were
insistent . . . [*The battle trumpet sounds twice.*] and they could
only respond. [*There are distant sounds of battle.*] The slaughter
was enormous; the battle went on and on, through the morning
and into the afternoon. The sun was high and hot when the few
still alive had to stop if they were to stay alive; and there was a

lull in the battle. [*Moves to the rear. Soldier enters from downstage left, beaten, battered, staggering; moves to center stage in great agony, pulling off some armor; drops his weapon and collapses. After a pause, the pilgrim enters from the audience.*]

SOLDIER. [*Tries to grab his weapon.*] Who's there?

PILGRIM. Relax; I won't hurt you. I'm one of the pilgrims.

SOLDIER. Pilgrims? Fools! Praying in the middle of a battle. [*He tries to laugh, but begins to cough and choke.*]

PILGRIM. [*Moves to the soldier and pulls out a canteen of water.*] Here, have some water. [*She sits next to him, holds up his head and gives him water; when he finishes, she drinks. The soldier tries to sit up, but his arm is wounded and he can't lean on it; he cries out in pain.*]

PILGRIM. You're hurt; here, relax. [*Begins to wash his wounds.*]

SOLDIER. [*Leans back on her*] Are any of your pilgrims still alive?

PILGRIM. Some . . . not many. [*Pause.*] What about your soldiers?

SOLDIER. A few. [*Pause.*] Why did you do it?

PILGRIM. [*Thinks a moment.*] Because we had to.

SOLDIER. Had to stand praying in the middle of a battle? Had to stand and be slaughtered? You're crazy!

PILGRIM. [*Pause*] Why did you do it?

SOLDIER. Do what?

PILGRIM. Fight.

SOLDIER. Why do I fight? What a question. You *are* crazy!

PILGRIM. Why?

SOLDIER. Because I'm a soldier. That's what I do. I have to fight.

PILGRIM. And end up like this? Beaten, wounded, your slaughtered friends around you?

SOLDIER. We had to . . .

PILGRIM. So, we are the same.

SOLDIER. The same?

PILGRIM. And both a little crazy. [*The battle trumpet sounds.*] Again?

SOLDIER. [*Rises painfully*] We will go on until we win.

PILGRIM. No one ever wins.

SOLDIER. [*Pause.*] But we will go on. Go home and pray for peace.

PILGRIM. At home there is peace. Here is where we must pray. [*Pause. Soldier starts to leave.*] Don't go.

SOLDIER. [*Pause.*] I have to go. [*The battle trumpet sounds; he leaves.*]

PILGRIM. [*Pause; reslings her canteen.*] So do I. [*Exits, following the soldier. The trumpet sounds and the fighting begins again.*]

NARRATOR. [*Returns to center-stage.*] The battle raged and raged. [*The trumpet sounds.*] And it still rages.

Suggestions for Discussion

1. Evaluate the actions of the priest. What do you think of his obedience to the king's orders? Why does he speak quickly and quietly when he tells the soldier not to go to battle? How could he have acted differently? What do you think of his encouraging the pilgrims to walk onto the battlefield to pray and risk death, yet at the same time not joining them in this action?

2. Now discuss the actions of the soldier. Why is he confused by the message of the priest? Why does he go anyway? Toward the end, why does he go back to battle even though he has seen the waste and pain of war?

3. Finally, consider the actions of the pilgrims. Do you think their acts are foolish, courageous, unavoidable? Do you agree that Christians must witness and pray to their God even at the very places where others worship idols? In this context, what do you think of people getting arrested for praying at nuclear missile sites?

4. Which behavior corresponds most to yours: that of the priest, the soldier, or the pilgrim? In what way?

OH YES — I GUESS

by James M. Drescher

PREFACE

This play is a satire which intends to present the contrast between what is generally taught and what is generally practiced — particularly concerning peace-making and military service. It was written in the time of the Vietnam War, but the issues it raises retain its significance and become ever more valid as we live with the threat of nuclear warfare.

PRODUCTION NOTES

The properties needed for the performance are one rocking chair, one small chair or footstool, one rectangular conference table, four rectangular straight back chairs, one Bible (preferably R.S.V.), three sheets of 8½" x 11" paper, two large business-size envelopes with 8½" x 11" paper enclosed, one badge or ribbon, and two spotlights to be used to focus on those people speaking. Play mood music before and during the presentation. A very effective visual device, if available, are slides or pictures of war and peace scenes projected on a screen by means of a slide or overhead projector. The pictures should serve as a background to the action and support the dialogue on stage.

CHARACTERS

MRS. JOHN SMITH, *mother of Jason.*
JASON SMITH, *draft-age youth except for the first two scenes*
SCOUTLEADER, *a middle-aged man*
MR. READ, *member of the draft board*
MR. WHITE, *member of the draft board*
MR. BLEW, *member of the draft board*

ACT ONE

SCENE 1

Jason is pre-school age. The stage is dark except for a spotlight on Jason and his Mother. Jason is seated on a small low bench or chair. Mrs. Smith is sitting on rocker. Jason has elbows propped on his knees and his chin cupped in hands. All the while Jason is staring and listening intently to his Mother who is reading in a reverent fashion passages from the Bible (RSV). These passages should be marked well so as to be readily found and read. She reads in a very deliberate, authoritarian way.
MRS. SMITH. Luke 10:27, 29, 37; John 3:16; John 15:9, 10, 12, 13; John 13:34, 35; Matt. 5:38, 44, 46; Matt. 5:3, 9; Exodus 20:13.

SCENE 2

Jason is a teenager. (Spotlight on Jason and Scoutleader). Each is dressed in scout uniform if possible. As spotlight goes on, scoutleader and Jason are standing facing each other. Scoutleader pins symbolic badge on Jason. After pinning badge, he steps back and asks Jason to repeat the scout pledge after him.
SCOUTLEADER. On my honor/I will do my best/to do my duty/ to God and my country,/and to obey the scout law,/to help other people at all times,/to keep myself physically

222

strong,/mentally alert,/and morally straight./ I believe a scout is trustworthy,/loyal,/helpful,/friendly,/courteous,/kind,/ obedient,/cheerful,/thrifty,/brave,/clean,/and reverent. Congratulations Jason! And I hope you will never forget to carry out the scout slogan: "Do a good turn daily."

JASON. Thank you.

SCENE 3

Jason is sitting in rocker reading a book. His mother walks in.

MOTHER. Here is a letter from the draft board, Jason.

[*She hands him a letter. Jason slowly opens it and reads aloud to his mother. Mrs. Smith stands next to him.*]

JASON. Dear Mr. Smith: Because of a recent Presidential order, it now becomes necessary for all those wanting to enter the Armed Forces to appear at an informal hearing to determine whether or not they can, in good conscience, be active participants in the military machine. As a result you are ordered to appear at your local draft board on Friday, 9 A.M.

SCENE 4

Jason is 20 years of age. He appears before a local draft board to be interrogated about his beliefs concerning participation in war. He sits facing three members of the Selective Service board who are seated behind a table. Each member of the board is holding a sheet of paper in hand. The stage is unlighted. The one spotlight is on Jason throughout. The other spotlight is shifted from speaker to speaker.

MR. WHITE. Your name is Jason Smith — is that correct?

JASON. Yes, sir.

MR. READ. Your parents' names are Mr. & Mrs. Joseph Smith — is that correct?

JASON. Yes, sir.

MR. BLEW. And your home address is R. D. 1, Paxboro.

JASON. Yes, sir, that's correct.

MR. WHITE. This hearing is not an attempt to embarrass or confuse you. Try to relax and be at ease. We want you to give us your honest answers so that we can evaluate the sincerity of your convictions. If you can persuade us that you are sincere and honest about your convictions, we will try to give you the classification you requested.

[*Jason nods his head in compliance.*]

MR. WHITE. [*Clears his throat and glances at paper which is in his hand*] Now because of our uncertainty about your background and former history, we want to ask you some questions about your somewhat bold assertions which you indicate typify your character and personality. As a matter of fact, your background seems to indicate you've led a generally mild, peaceful life.

JASON. I suppose one could say that — yes.

MR. BLEW. Mr. Smith, have you ever assaulted anyone?

JASON. [*Showing surprise*] No — of course not. That's against the law, isn't it?

MR. BLEW. Not even ever involved in a case of simple assault on a neighbor or classmate? Can you recall any time this has happened?

JASON. [*Slowly*] No, sir, I can't.

MR. WHITE. Well, well, either you have a very short memory or you've led a very sheltered life. However, let me ask you this question — What would you do if a drunk swore at your Mother?

JASON. Why, I'd slap him in the face and demand an apology.

MR. BLEW. Aha! Now we're getting somewhere.

MR. READ. Would you kill him? [*Spoken hastily and abruptly*]

JASON. [*Blankly*] Kill him — for an assault?

MR. WHITE. Suppose he attacked you with a deadly weapon?

JASON. Well now — that of course would be different.

MR. READ. Well . . . What would you do?

JASON. I suppose I'd try to get the weapon from him . . . and . . . if there wasn't a policeman around, I'd try to disable him in some way.

MR. READ. [*Eagerly*] Kill him perhaps?

JASON. I suppose if I had to, but that's a pretty serious thing.

MR. WHITE. [*Gently*] Mr. Smith, what one thing do you think is most important in preserving world peace?

JASON. [*Abruptly*] Military strength . . . of course . . . We must have military superiority.

MR. WHITE. What would you use to kill the drunk who assaulted your Mother?

JASON. Anything I could get my hands on . . . I guess.

MR. WHITE. Mr. Smith . . . Don't you carry a gun with you at all times for your protection?

JASON. No . . . of course not . . . Isn't it illegal without a permit?

MR. READ. Then how would you protect your mother from those assaults?

JASON. [*Tartly*] As a matter of fact, neither my mother nor I were ever threatened or attacked in the manner you suggested, but [*pause*] if someone did and I had a gun, I suppose I'd use it. Isn't that O.K.?

MR. BLEW. Suppose you had an automatic rifle . . . Would you be willing to kill his wife and their children, his mother, and his neighbors? Would you be willing to burn down their houses, defoilate their crops or spread disease germs among them . . . [*Impatiently*] Well, would you?

JASON. [*Outburst*] Please! . . . Please! . . . Stop! . . . Stop! . . . No! . . . No! . . . That would be awful — of course I wouldn't. That would be murdering a lot of innocent people. [*Jason props his head in his hands while his arms are propped on his knees. There is about a half minute pause.*]

MR. WHITE. [*Weary voice*] Mr. Smith, suppose you tell *us* why you think you qualify as a sincere combatant.

JASON. [*Sullen but firm voice*] You see I am presently a sergeant in the Reserve Officers Training Corps at the University. I volunteered. Doesn't that count for something?

MR. READ. What did you learn in Reserve Officers Training Corps?

JASON. We learn the manual of arms, how to salute, and how to take a rifle apart. We sponsor social events. Our band plays at various social functions.

MR. READ. Do you have outdoor weekend training exercises?

JASON. No, sir. They tried to, but . . .

MR. READ. Do you steal from neighboring farmers and villagers and rape their daughters?

JASON. [*Very insulted*] No — of course not!

MR. READ. Do you kill people who are unknown to you and who never did you any harm?

JASON. Oh, no! The college wouldn't permit that.

MR. WHITE. [*Businesslike*] Now Mr. Smith . . . Let's get to the main point of this interview. You are facing being drafted for a two-year term. If you are permitted to serve in the armed services, it would require you to surrender your personal conscience and responsibility. As far as I know, the military is the only organization which requires such rigid allegiance. During this period the country may go to war. Why do you think you are conscientiously able to participate in armed conflict?

JASON. [*Convincingly*] Well, in this case, the country to which you are referring is threatening our way of life. Perchance they may invade us. I would be protecting our way of life. We *must* meet force with force. We *must* give them some of their own medicine. After all, if *we* don't stop them, who will?

MR. WHITE. Very good. Now you are sounding a bit more convincing. Let me ask you . . . What do you mean by "our way of life?"

JASON. Freedom, liberty, freedom of religion, freedom of speech freedom of press and freedom of enterprise.

MR. READ. What do you mean freedom of enterprise?

JASON. I mean choice of jobs and occupations.

MR. READ. Oh, I see.

MR. WHITE. Getting back to your other comment. What do you mean when you said we must meet force with force? Is there any other way?

JASON. [*Slowly*] Not really . . . I guess.

MR. WHITE. Did you ever hear about non-violence or pacifism.

JASON. Just a little bit in my Sunday School class. But I never gave it much thought.

MR. BLEW. Are you saying that you would be willing to drop anti-personnel bombs on civilian populated areas, killing or injuring thousands of women and children?

JASON. [*Slowly*] Well . . . I guess . . . If I was so ordered.

MR. BLEW. And would you conscientiously help enforce a food blockade, thereby causing children to starve and babies to be born dead? Would you drop Napalm on villages and crops causing the land to become uninhabitable?

MR. READ. And you mean you would help spread gases and disease germs which would cause horrible agony to old men, women, and children?

JASON. [*Shouting*] Please . . . must you keep bringing up the subject of women and children? I thought in a war soldiers fight soldiers. Well, . . . don't they?

MR. WHITE. Supposedly so, but today's modern weapons are so destructive and their capabilities are so great that it's difficult to limit them. Take Hiroshima and Nagasaki for example.

JASON. Well, that is a bit different . . . I guess.

MR. BLEW. One more final question — you realize that the first casualty in any war is truth. Would you be willing to lie and cheat if told to do so?

JASON. Well . . . I guess . . . if it helped the cause.

MR. READ. How do you feel about torturing prisoners in order to get the desired confessions?

JASON. That's against the universal rules governing warfare, isn't it?

MR. READ. Yes, in a sense, but in time of war, anything that seems expedient goes.

MR. WHITE. O.K. That's all for now, Mr. Smith. Within about a week you will receive a letter from us indicating your acceptance or rejection for the classification you seek.

SCENE 5

Spotlight on Jason who is sitting on a rocking chair slowly taking a letter out of an envelope. He reads it slowly and distinctly.

JASON. Dear Mr. Smith, Our board came to the conclusion that you do not possess those resolute convictions that a fighting man needs to kill his fellow human being. At this point, we feel that your early home and Sunday School training have left a deep impression upon you which you apparently find difficult to erase. Yet, these things must be completely removed if you are to become a good military man. Of course the military can do much in training you to kill and destroy, but you will need to face up to the part that your convictions play. Also we, the military, can instill a great deal of hate, which is so necessary for war, and which it is apparent you lack. However, you must have a will to hate also. Furthermore, we are not yet persuaded that you are willing to surrender your own conscience and give absolute loyalty to the military. We sense that you may even feel, at times, that you should obey God first rather than the military machine. You understand that the military demands absolute loyalty—don't you? Therefore, we cannot give you your desired classification. We suggest that you seriously think about what you really believe. We think you will be a much happier and effective person in society if you take a definite stand regarding your alleged convictions. In five weeks you will be ordered to reappear for another hearing. At this time, we hope you can convince us that you *can* conscientiously be part of an organization whose job is to kill and destroy. Of course, in the meantime, you have the right to appeal your case. [*As the curtain closes, Jason rises slowly from rocker and walks, with head drooping, away from audience toward back center of stage. He reaches back of stage at time curtain is closed.*]

Suggestions for Discussion

1. Have a panel discussion on military recruitment, registration and the draft, and/or military service. Consider including a veteran, an army officer, a former draft board member, a conscientious objector, and a draft-age youth.

2. Have a general question and answer period with the audience.

3. Let the audience divide into "buzz groups" to discuss the play and related subjects. Here are suggestions of what they may wish to focus on:
   — Where do young people get their information about the military? Is this information adequate? How does it differ from that given in the play?
   — How is your position on military service linked to your faith? Do you share the view that fighting a war today is incompatible with faith in Christ? If not, how do you feel about those that hold it? If you agree, how would you communicate that view to those who do not have it?

HIS OWN HOUSEHOLD

by Arleta Unzicker

CHARACTERS

TOM SOMERS, *veteran of World War II*
CAROL SOMERS, *his wife, a kindergarten teacher*
PRASAD, *adopted son, age 18, native of India*
DANIEL, *grown son, veteran of the Viet Nam War*

The scene shows the dining-living room of the Somers home in Glenwood Springs, Colorado. It is a Saturday morning in the summer of 1980.

Before the curtain opens, a voice is heard singing "How Beautiful are the feet of them that preach the Gospel of Peace." The characters seem as unaware of the music as they are of the peace implications of the Christian Gospel to which they have been committed for many years.

The music continues as the curtain rises and for several more moments before anyone speaks.

As the play opens, Tom Somers reads the newspaper while Carol clears the table and exits with the breakfast dishes. She leaves one place setting and a pitcher of grape juice on the table. Near the table is a buffet with a mirror above it. At right are a sofa and other pieces of traditional living room furniture. The homey atmosphere results more from the plants here and there than from any decorating taste. [Carol enters.]

TOM. [*Restlessly.*] How long can he sleep?

CAROL. Well, 9:00 o'clock is rather late for us, but it's not really so bad for him, is it? He gets up at six five days a week. I guess he can sleep late on Saturdays. [*Pause.*] And it's his birthday. Remember?

TOM. Yes, well, I guess he's entitled to some privilege on his birthday. [*They smile at each other, giving the impression that they enjoy talking about their family.*] He's going to have to register. The paper is all about the draft registration. I thought I could have one son get on with his life without the draft.

CAROL. It's just registration, isn't it?

TOM. Oh, yes. Just the same, you never know.

CAROL. This may sound unpatriotic, but I think we've contributed our share so we can have a free country. You in World War II, and Phil and Dan in Viet Nam.

228

TOM. I'm proud of it, but plenty of others gave more — their lives. It burns me up the way these antidraft people, "doves" and whatnot don't believe in defending our country. But they sure like to live here! [*During the end of Tom's speech, the sound of someone coming down the stairs is heard. Prasad enters from center back. He is energetic, jovial, and light of step. Though he is clearly Indian, his manner and speech are typically American since he has lived in the United States since the age of three.*]

PRASAD. Morning.

TOM. Morning, Son.

CAROL. Happy birthday, Prasad.

PRASAD. Thank you. Thank you. [*He heads for the kitchen.*] Anything around here for breakfast?

CAROL. [*Restraining him by putting her hand on his shoulder.*] Sit down. I'll get it. Would you like one egg or two?

PRASAD. I can't have three?

CAROL. Well, yes, of . . .

PRASAD. No, no. Make it two.

CAROL. Well, if you want three . . . [*Both smile as she realizes he was teasing. Carol exits. Prasad flits around the room, stopping at the mirror to comb his hair, looking at plants — anything to be doing something with his excess energy.*]

TOM. [*Good-naturedly.*] Why don't you sit down? You're making me nervous. [*Prasad grins at his father and heads for a chair and sits.*]

PRASAD. There's nothing quite like construction work to make a guy appreciate weekends. School always made me glad for Saturdays, too. But I think I'd rather have school than construction work. I know I would. After construction work, college sounds pretty nice. [*Prasad fills his glass with grape juice for a pitcher on the table. He drinks and then refills his glass. He sips the second glassful slowly. Tom folds his newspaper and takes off his glasses. He is now seeking conversation.*]

TOM. So you don't think you like construction work?

PRASAD. It's all right. [*Carol enters with breakfast.*] Thanks. This looks a lot better than the cornflakes I fix myself every morning. [*To Tom.*] It's nice to see all that lumber and stuff turn into a house. But such a pain before it happens. Pounding all day long. Baking in the hot sun. When you're hot and tired and thirsty it's hard to be excited about this beautiful house you're building. I mean it isn't romatic. You never think about this finished product putting its loving wooden arms around a man and his wife and holding up a baby's stumbling feet. [*He sees the bemused amazement on his father's face.*] I didn't make that up. It's from something I had to memorize in the sixth grade. I don't even know who wrote it.

TOM. [*Studying his son while he eats.*] Actually, I think the job's done you good. For a couple a months you moped around so that your mother and I thought we'd have to get you a good check-up. Thought you were sick.

PRASAD. I wasn't sick. Just thinking over some things. Now I've made up my mind about some things and I feel better. [*He sees that his father is waiting for him to say more.*] Haven't you ever made a decision and felt so good about it you felt confident you could go on to make the right decisions about everything else that comes up?

TOM. [*He ignores the question but leans forward curiously.*] Just what decisions are you talking about?

PRASAD. What to major in. Whom to marry.

TOM. When did all this happen?

PRASAD. It didn't happen. But when such things do come up, I'll be able to decide.

TOM. [*He waits for Prasad to go on, but Prasad continues eating instead.*] Well, what then is the biggie?

PRASAD. You know I have to register. Well, I've decided to request classification as a conscientious objector and do some kind of alternative service. [*Tom is stunned. Carol, who has picked up the grape juice pitcher and the salt and pepper shakers, decides this is not the time to be in the kitchen and sets them back on the table.*]

TOM. Tell me I didn't hear you right.

PRASAD. [*Quietly*] You did hear me right.

TOM. How could you do this to us? When I'd hear about all them draft dodgers and draft card burners, I never thought I'd have a son like them.

PRASAD. I'm not dodging the draft and I'm not going to burn my draft card.

TOM. Might as well. What are you going to do, be an orderly in a hospital and carry bed pans? Nobody'd shoot at you that way, that's for sure.

PRASAD. I don't suppose orderlies are commanded to shoot at people either. Some people always assume that people who refuse to fight in war are cowards. Maybe they just don't believe in killing people. Maybe they just don't want any part in the whole senseless, bloody mess.

TOM. Who's been filling your head full of this nonsense — that Mennonite history teacher? Or maybe it was the atheist? What does he teach?

PRASAD. Biology. But he's not an atheist. He's an agnostic.

TOM. Same difference. Harold Moffat got on the school board on purpose to get Byler kicked out . . .

PRASAD. No, Byler's the Mennonite. You mean Mathies.

TOM. Mathies. He's still there. They put him on tenure. Between the Mennonite and the atheist . . .

PRASAD. Agnostic.

TOM. . . . it's hard to say which can do more harm to the kids.

CAROL. You don't have to worry about Byler. The Mennonites are nice people.

TOM. Sure. Ralph Corwin lives over there beside their church. He says they sing nice. But that doesn't mean they don't have some crazy ideas.

PRASAD. Byler and Mathies are just the two best teachers in the school. That's all. I suppose Harold Moffat thinks Mr. Terney is a good teacher because he goes around with a New Testament in his breast pocket.

TOM. Careful now. You should admire him for that.

PRASAD. I wish I could admire him. He can't keep order. He can't explain anything. He won't say what he thinks. If someone tells him the moon is made of blue cheese, he says [*Imitating*,] "Yes, it sure is. That's right. You bet." He has a motto on his desk that says "Prayer changes things," but I can't see that it changes anything for him — at least not for the better. I don't like people to know that he goes to our church.

CAROL. The church is for people with problems, too.

PRASAD. Sure, but shouldn't it help them solve their problems — not just pretend it does and hope people are fooled? [*The conversation isn't going the way any of them want it to, and they all look miserable.*]

TOM. [*To Prasad.*] You are sure this, this conscientious objector thing is what you want? [*Prasad nods. To Carol*] I'm going to call Dan to come over. Maybe he can talk some sense into him.

CAROL. He's coming tonight for the birthday supper.

TOM. I want to get this settled before then. [*Exits center back. Music of "How Beautiful are the Feet" is heard. Carol goes to the table, gathers up dishes and heads for the kitchen. Prasad helps her. Both exit at left. After a few moments Tom enters from the center back. He sits on the sofa. Carol enters from the left. Music stops.*]

CAROL. Is he coming?

TOM. Yes, thank goodness.

CAROL. [*Sits on arm of sofa.*] Well, don't keep him long. You know he always reserves Saturdays to spend with Judy and the children.

TOM. They'll just have to understand. [*Prasad enters from left.*] Prasad, tell me, was it Byler who talked you into this?

PRASAD. No, Dad. He really didn't. Our best teachers don't try to make us think one way or another. They try to get us to think things through and come to our own conclusions. I had two of Mathies' classes, but I still believe in God as Creator.

TOM. And you took one history course of Byler's and you're a pacifist.

231

PRASAD. It's not like that at all. I didn't even know from sitting in his class that he was a pacifist. I knew he was anti-war, but who isn't except for some generals and Pentagon people.

TOM. Then how did it happen?

PRASAD. You won't get mad at me if I tell you?

TOM. I'll try not to.

PRASAD. It started gradually. I remember asking Dan about Viet Nam. He kept trying to change the subject. Finally, I asked him why he didn't want to talk about it. He said that when you have horrible nightmares you get over the terror because you know they're not real. But when your nightmares turn out to be real, then you don't want to keep reliving them. You don't talk about them because you want to forget. Then he told me a story. There was this nurse in the battlefield hospital where he worked for a while. She was doing whatever they do to some tubes on the chest of a Viet Cong POW and didn't see him reaching for the scissors hanging on his belt. He grabbed them and tried to stab her. When she pulled back, in self-defense, she yanked the tubes from his chest. Two MP's grabbed him and took him out. When the nurse went to see, they gloated, "See how we took care of him." They had skinned him alive.

CAROL. He never told us that.

PRASAD. He had never told anyone. He said the incident haunted him for months, even years. And it was only one of dozens of nightmares he lived through in the name of preserving our freedom. I started thinking about what I'd do if I was ever called up, but I couldn't resolve it for a long time. Then I had to write a paper for my American Lit class. We had to choose a topic and write what various authors had to say about it and then write our own ideas on the subject. I chose war. My English teacher suggested Thoreau. He went to jail rather than pay tax to support the Mexican War and slavery. He suggested Mark Twain's account of how he felt after killing an "enemy" in the Civil War. Oh, let's see. There were others. Lincoln in his Second Inaugural, James Russell Lowell, and some modern poets. Then I went to Mr. Byler . . .

TOM. Uh-huh.

PRASAD. . . . and talked to him about my paper. I just went to him because I could always talk to him. He listened. He always had time. He seemed really interested. He asked me all about my paper and finally asked me what I thought about participating in war. I said I didn't think it was right, but I didn't want to go to jail. I said I guess I'd have to go to Canada. Then I asked him what he would do, and he told me what he did do, about 1958. [*Doorbell Rings.*] He suggested I read the New Testament, which I did. Several times, Dad.

DAN. [*Entering from the right.*] Hi, Mom, Dad. [*They ad lib*

232

replies.] Missing your kindergartners these days, Mom?

CAROL. I wouldn't be honest if I didn't admit to liking vacations.

DAN. [*To Prasad.*] My kid brother, eighteen years old. [*He claps him on the shoulder and they scuffle good-naturedly.*] Every time I wanted to go shoot baskets or go rafting down the canyon, no, I had to watch my little brother.

PRASAD. [*In mock penitence*] Can you ever forgive me?

DAN. Oh, you've been more than worth it. How could I have got along without a brother named Prasad? In college when I would tell my friends about my family I'd say; "I have an older brother Phil. He's married. Then I have a sister Cathy who's in high school. Then I have a little brother who's in kindergarten. His name's Prasad. I always had to repeat it. It never failed. [*They all laugh.*]

TOM. [*He stands up, goes to his sons and takes each by the arm briefly.*] We have a few things to talk about. Let's go to the table. [*He sits at the table. He pulls up a chair at his left for Carol. Prasad sits at Carol's left.*]

DAN. [*Still in a jovial mood and not knowing what to expect.*] Do I get to be Sir Galahad?

TOM. Cut the jokes for now. I don't understand them anyway. [*He is making a deliberate effort to be calm and quiet.*] Dan, you know Prasad is going to have to register. Now he has just informed us that he is a conscientious objector. [*He looks at Dan for a reaction, but Dan is non-committal.*] This is contrary to everything we've always been taught — that we need to defend our country. What if everybody did this? The Communists would take over the world. Then what would happen to the Christians? We wouldn't be able to live according to our beliefs.

PRASAD. I'm not sure we all are now.

TOM. I just want you to believe and do what's right. We didn't rescue you from heathendom to have you turn your back on our country and what we've taught you.

PRASAD. You didn't exactly rescue me from heathendom. You got me from a Christian orphan's home. There's a good chance I'd have been taught Christian beliefs and come to accept them as my own even if I'd grown up in India.

DAN. [*Gently, because he doesn't want to add to the hurt feelings.*] Dad, what is it about our country that needs military defense?

TOM. Not you, too? What kind of question is that? Why, our whole way of life. We can't be dominated by a godless government.

DAN. Did Jesus teach that we must have political freedom in order to follow Him? There are lots of Christians in the Soviet Union. In Poland I hear the churches are packed. When the Pope visited there, two and one-half million people turned out to hear him.

233

Looks as though the faith of Christians behind the Iron Curtain is more precious to them than it is to many Christians in the free world.

TOM. Maybe you'd like to live there.

DAN. No, I rather live here, of course. There are things about this country I think are worth preserving, but not with military strength. Not by killing people or destroying buildings and forests and farmland. I believe Jesus taught his followers to go about doing good — teaching, healing, reconciling. all people everywhere, treating every person as a members of God's household, or potentially so. To me, that's got to rule out killing even a Communist for oil or ideology or self-defense. I think we must obey God and leave our destiny to His mercy.

TOM. Put yourself in the line of fire and ask God to protect you?

DAN. That's not what I said. That's what's been done over and over again. We decide war is the way to settle something and then we ask God to protect us and give us victory. I'm saying our first responsibility is to obey Christ and love our enemies and all that implies, and leave the consequences of that obedience to God.

TOM. That'd take a lot of faith. [*He speaks hesitatingly, no longer confident that he has an argument.*] I don't know, I — I always thought we had to have strong Christian nations, and then, well, then God would help us against the Godless ones, so — so the Christians in those countries can live for the Lord, too. God and my country — they go together, don't they? [*He looks from one to another. No one answers.*]

CAROL. They haven't rejected either, Tom. Or us. They've just taken what we've taught them a little futher than we have. And maybe they're right.

TOM. You, too.

DAN. I think you've analyzed it accurately, Mother. When I went to Viet Nam I was only 19. I hadn't taken my Christianity very seriously. But I wasn't there long when I began to do a lot of thinking. And praying. I came to the conclusion that the only position for a Christian was pacifism. When other veterans came home they were troubled that they didn't feel appreciated, that they had gone through all that misery only to have the people at home feel the whole involvement was unjustified. My problem was different. I was shocked by how many Christians still thought it was a duty to fight when their country calls them. I had to try to understand that Christians are at different levels of growth and commitment, that some aren't forced into the soul-searching that others are, and that there are, simply, honest differences. [*He looks at his parents with a sudden wave of compassion. He rises, goes to stand behind his parents, puts an arm around each and kisses his mother.*]

234

DAN. Even if we don't always agree, we'll never stop loving each other. [*Pause.*] I'll be back with Judy and the kids tonight. See you then. [*Tom and Carol follow Dan and Prasad as far as the center of the stage. All ad lib goodbyes. Prasad exits with Dan at the right.*]

CAROL. We need to allow them their differences — we're still a family. Just like people everywhere are members of God's household.

TOM. [*Not convinced, but trying to sort things out.*] And if they aren't we don't kill them off — we try to bring them into our household. [*Music of "How Beautiful are the Feet" is heard again.*]

Suggestions for Discussion

1. How would you feel about someone in your family wanting to be a conscientious objector? About his refusing to register for the draft? About his enlisting in the military?

2. How would you try to work things out if he chose an option with which you were not pleased?

3. Invite several Vietnam veterans to speak about their experiences during the war.

4. If you are a veteran, how do you feel about COs? If you are a conscientious objector, how do you feel about those who have fought in wars?

5. Prasad explains how he has developed his conviction. What has lead to his choice not to let himself be drafted?

6. Listen to 18 year-olds in your congregation who are now facing registration. Where can they turn for draft counselling? What has influenced them in their decision making process?

A LETTER FROM FREDDY

by James M. Drescher

CHARACTERS

FREDDY, *17 year-old college student*
FREDDY'S FATHER
FREDDY'S MOTHER
A CLERGYMAN, *interviewee*
A LAWYER, *interviewee*
RETIRED MILITARY OFFICER, *interviewee*
RETIRED PERSON, *interviewee*
TEENAGER, *interviewee*
TV ANNOUNCER/INTERVIEWER
  [*The interviewees planted throughout the audience.*]

The properties needed for the play are a single bed (cot), a newspaper, coffee cups, kitchen table and chairs, a coffee pot, a lunch pail, a letter in an envelope, a portable microphone, a Bible (for the clergyman), and an alarm clock.

The general setting is any home, anywhere in the U.S.A.

SCENE 1

The scene opens with Mother setting the breakfast table with coffee cups. Father walks in.

FATHER. Good morning, Dear. Coffee sure smells good! Is the paper here yet? [*Mother gets the newspaper and hands it to her husband as she pours some coffee.*]

MOTHER. I wonder when we are going to hear from Freddy.

FATHER. It has been a while, hasn't it? I sure miss him. I guess he's busy with his studies and extra-curricular activities. [*Father opens the newspaper and slowly reads the headlines.*] "Congress Votes $30 Billion More For Military Budget. President Says More Bombs Needed." What great news to wake up to!

MOTHER. Sure is depressing, isn't it? You'd think with such an overkill capacity already in existence someone would put an end to the arms race.

FATHER. [*Turning newspaper page, reads audibly.*] "President Reinstates Draft Registration." It says all 18 year-old males are supposed to register for the draft.

MOTHER. Freddy will be 18 next month. I wonder what he plans to do about registration. [*Father puts the newspaper away and finishes drinking coffee. He rises and heads toward door.*]

FATHER. Well, I've got to get to work. See you tonight. [*He kisses his wife goodbye, picks up his lunch pail and goes out the door.*]

SCENE 2

Evening of the same day. Father enters kitchen with lunch pail and greets his wife with a kiss. He sets his lunch pail on the table and sits down.

MOTHER. How was your day at work?

FATHER. Busy as usual. Any mail? [*Mother hands him a letter.*]

MOTHER. Yes, a letter from Freddy.

FATHER. Great. It's about time. [*Father opens the letter and reads aloud.*]

Dear Mom and Dad,

I guess you thought I'd never write, but honestly I've been so busy with term papers, tests, and required reading. I really like college and I miss being home.

As you realize, in about two weeks I'll be 18 years old. I am faced with a big decision about registering for the draft. I need your advice. I feel like I'm caught in the middle. Throughout my life you have taught me to practice the way of peace, love and non-violence. Yet, in thinking about this, I realize that you, with your tax money, are supporting the very organization which you don't want me to join. It seems to me that a great inconsistency exists here. If I am not expected to give my body to this military machine, why do you support it with your hard-earned money? It seems to me, if it is wrong to participate with our bodies, it's also wrong to contribute money to keep the machine functioning. What do you think? What should I do? Can you understand my dilemma? Let's make a deal. I won't join the military if you won't contribute money toward the support of it, ok? Since I need to make a decision in a few weeks, I hope I'll hear from you soon.

Love, Freddy

[*After finishing reading the letter, Father sits with his head in his hands for about one minute before speaking. Then he looks up and says:*]

FATHER. It was good to hear from Freddy. But wow! What a hard deal he proposed. He must have been doing some heavy thinking.

MOTHER. Doesn't give us much choice, does it? . . . If we don't want him to join the military, that is.

237

FATHER. I've got to have time to think about this proposal. Quite a deal . . . I don't feel like eating . . . I'm going to bed early. I need more time to think about Freddy's proposal before I write a response to him. How do you feel?

MOTHER. I'm wondering about what our relatives and friends would say if they found out that we were war tax resisters.

FATHER. If it's our belief and conviction, what does it matter? We can explain.

SCENE 3

Father is lying on cot, tossing and turning in his sleep, mumbling phrases unintelligible to the audience. He dreams that he is a TV announcer/interviewer and that he is walking through the audience asking persons the following question: "Should a person who is conscientiously opposed to participating in war be obligated to pay war taxes?" Meanwhile, a person with microphone in hand explains the dream and then proceeds out into the audience and asks the pre-selected persons [clergyman, officer, retiree, lawyer, and teenager] the above question.

ANNOUNCER. *[To audience]* Freddy's father is having a dream in which he is a TV interviewer. In this scene he interviews 5 persons from the audience. *[Announcer steps off stage into audience and goes first to clergyman.]*

ANNOUNCER. Sir, what is your occupation?

CLERGYMAN. *[Dressed in a business suit and carrying a Bible.]* I'm a minister of God's church on Main Street.

ANNOUNCER. The question is: "Should a person who is conscientiously opposed to participating in war be obligated to pay war taxes?" What do you think?

CLERGYMAN. *[Very piously]* The Bible says: Render to Caesar what is Caesar's and to God what is God's. I think the Governments are ordained of God. I feel I am not responsible for what the Government does with the money I am obligated to give them.

ANNOUNCER. Thank you. Just a side question. Would you feel the same if you live under a Nazi or communist government? *[He moves on to next interviewee, the lawyer.]* Now sir, what is your occupation?

LAWYER. I'm an attorney.

ANNOUNCER. Would you kindly respond to the question? Should a person who is conscientiously opposed to participating in war be obliged to pay war taxes?

LAWYER. *[Speaks deliberately.]* It's illegal not to pay your taxes. Law is law. Law is the basis of any organized society. It just wouldn't work to let individuals decide which taxes they want to pay. Of course, the 1st Amendment of our constitution does assure citizens free exercise of religion. It depends on how you look at it, I guess. One way or another, the IRS usually gets the money owed to them. However, there do seem to be many loopholes in the tax laws for the real wealthy and huge corporations. Perhaps, in fairness, conscientious objector status should be extended to tax payers. [*The announcer moves on to the career military officer.*]

ANNOUNCER. Now, sir, what is your occupation?

OFFICER. I'm a career military officer, retired after 20 years.

ANNOUNCER. Would you care to respond to the question which is being asked?

OFFICER. Yes, I sure would. It's bad enough if people don't fight for their country. It would be that much worse if there was no money for weapons and supplies used in war. I think all the war tax and draft resisters should be jailed.

ANNOUNCER. Now let's move on and ask a few more people about their viewpoint. [*He repeats the original question.*] As a young person, would you like to give us your opinion?

TEENAGER. Yes, that argument about consistency and constitutional assurances makes sense to me. After all, don't we have freedom of religion?

ANNOUNCER. [*He moves on to final interviewee, a retired citizen.*] Do you remember the question?

RETIRED CITIZEN. Yes, I just never thought much about this whole issue. Taxes are American as apple pie. Our government can't function without money. Taxes are not evil in themselves. It boils down to how they are used. Most of us retirees need tax relief — not more taxes. Obviously, money which is used for the military cannot be used for programs for the sick, elderly and other needy persons.

ANNOUNCER. Thank you, sir. There you have it, folks. A sample of people's opinions about the question "Should a person who is conscientiously opposed to participating in war be obligated to pay war taxes?" And now back to our sponsor.

SCENE 4

Father wakes up when alarm clock rings. He sits on the edge of the bed, head in hands. After about one minute he gets up and goes to the breakfast table.

MOTHER. You sure tossed and turned last night.

FATHER. Yes, I didn't get much sleep. Just couldn't get Freddy's question off my mind. I had a most unusual dream. I dreamed I was a TV talk show host and that I was asking persons in the audience about paying war taxes. I can't remember many details but I do recall each person was quite persuasive in his opinion.

The dream wasn't very helpful to me in making my decision about war taxes. Oh, what a night!

MOTHER. After you went to bed last night, Freddy called and said he is coming home this weekend.

FATHER. Good, then I won't need to write a letter to him.

SCENE 5

Several days later.

FATHER. I'm glad I didn't need to write a letter in response to your inquiry about the payment of war taxes. I've thought a great deal about it. It's a bit complicated.

FREDDY. To me it seems like a real pertinent issue.

FATHER. [*Sounding defeated.*] But it's not practical.

MOTHER. [*Lamenting.*] We've worked so hard and long to get what we have—a car, house, and nice furniture. We could lose our property. It's so risky.

FREDDY. So is going to war or having a nuclear holocaust. [*Freddy and father rise, look at each other in the eyes. Father extends his hand, shakes hands with Freddy.*]

FATHER. It's a deal. I've made up my mind. I won't pay if you don't go. My conscience won't let me pay for death and destruction. I feel it's the least I can do for you and your children. What do you say Mother?

MOTHER. OK, I'll take the risk for peace with you. [*As the curtain closes, Freddy walks off stage with his arms around the shoulders of his parents.*]

Suggestions for Discussion

1. What would you have answered if the interviewer had asked you the question, "Should a person who is conscientiously opposed to participating in war be obliged to pay war taxes?"

2. Is your attitude about military service the same as it is about taxes that pay for past, present, and future wars? Explain why or why not.

3. Stop the performance after Scene 4. Then divide the audience into small groups and let them roleplay the dialogue they think will happen once Freddy comes home. After about 10 minutes, discuss the suggestions about how to end the play. Then perform Scene 5 as one possible option.

4. Invite a person to speak who has resisted war tax payments. Ask him or her to share experiences and to present a list of legal and illegal options for such witness.

5. Comment on the following statement by Harold R. Regier: "I'd rather explain the folly of war tax resistance to those who misunderstand than explain my silence and inaction to my children and grandchildren should nuclear ovens become our graves."

World Hunger and Human Rights Violations

Like the threat of nuclear war, world hunger is easiest to deal with by resorting to psychic numbing. As long as we do not focus on the problem, we can pretend that it does not exist, or that nothing can be done, or at least that we are not required to act. This escape from responsibility is even more obvious in the case of world hunger than war, because all-out nuclear war is only a potential threat whereas death from starvation occurs daily. Hunger is probably the ugliest feature of the human community, particularly in view of the contrast between affluent and poor nations, or the juxtaposition of very rich and very poor, both here and abroad.

Our attitudes have to change profoundly. We need to admit that world hunger is indeed our problem, acknowledge that it can be remedied, and find ways to end it.

Hunger is our problem for several reasons. First of all, we don't need to seek very far to find it. Malnutrition and poverty is spreading in the United States. With the shift in the national budget toward greater military appropriations at the expense of human services, the numbers of the needy keep increasing. Ours is one of the wealthiest nations on earth, yet it cannot — or chooses not to — feed the hungry.

But our responsibility does not end at national borders. We live in a global community. It is indeed appropriate, like in the play "And Marybai is Hungry," to speak of starving people everywhere as "neighbors." We know of their plight, and we are called to act. "For I was hungry and you fed me, I was thristy, and you gave me a drink . . . ."

A third reason why world hunger is *our* problem is that we are an indirect cause of that condition. People starve not only because their soil fails to produce or a climatic change has ruined the crops for a particular year. More often than not, they starve because they are forced to plant crops for export rather than for the needs of their own families.

Human rights violations must be our concern for the same reasons. The call to feed the hungry is followed by the call to care for the sick, the naked, and the imprisoned, be they in the US ghettos and high security prisons, or in the African homelands, or in torture chambers anywhere in the world. Here again, US involvement has often aggravated the situation. Torturers working for right-wing governments in Argentina, El Salvador, and pre-revolutionary Nicaragua were trained in Washington D.C. and often received further instruction from US forces in the Panama Canal zone.

Military dictatorships today receive economic and diplomatic backing as long as they promise to keep their country "free of communists." The idea is that "the enemy of my enemy is my friend," regardless of drastic human rights violations.

The responsibility of Christian peacemakers is to be informed, pray, educate, and act to end injustices. Drama, in this context, can help make people aware. Once again, it is crucial not to leave the audience with a sense of impotence, but rather to follow up the presentation with suggestions for individual and community action.

TO FEED THE HUNGRY

by Ingrid Rogers

PRODUCTION NOTES

World hunger is a difficult theme to develop within the limits of a short play. How could the tone ever be grave enough to suggest the horror of the situation? Where is the actor who could adequately portray a starving child or adult? How can we appropriately point to the shamefully uneven distribution of wealth without getting stuck in unproductive guilt feelings?

In view of these difficulties it seemed appropriate to use a light tone, to show tragedy behind the veil of comedy. The two actors in the play could both be either clowns or bums, or you may wish to make just the first speaker a clown. (The actors should probably use their own names in place of "Tim" and "George." Of course, the roles could be played by women as well.) The idea is to appeal to the audience: to inform while allowing to identify, to amuse but also to shock, to bring about a wish to act rather than resign.

George enters with a grocery bag. He sees Tim sitting on a bench.
GEORGE. Hi, Tim! What are you brooding about?
TIM. I am hungry.
GEORGE. Hungry? Why don't you just eat something?
TIM. I don't have anything to eat, George.
GEORGE. Oh. Well, here. Have an apple. [*Holds out his bag of apples.*]
TIM. Yeah, you see, that's part of what worries me.
GEORGE. Hey, what's the matter? There's nothing wrong with my apple!
TIM. It's not your apple. I mean the fact that I can just go get something to eat if I want it.
GEORGE. I can't see anything wrong with that either.
TIM. Okay, look. Here I am, hungry, but I certainly can do something about it if I choose to. It just dawned on me how many people don't have that choice.
GEORGE. That's true!
TIM. So that's why I have decided not to eat anything for a while, just to see what it feels like to be hungry.
GEORGE. [*Aside*] He's nuts!
TIM. And you know, we have so much that it doesn't even mean much to give something away — there is always more.

GEORGE. Makes it nice that way, doesn't it? When you are rich, you can be generous. That's one of the things I like about being rich!

TIM. But you see, the gift doesn't really mean anything then. You'll never miss it! [*George looks at his apple, frowning.*] I don't mean your apple. That was sweet of you to offer it to me. [*George nods and grins.*] Now picture me not just hungry, but actually starving.

GEORGE. My word, what are you up to?

TIM. Not in reality! Come on now, use your imagination!

GEORGE. Ah . . . all right.

TIM. Well, what would you have done?

GEORGE. I guess I would send you to the doctor and recommend a special diet or something.

TIM. What if I didn't have any money for the doctor or the diet or food, period?

GEORGE. I don't know . . . Why wouldn't you have money? Wouldn't you be working and getting an income?

TIM. I would be working, but not for enough money to feed my family. The profits of the crops of the land I help cultivate would go to the man who owns the land.

GEORGE. And he would be rich?

TIM. Very rich.

GEORGE. So why doesn't he help you?

TIM. It's not in his interest.

GEORGE. What a rat!

TIM. What do you mean?

GEORGE. I mean he's obnoxious, living off what you have produced, practically watching you starve!

TIM. Right.

GEORGE. Now what has all this got to do with my apple?

TIM. George!! Your apple is fine! But let's say it were a banana.

GEORGE. A banana? [*Looks at the apple.*]

TIM. Yeah. You pay about ten cents for a nice golden banana. You know how much of this the people get that have grown and picked it?

GEORGE. No idea.

TIM. About one hundredth of a cent.

GEORGE. Where do the other 99 hundredths go?

TIM. To the land owner, the shipping company, and the grocery stores.

GEORGE. Wow. . . . So what can I do about it?

TIM. Remember what you called the rich guy earlier?

GEORGE. A rat. I called him a rat. I meant it, too.

TIM. Well, we are sort of in his situation.

GEORGE. [*Stunned*] Who—I? You? We?

TIM. We have everything, they have nothing. We use their labor so that we can have cheap bananas, or a nice standard of living. We watch them starve, or we just don't look; and when they rebel we call them communists and pay their government so they can be shot. [*Both sit quiety for a while. Then George gets up and puts the bag of apples in Tim's lap.*]

GEORGE. Here.

TIM. What's this?

GEORGE. I don't want them. I'm not hungry anymore either.

TIM. George, I've got an idea.

GEORGE. Really? I'm so depressed, I'm not even sure I want to hear.

TIM. Sit down. Remember how you acted when you first learned I was hungry?

GEORGE. Yeah. I gave you an apple and then you didn't want it.

TIM. [*Smiles, puts his arm around George*] Well, you saw what I needed, and you acted on it, right?

GEORGE. I guess so.

TIM. Okay. Now I'm thinking, what if we just let people know what's going on? I mean, like I told you.

GEORGE. Gosh, if there's anything I can do . . .

TIM. Sure, we'll make them aware, you and I.

GEORGE. And once they know, they'll help change things, won't they. Will they? Won't they? Won't they? [*George runs beside Tim as they exit.*]

Suggestions for Discussion

1. *Bread For the World*, 32 Union Square East, New York, NY 10003, has readings, prayer services, study courses on world hunger, and action suggestions. Write to them for a list of available resources.

2. Fast for one day each month, one meal per week, or whatever length of time and frequency you want to commit yourself to. Invite friends to join you, and help each other keep that commitment. Give the money saved to relief work.

3. Check your congressmen's voting record for bills concerning economic aid. Write to them expressing your feelings about the strong shift towards military aid and away from aid to the world's poor.

4. Oppose infant formula advertising and sales in developing countries.

5. Brainstorm about ways to reduce consumption of food and resources. Draw up a plan of action for yourself that you feel you can stick to. Urge the other members of your group to hold you accountable.

6. Teach a course on world hunger using study material from *Bread for the World* (address listed above).

AND MARYBAI IS HUNGRY!

by Jean Moyer

CHARACTERS

Four narrators who speak from the four corners of the church:
N1 *right front;* N2 *left front;* N3 *right back;* N4 *left back*

The five people around the table:
MARTHA; JOE; ALICE; SAM; MARGARET

BUSINESS EXECUTIVE
CLERGYMAN
TWO PEOPLE FROM AUDIENCE
MARYBAI

A table and chairs are at the right of the stage or chancel area. A young girl (Marybai) is standing at stage left. She stares listlessly over the heads of the audience and at times may place her head in her hands in a gesture of despair. Marybai is in a world of her own and does not react to any other words or action. She should be dressed in a simple costume of a Third World country.

During the opening speeches the following come up the center aisle: Margaret pushing a full shopping cart; Joe and Alice carrying trays of food; and Sam and Martha, wearing party hats and carrying a cake and a bucket of fried chicken. They walk quickly, their mood one of lightheartedness. Greeting each other as they meet at the front, they gather around the table, place their food on it, and talk together as they begin to eat.

NI. The shopping carts go rolling by;
    Despite inflation they're piled high
    With food to tempt your taste and eye.
                    N3. And Marybai is hungry.
N2. We'll fill our shelves with goods galore
    With bargains from our local store
    And when they're empty, we'll buy more!
                    N4. And Marybai is hungry.
N1. Let's to MacDonalds for a snack
    To dine on french fries and Big Mac.
    (How many billions? I've lost track!)
                    N3. And Marybai is hungry.

N2. So pop the corn and broil the steak;
   Let's blow the horn and bake a cake —
   We're celebrating . . . no mistake!
                              N4. And Marybai is hungry.
N1. What do we have to celebrate?
   Why, life is good — the food is great!
   So live it up 'fore it's too late!
                 N3. [*With great intensity*] But Marybai is *hungry!*
N2. Who is Marybai . . . that strange-sounding name that keeps
   interrupting our cheerful little rhymes of food and plenty?
N1. The name is that of a young woman from a province in
   Bombay, India, as described in the chapter "The Face of Hunger"
   from I.W. Moomaw's book *Crusade Against Hunger.*
N2. But she could be one of the six million facing death in the
   Sahel region of Africa —
N3. a statistic from the 1,700,000 who are dying of hunger in
   Ethiopia —
N4. a face among the seven million who are starving in
   Southeast Asia —
N1. a child from Pakistan described by Brother Moomaw as one
   who watches with big solemn eyes, showing no mischief or joy,
   like a little old man or woman with sunken cheeks, swollen
   abdomen, and spindly legs that speak of misery and deprivation.
N2. If anyone in our community were in need of food, the church
   would do everything they could to see that his or her needs were
   met.
N3. The words of Christ, "I was hungry and you fed me," would
   move us to share a pot of soup . . . a basket of potatoes . . . a jar
   of home-canned peaches without hesitation.
N4. But what about the hungry, thousands of miles away . . .
   those unreal millions we have never met but whose sad faces
   catch our eye occasionally during the seven o'clock news?
N1. We shrug our shoulders, deeply sigh,
   Feel overwhelmed — and pass on by.
N2. We never think that we might try
   To touch . . . to share : . . to love.

*The action shifts to the people around the table as they talk
together.*
SAM. Pass the syrup please, Martha.
MARTHA. Go easy on the sweet stuff, Sam. It's up to $1.80 a
   bottle!
MARGARET. Isnt' it awful? I just shake . . . I mean literally shake
   every time I get to the checkout counter. I dread it when that
   long white paper with those numbers jumps out at me. Things
   get worse every week!

MARTHA. Sure, it's bad, but a body has to eat! They've got us over a barrel. They know we'll pay for it!

SAM. You ought to be like Joe here. He's on a diet again.

MARTHA. Hey, fella. Didn't all those broiled steaks and raw turnips do the trick?

JOE. Naw . . . I got too hungry at night and I'd fill up on ice cream and donuts before I turned in.

ALICE. I bet you filled your donut holes with cottage cheese before you ate them!

JOE. Yeah, with a cherry on top and a lettuce leaf on the side. Made me feel less quilty that way! [*Laughter*]

SAM. How many diets does this make for you, Joe?

JOE. Oh, maybe four or five.

MARGARET. [*Standing.*] Hey, how about me running down to (*insert name of local fast food place*) for some more shakes and fries? Anybody like more? [*The next four speeches overlap*]

MARTHA. Listen, I'm full up to here!

ALICE. No, thanks . . . but while you're up would you get me the ketchup?

JOE. Boy, you're ambitious!

SAM. None for me, but you're a good kid to offer!

ALICE. I don't know what's the matter with this fried chicken. It just doesn't taste as good as it usually does.

SAM. Well, don't throw it away. There are plenty of hungry people who'd love to eat that chicken. I hate to see food going to waste.

ALICE. If a hungry person were here, I'd *gladly* give it to her!

MARGARET. Well, thank God, there's nobody here who's hungry. Did you see those children on the CBS news last night? [*Some respond affirmatively*] I could hardly watch them. It nearly made me *sick*!

SAM. Yeah, I really pity those starving people you hear about, but listen . . . there's *nothing we* can do about it, so why worry?

MARTHA. We've got enough to worry about, what with the energy crisis, the arms buildup, inflation, and all.

JOE. Still . . . when you see a kid starvin' you gotta pity him . . . but you're right. There's not a blame thing we can do. It's hard enough watching out for *yourself* these days.

ALICE. Hey, let's not talk about things like that. You're spoiling the party!

MARGARET. Right, Alice! Let's cut the gloom!

SAM. While you have the knife out to cut the gloom, how about cutting the cake?

Mood changes abruptly, everyone happy again, talking and laughing softly, eating cake as it is passed.

N1. There's *nothing* we can do about it . . . .
There's nothing we can do about those hollow eyes,
the arms like sticks,
the bloated bellies.
So why worry?
After all, just who *is* my neighbor?
N2. Am I my brother's keeper?
N3. O Lord, I thank thee that I am not like other men . . .
N4. For health, and strength, and daily food,
We give thee thanks, O Lord.
N1. [*Irritated and deliberately.*] You *didn't* answer my question .
Who is my neighbor?
N2. A lawyer asked that long ago.
And by this time you ought to know!
N3. You ought to know . . .
N4. You ought to know . . .
N2, 3 & 4 together. [*Intense whisper*] You ought to know!

Darkness, with one spot on Marybai who sinks to the ground in exhaustion. Action freezes around the table. A business executive, well-dressed and carrying a briefcase, enters, sees the body, and stops.
BUSINESS EXECUTIVE. [*Sees the body, kneels, shocked.*] Oh my Lord, what's this? Woman . . . are you . . . [*Lifts head, then drops it again*] She's still alive, but I just don't see how I can afford to help her. [*Shakes head*] Too bad . . . too bad . . . another victim of tragic circumstances. [*Sighs and stands up. Addresses audience.*] If only those people would have the foresight to practice birth control and get rid of their fool superstitions and customs. They're such an ignorant bunch! Well, there's nothing I can do about it. [*Pause, looking at Marybai.*] It's probably better in the long run if she dies . . . prevent a new pack of kids to come into the world to perpetuate this misery. Old Malthus was right about excessive world population. We've only got so many lifeboats, and I don't want any more people swarming into mine! [*Looks at her again, starts to kneel, then catches himself.*] Still, when you meet up with one of these poor devils in person, you wish you could . . . [*briskly*] Mustn't become emotional about this. I need to think about our own economic health and welfare. [*Looks at watch*] Oh, Lord, if I don't start moving I'll be late for the board meeting!

He hurries off. After a few moments of silence, a clergyman enters in clerical garb.
CLERGYMAN. Oh, my God! [*He quickly kneels and shakes Marybai gently as though trying to revive her.*] Lady! Lady! Can

251

you hear me? [*Stops and holds her face between his hands, looking at her intently*] Do I know you? I feel as though I do. [*He turns away.*] You've been on my mind many times lately . . . many times. I've read about you in the paper. I've watched you on TV . . . I've been vaguely aware of you at banquets and potluck dinners . . . sometimes when I read the words of our Lord your hazy image starts to haunt me. [*Looks at her again, intense, upset*] But never before have I looked you in the *face*. [*Frustrated he speaks to her as though she can hear.*] I *know* I should be doing something to help you. I *know!* But where do I start? There are millions more like you, you know. Millions! I suppose we *could* take an offering . . . but really, I hate to tell you this, but my people don't want to hear about you. You're depressing. The other night at the church supper someone turned to me and said . . . Oh, never mind! [*Quickly turns away, greatly agitated*] What am I doing? I'm forgetting that my first task is to preach the salvation of souls. My people need me to do that. [*Looking at her again, almost tenderly*] I wonder, child . . . are *you* saved? Now that we've met, I *know* I should do something more . . . but I . . . forgive me. I can't be late for the church council! [*He hurries off. There is a long pause.*]

N2. Well, isn't there more? Shouldn't the Samaritan be coming in about this time?

N1. Yes, where's that good neighbor . . . the one who shows compassion?

[*N3 & N4 overlap the next speeches louder and more intense.*]

N3. The Samaritan? Where's the Samaritan?

N4. Where is he? Bring on the Samaritan?

N2. [*Slowly speaking directly to the audience, with hesitation, but with deep feeling*] Could he or she be here? . . . could you be the Samaritan . . the one who shows compassion? The one who feeds the hungry? The one who binds up the wounds of Marybai and gives her a chance to live?

VOICE FROM AUDIENCE. [*Person stands as he or she speaks.*] But how? I'd just like to know how? How do you expect one person, or even all of us [*gestures to include audience*] to do any good in the midst of this terrible starvation and poverty?

VOICE SHOUTS FROM AUDIENCE. We're not God. We can't help it when the Monsoon rains don't come or that the Sahara Desert is moving southward. That's beyond our control!

FIRST PERSON FROM AUDIENCE. You're right. It's overwhelming and beyond us! That doesn't mean we don't feel very sorry for those poor souls, but how can any of us be of help?

N1. [*Quietly, gently*] You have helped already. You have asked "how?"

N2. You have looked at one face from the multitude of the hungry, and like Jesus, you have felt compassion.

N3. You have not said "I wash my hands. This is none of my affair. I have no responsibility here."

N4. Despite your helplessness, your frustration and your reluctance, you have asked "how?" It is a beginning.

During the following speeches the people around the table come to life and listen intently as they gather together their dishes.

N1. The Chinese have a saying: The journey of a thousand miles begins with one step.

N2. And the Quakers have noted that just one pinprick in the umbrella of darkness will let in some light.

N3. I am one person. I cannot begin to do everything. But just because I cannot do everything, let me not neglect to do that which I *can* do.

N4. And there are ways we can help, if we will. Some may seem like little ways; others involve sacrifice and a willingness to alter our lifestyles when needed.

N1. But they are ways we must consider if we believe that we are one family under God; that all of us living in this global village are united by thread of common needs; that we are interdependent and responsible for one another; that truly we are called to be our brother's and sister's neighbor.

N2. [*Slowly*] Bread for ourselves is a material concern.

N3 & 4. Bread for our brothers and sisters is a *spiritual* concern.

The people at the table notice Marybai. They leave the table and surround her with love and concern during the singing of "Because I Have Been Given Much" #340, Brethren Hymnal, sung by the congregation or by a soloist. They leave with Marybai during the singing of the hymn.

Because I have been given much, I, too, must give;
Because of Thy great bounty, Lord, Each day I live
I shall divide my gifts from Thee With every brother that I see
Who has the need of help from me.

Because I have been sheltered, fed, By Thy good care,
I cannot see another's lack And I not share
My glowing fire, my loaf of bread, My roof's safe shelter overhead,
That he, too, may be comforted.

Because love has been lavished so Upon me, Lord.
A wealth I know that was not meant For me to hoard,
I shall give love to those in need, Shall show that love by word and deed,
Thus shall my thanks be thanks indeed.

Suggestions for Discussion

1. In groups of five, share your reactions to the play.

2. Why is the story of the Good Samaritan appropriate in this context?

3. Discuss how in the past you have been part of efforts to eliminate world hunger — as a citizen, as a community member, and as an individual. Ponder how these attempts can be continued and increased.

4. How can we change our pattern of life? Can we consume less, waste less, drive or aircondition less?

5. For further activities, see the suggestions following the previous play, "To Feed the Hungry."

NABOTH'S VINEYARD

by Dorothy Friesen

CHARACTERS

EXECUTIVE OF USBI (*United States Banana Importers*)
PRESIDENT OF THE PHILIPPINES
READER
JOSE, *a farmer*
CARLOS, *Jose's friend*
THE PRESIDENT'S WIFE
BARRIO CAPTAIN
CATHOLIC PRIEST
CANVASSER FOR USBI CORPORATION

PRODUCTION NOTES

Often stories from the Old Testament have startling parallels to events in our own time. This play draws the analogy between the story of Naboth (I Kings 21) and current events in the Philippines. The play consists of five short scenes separated by readings from the Bible. Use blocking and, when possible, lighting accordingly.

From a podium, the USBI Executive and the President are looking over the countryside.

USBI EXECUTIVE. Yes, Mr. President, this Mindanao land certainly is rich and fertile, just what our corporation is looking for to grow bananas. But what about these rice fields here? Who do they belong to? Can we just take them over without problems?

PRESIDENT. Oh, no problem at all. None of these people have title to this land. They just moved onto it, cut down the trees and started planting rice. Some of them are tribal groups — they are satisfied with anything. We'll just give them an airplane ride to Manila, take them to a fancy restaurant, and they will sign away any ancestral rights they might have.

USBI EXECUTIVE. Well, it sounds good. I think we have a deal. I'll make sure you get your part in this, if you know what I mean.

PRESIDENT. I know what you mean. This will be a good investment for me. [*He catches himself.*] I mean, for the country.

READER. [*He reads from the Bible.*] First Kings twenty-one: Now Naboth the Jezreelite had a vineyard in Jezreel, beside the palace of Ahab, king of Samaria. And Ahab said to Naboth, "Give me your vineyard, that I may have it for a vegetable garden, because it is near my house; and I will give you a better vineyard for it; or, if it seems good to you, I will give you its value in money." But Naboth said to Ahab, "The Lord forbid that I should give you the inheritance of my fathers."

Jose and his friend Carlos are hoeing in the area that the USBI Executive and the President of the Philippines are surveying.
JOSE. It will be a good harvest this year, thank God. Maybe I will even have enough money to send my children to school.
CARLOS. But Jose, this may be our last harvest, if we even get a chance to harvest this rice. An American corporation wants to move in here and grow bananas. You know, they said if we don't voluntarily move they will spray our crops with poison. All that work, all that money will be for nothing.
JOSE. [*Assertively.*] But I won't move. God gave our people this land to use to feed our families. How can anyone take it away from us? We are already a poor country. Why would rich foreigners take even this from us? They will have to kill me first. I won't move.
READER. And Ahab went into his house vexed and sullen because of what Naboth had said to him; for he had said, "I will not give you the inheritance of my fathers." And he lay down on his bed, and turned away his face, and would eat no food. But Jezebel his wife came to him and said to him, "Why is your spirit so vexed that you eat no food?" And he said to her, "Because I spoke to Naboth the Jezreelite, and said to him, 'Give me your vineyard for money; or else, if it please you, I will give you another vineyard for it'; and he answered, 'I will not give you my vineyard.'" and Jezebel his wife said to him, "Do you not govern Israel? Arise, and eat bread, and let your heart be cheerful; I will give you the vineyard of Naboth the Jezreelite."

The President is in a corner, frowning. His wife walks in, beautifying herself, and notices him pouting.
PRESIDENT'S WIFE. What's the matter? You look depressed.
PRESIDENT. I want to develop this country, get it moving on the road to progress and prosperity. We desperately need foreign capital. Banana sales to Japan would bring a lot of money into the country for us to build hotels and buy consumer items from the West. But these backward people in Mindanao won't sell their land. They are appealing to a decree I made a few years ago about ancestral land and the rights of the tiller. So what am I to do?

PRESIDENT'S WIFE. Well, aren't you the president? Don't you have the power to declare martial law? Can't you change decrees? Isn't the army supporting you? Can't you appoint me Governor of Metro Manila and Minister of Human Settlements and Ecology? Given these facts, you shouldn't have anything to worry about. I'll make sure this deal goes through.

READER. So she wrote letters in Ahab's name and sealed them with his seal, and she sent the letters to the elders and the nobles who dwelt with Naboth in his city. And she wrote in the letters, "Proclaim a fast, and set Naboth on high among the people; and set two base fellows opposite him, and let them bring a charge against him, saying 'You have cursed God and the king.' Then take him out, and stone him to death." And the men of his city, the elders and the nobles who dwelt in his city, did as Jezebel had sent word to them. Then they sent to Jezebel, saying, "Naboth has been stoned; he is dead."

Jose hoes silently, stage left. The spotlight shifts to Canvasser and Barrio Captain, stage right.

CANVASSER. Well, I'm having a lot of trouble getting the local people to sign over their land, even though I'm waving hundred-peso bills in their faces. Jose has refused to sell, and the others are supporting him.

BARRIO CAPTAIN. We just have to get those land transactions completed. We are under a lot of pressure from the First Lady. It could mean my job if I don't comply with her wishes.

CANVASSER. Why won't Jose sell? He must be a subversive. Perhaps he's a communist or a sympathizer.

BARRIO CAPTAIN. Well, I don't think he is, but that would be a good excuse to get rid of him. We'll just kill him and say that he was shot in an encounter between the military and the communist New People's Army. The other farmers will sell once they see what happens to Jose.

READER. As soon as Jezebel heard that Naboth had been stoned and was dead, Jezebel said to Ahab, "Arise, take possession of the vineyard of Naboth the Jezreelite, which he refused to give you for money; for Naboth is not alive, but dead." And as soon as Ahab heard the Naboth was dead, Ahab arose to go down to the vineyard of Naboth the Jezreelite, to take possession of it. Then the word of the Lord came to Elijah the Tishbite, saying, "Arise, go down to meet Ahab king of Isreal, who is in Samaria; behold, he is in the vineyard of Naboth, where he has gone to take possession. And you shall say to him, 'Thus says the Lord: "In the place where dogs licked up the blood of Naboth shall dogs lick your own blood." ' " Ahab said to Elijah, "Have you found me, O my enemy?" He answered, "I have found you, because you have sold yourself to do what is evil in the sight of the Lord. Behold, I will bring evil upon you; I will utterly sweep you away, and will cut off from Ahab every male, bond or free, in Isreal; for the anger to which you have provoked me, and because you have made Israel to sin. And of Jezebel the Lord also said, 'The dogs shall eat Jezebel within the bounds of Jezreel.' There was none who sold himself to do what was evil in the sight of the Lord like Ahab, whom Jezebel his wife incited.

PRESIDENT. [*By himself, looking over banana fields.*] At last these fields are changed over to bananas. This will mean lots of dollars for the country . . . and for me, too. [*Priest approaches.*] Oh no, look who's coming. My chief critic from the Catholic church. So, you foreign meddler, what are doing here? Why are you and your subversive cohorts causing so much trouble in the country?

PRIEST. You are responsible for Jose's death. The blood of the starving and malnourished children, the sons and daughters of the farmers who have been driven off the land, is on your hands. The blood of the victims of your soldiers' atrocities is on your hands. Injustice will not go on forever unpunished. Your family will pay for this eventually, particularly your wife. The people know what she is doing. We are not foreign meddlers and subversives. We are people of God entrusted to write and speak the truth about what is happening in the Philippines.

READER. And when Ahab heard those words, he rent his clothes, and put sackcloth upon his flesh, and fasted and lay in sackcloth, and went about dejectedly. And the word of the Lord came to Elijah the Tishbite, saying, "Have you seen how Ahab has humbled himself before me? Because he has humbled himself before me, I will not bring the evil in his days; but in his son's days I will bring the evil upon his house." [*Reader closes the Bible and steps forward.*] The story in the Philippines is not completed. In the tangle and confusion of conflict, structural violence and military violence, anything is possible. The blood and gore that came to accompany the fall of Ahab's house in Israel may not be avoided in the Philippines. When the writers of this play suggested that a Philippine religious magazine print this scripture, the editor looked horrified. "We would have this magazine closed down in a minute," he said. "We even have to censor the Bible to survive here." Our friends with censored Bibles in the Philippines need our prayers. But let us pray for ourselves, too. For if we in North America spiritualize and sanitize the bloody earthiness of God's struggle against evil, we too read a censored Bible.

Suggestions for Discussion

1. In your own words, clarify the parallels between Naboth's experience and the situation in the Philippines.

2. Explain the last sentence of the play. Do you agree that we tend to read "a censored Bible?" In what way? What do we choose not to accept?

3. Do you know of imported items that have been grown on land which could have produced food for a starving population? Are you aware of U.S. corporations whose interests and investments abroad contribute to world hunger? Write to CROP and Bread for the World for information.

4. Investigate hunger in your own community and take steps to help.

Fear, Apathy, and Hopelessness

Peacemakers need a deep faith as a source from which to act. Without this faith, well-meant efforts to make changes soon seem vain because the obstacles appear too high, the tasks too immense, and the forces of opposition too strong. Part of this faith has to be that people can indeed live peacefully together on earth. Although human beings have chosen to sin by failing to love God and their neighbors, and although we may keep failing this way, the *potential* of making a different choice is in all of us. Jesus overcame hatred with love, and we are called to do the same. If we take seriously the belief that Jesus ushered in the kingdom of God and asked us to partake in it by loving God and our neighbor, then we must also believe that the change in human nature from basic egocentrism motivated by greed and self-interest to an awareness of human interdependence and brotherhood is possible and necessary. Christians have the promise of the kingdom, and this promise leaves no room for resignation, apathy, hopelessness, or fear.

Several mental attitudes get in the way of making effecive changes. One is the idea that we need to confront the world's problems as individuals. Often people, when alerted to social ills, have a strong desire to remedy them and for a while may invest much energy, only to realize very quickly that they are not getting anywhere. The result is all too often a sense of isolation, disappointment, "burn-out," maybe even hostility and advocacy of change through violence. The alternative to this individualistic approach is to live in community and to make the peace witness an expression of a body rather than a single person. As in the days of the early church, the Christian pacifist community has to become the alternative to a sick society. If we then respond to the call to make peace, the community undergirds us and gives us strength for the task.

Without a nurturing community, individuals stumble into pitfalls that hamper peacemaking efforts. Some people may want to withdraw from the challenge of peacemaking because they have no hope that human beings can change, or because they feel that it is "too late," that we have missed our chance. Others react with apathy. They believe that human beings need not hold each other accountable. A third group wants to avoid picturing the horrors of nuclear holocaust or world hunger and accordingly resorts to psychic numbing. People in this group will force themselves not to think about evil because they fear the knowledge, fear the sense of powerlessness, fear the terror itself. Whatever the mental attitude may be—fear, apathy, or hopelessness—all are alike in that they prevent change from happening. They are thus attitudes that peacemakers have to counteract.

The three plays in this section work on these problems. In "A Candle in the Dark," a couple has chosen to live with and even contribute to the build-up of weapons because it means job security and—in the case of the husband—because this is seen as protecting our way of life. Over the course of the play, the wife comes to face up to her fears and verbalizes them. The intention of "Alligator," in the author's own words, is "to help heal us of the numbing, the hopelessness, the horrible fear that we squelch and squash. I believe that we can be rid of that fear or at least learn to live with it . . . . We can realize that, horrible as it is, the worst part of a holocaust is the separation from God that it entails." "Genesis" affirms that neither preaching doom nor avoiding the issue are correct approaches to bringing about change; rather, evil has to be recognized as such and then directly confronted in the faith that it can be overcome.

ALLIGATOR

by Don Yost

CHARACTERS

MEG, *thirty years old*
TOM, *Meg's husband*
ROBBY, *their five year old son*
JENNY, *Meg's best friend*
WISARD, *a voice in Meg's dream*

SCENE 1

The stage has large areas of darkness. There is a white, single bed.

ROBBY. [*From offstage.*] Daddy. Daaaadddy. I'm ready for bed. Come on.

TOM. [*From offstage.*] All right. OK. Hop in bed. I'll be up in a minute. [*Robby enters with a stuffed bear and climbs in bed. His father comes in.*]

TOM. Did you use the bathroom? [*Robby nods.*] You got your drink? [*He nods again.*] All right. Check under the bed for monsters. No monsters. Fluff up your pillow . . . there. Snug up the blankets tight and warm. And here's your kiss. Good night guys.

ROBBY. Aren't you going to kiss Fozzy Bear?

TOM. Right . . . a kiss for Fozzy Bear. Sleep tight.

ROBBY. You forgot to check the closet.

TOM. Do we have to go through this *every* night?

ROBBY. Please?

TOM. You're getting a little old for this, Robby. All right. Check the closet. Helloooo. All you ugly old monsters better get out of here. Nope, no monsters in the closet. Goodnight, son.

ROBBY. Would you stay with me for a little while? I'm scared.

TOM. Robby, I checked under the bed and in the closet.

ROBBY. But I'm scared.

TOM. There's nothing to be afraid of. Be a big boy and go to sleep.

ROBBY. Just for a minute?

TOM. I've got a lot of work to do. I'm going to be up half the night as it is.

ROBBY. [*Sitting up in bed.*] But what if . . .?

262

TOM. Lie down. That's an order. Go to sleep. [*Robby obeys. Tom walks to the door and turns out the light.*] Good night. See you in the morning. [*Tom leaves. Robby shuts his eyes tightly and pulls the blanket up over his head. Four figures enter from each of four directions. They are dressed in dark robes with hoods up over their heads. No human flesh or facial features can be seen. Their movement is slow, ritualistic, cruel, irrefutable. They meet at the four corners of the bed. After a pause, they lift up the bed, carry it upstage, and vanish into the darkness.*]

SCENE 2

The livingroom of a comfortable suburban house. There is a couch, a coffee table in front of the couch, a floor lamp, and a desk and chair. Meg sits on the couch, reading. Tom enters as if from Robby's room.

MEG. That was quick. Is Robby asleep?

TOM. I didn't stay. [*Begins working at the desk.*]

MEG. He gets scared up there by himself.

TOM. Look, Meg, I've got this proposal to finish by eight o'clock tomorrow morning.

MEG. I'll go stay with him.

TOM. The boy is five years old. You'll probably just disturb him.

MEG. Did he seem scared when you left?

TOM. He's all right. Give it ten more minutes. If he's scared, he'll come down . . . he always does. [*Meg goes back to reading. One of the robed figures begins making its way out of the darkness upstage into the consciousness of the audience. Meg and Tom do not in any way acknowledge its presence.*]

MEG. [*After a long pause.*] Do you want something hot to drink?

TOM. No thanks. [*The figure enters the lighted area of the stage, walks to a point just behind Meg and stops.*]

TOM. I can't find the last page of this budget.

MEG. What's it look like?

TOM. It has numbers on it. It's a white sheet of paper with numbers. [*The figure moves to the opposite end of the couch and then to a point just behind Tom.*]

TOM. I had it in the first drawer.

MEG. I haven't seen it. I stay out of your papers . . . you know that.

TOM. [*Still looking*] I'll bet Robby used it for drawing paper. [*The figure reaches over Tom's shoulder and picks up several papers, then drops them to the floor. There is no response from Tom. The figure picks up the typewriter.*]

Oh . . . I'm sorry. I found it. It was right here under the typewriter. [*Starts using a pen. The figure drops the typewriter.*]

TOM. Are you going to check on Robby? [*The figure walks to the coffee table and overturns it.*]

MEG. I guess not. You're right . . . he'd be down by now. [*The figure removes the book from Meg's hands.*]

MEG. [*Sighs*] I can't believe the garbage that comes between two covers these days. I checked out three novels on the best-seller list and there's not one worth reading. I'm going to make some mint tea. Are you sure you don't want any? [*The figure pushes over the floor lamp. Stage lights go to nearly zero.*]

MEG. [*Stifled*] No!

TOM. It's no use. I might as well go to bed. I'm not getting anything done.

MEG. I . . . thought . . .

TOM. I'll get up early tomorrow morning. What about you? You ready for bed?

MEG. [*Subdued*] Turn down the furnace. I'll let the cat out. [*Tom and Meg exit. The figure follows them.*]

SCENE 3

Two stools are placed ten feet apart, downstage and to one side of center. Meg sits on the stool nearest to the center. Tom sits on the other stool. The figure stands between and behind them — just barely visible once the lights are on. The conversation between Meg and Tom takes place as though in a double bed. They have matching blankets. To the other side of center stage is a desk and chair. Wisard is seated in the chair — invisible until the conversation includes him. Meg shifts position. Pause. She shifts again.

TOM. Why don't you fix the tea you were talking about?

MEG. I didn't know you were awake. [*Pause.*] Am I keeping you up?

TOM. I've got a headache.

MEG. Did you take something for it? [*Tom remains silent. Meg shifts position again.*]

TOM. What's your excuse?

MEG. What time is it?

TOM. [*Squints out from beneath the blanket*] A quarter after one. I'm cold.

MEG. You want another blanket?

TOM. I can't concentrate enough to work on that proposal and I can't forget it enough to fall asleep.

MEG. How much do you have left to do?

TOM. There isn't that much if I could just sit down and do it. The first section of the methodology needs rewritten.

MEG. Want to talk about it? Would that help?

TOM. I want to go to sleep.

MEG. Maybe if you took a hot bath . . . [*There is a long pause.*]

TOM. Why aren't you asleep?

MEG. I don't know. [*Pause.*]. . . . It's Jenny.

TOM. She called?

MEG. I saw her at Hooks.

TOM. And . . .?

MEG. She lost eight pounds by eating pineapple — as much as she wants. [*Tom waits for Meg to continue.*] She was buying sleeping pills. I saw them. Two bottles,

TOM. You mean . . .?

MEG. She told me she's going to keep them, not use them. Keep them in a cupboard over the refrigerator . . . in case . . . . She says that she'll feed them to her kids. That it's better than watching the skin burn off their bodies . . .

TOM. Meg, don't.

MEG. They say there will be a twenty minute warning. [*Tom remains silent.*] What would you do in those twenty minutes, Tom? What would you say to Robby?

TOM. There's no use thinking about it. Go to sleep.

MEG. That's where Jenny is all wrong. With sleeping pills there would still be twenty minutes. Do you know of anything faster?

TOM. Faster?

MEG. Poison.

TOM. You're talking about murdering your son. Don't be stupid.

MEG. You know what's strange? I'm not even afraid. All I feel is this big empty place, but . . .

TOM. Fear.

MEG. I'm so detached. [*Long silence*] It's like the alligator dream. '[*Tom does not respond.*] The one . . .

TOM. I know.

MEG. I just stood there. I couldn't stop watching.

TOM. Meg, please. I have to get up early.

MEG. [*Staring hard*] The alligator pushed open the gate with it's nose and started towards me.

TOM. We've been through this before.

MEG. But I remembered a new part. I would have been safe . . . the fence was strong enough . . .

TOM. [*Liturgically*] It was a wrought iron fence with spearheads on top of each post. And your dad . . .

MEG. . . . sawed off the legs of our new bunkbed. . .

TOM. . . . because he thought you had the nightmare from being afraid of the height.

MEG. I never told you about the latch . . . did I?

TOM. I don't remember. [*Yawns*]

MEG. I stood there. I knew it was too late to run. I watched the alligator push open the gate and slide through. But I never remembered till now. The reason the alligator was loose is because someone . . . someone forgot to fasten the latch at the top of the gate. I wonder why. Who . . . could have done such a thing? [*A light reveals Wisard. Meg jumps and yells as she notices him.*]

WISARD. I'm sorry. I just couldn't help overhearing. You're asking the wrong question. You realize that? [*Meg looks puzzled and wary.*] It's got nothing to do with the gate.

MEG. The gate?

WISARD. The question is: Who made the alligator and why?

MEG. . . . I don't know.

WISARD. Why is there such a thing as the alligator?

MEG. . . . I don't know.

WISARD. Think. [*Meg leaves her stool. Sometime later, Tom and the figure disappear as discreetly as possible.*]

MEG. Why was there a gate? Why did the fence have a gate?

WISARD. Who made the alligator and why?

MEG. Who took the latch off the gate?

WISARD. Did you?

MEG. [*Startled*] I'm too little. I can't reach that high.

WISARD. Your father can reach that high. Your mother.

MEG. Get the alligator back behind the fence.

WISARD. Are you kidding? The alligator is out. The question now is . . .

MEG. It doesn't matter.

WISARD. What *does* matter, then?

MEG. The gate.

WISARD. If the gate is latched, it's as good as a fence.

MEG. The alligator.

WISARD. What do you want to know?

MEG. Who's responsible. [*Almost yelling*] Who left the gate unlatched and why.

WISARD. Was it ever latched? You're assuming that at some point the gate was latched. Do you ever remember seeing the gate latched? [*Meg remains silent. The Wisard waits.*]

MEG. It was *you*, wasn't it? *You* unlatched the gate.

WISARD. I never unlatched the gate.

MEG. But you never latched it!

WISARD. Ahhh. You're right. I never latched the gate. I will freely admit to that.

MEG. [*Suddenly worried*] Who are you?

WISARD. On the other hand, neither did you.

MEG. Huh?

WISARD. Neither did Tom. So are you going to hate him? Julius Ceasar didn't latch the gate, nor did Ceasar Chavez. Stevie Wonder didn't. Colonel Sanders, Ronald Reagan, Captain Kangaroo, Martin Buber didn't . . . Betsy Ross, Betty Friedan . . .

MEG. [*Angry*] Stop it!

WISARD. You wanted someone to blame.

MEG. Maybe I can get around the alligator. Maybe I can get past it and run through the gate . . . and latch the gate behind me. I'll be safe on the other side.

WISARD. There is no latch.

MEG. [*Winces*] That's a lie.

WISARD. [*An airport announcer*] The gate swings both ways. There never was a latch. There never was a latch. [*Meg stares into darkness*] Their jaws are a grave, wide open, To devour your harvest, To devour your sons and your daughters.

MEG. Both ways?

WISARD. All that I have feared has come upon me.

MEG. What? [*Begins backing away.*]

WISARD. Wormwood and gall.

MEG. [*Wraps up in her blanket.*] Who are you?

WISARD. Summon the wailing women to come . . . that our eyes may fill with tears. [*Meg exits.*]

WISARD. Eli, Eli, lema sabachthani. [*To himself.*] Father, Father, why have you . . . forsaken us? [*Darkness. Wisard exits.*]

SCENE 4

The livingroom is restored to order. Meg enters, preparing for Jenny's visit. The doorbell rings.

JENNY. [*Enters on her own. She lays her coat over a chair.*] The cats are away?

MEG. Tom's mother picked Rob up to take him shopping. Are you hungry?

JENNY. Starved.

MEG. I don't have *fresh* pineapple.

JENNY. Oh, no. That was yesterday. Today it's radishes. All the radishes I want. Radishes sliced, radishes diced. Radishes boiled, broiled or baked. Tomorrow's much better, though. Tomorrow it's rutabagas.

MEG. Coffee?

JENNY. Just coffee.

MEG. I . . . I wanted to see you . . .

JENNY. Let me guess. You want my advice. You . . .

MEG. Be patient. Can you, please?

JENNY. My lips are sealed . . . except to sip.

MEG. [*Finally.*] I admire you now. [*Jenny waits for Meg to continue.*] . . . For the pills.

JENNY. I wasn't sure you'd ever speak to me again.

MEG. Am I that transparent?

JENNY. What do you admire about the fact that I keep two bottles of sleeping pills in my kitchen cupboard?

MEG. You've faced it.

JENNY. I have not faced it. I'm desperate, that's all. Anyway, I made up the whole thing.

MEG. Last night . . . I was afraid to go to sleep. I was afraid it was the end. I lay there and tried to go to sleep . . . I . . . finally I did. I started drifting into sleep, but it felt like I was falling into a black . . . hole. I jerked awake and found myself yelling.

JENNY. So you think the black uglies have got you.

MEG. I don't know. I'm just telling you the symptoms. [Silence] I don't want to see a flash of light, Jenny. I don't want to burn and die . . . .

JENNY. It isn't dying, Meg. We'll die, holocaust or not. What we fear about holocaust isn't the death of it . . . . It's the waste.

MEG. Waste?

JENNY. Try to collect, to measure all the effort, patience, love, time . . . think what it takes to get through one week of caring for Robby. Think what more it will take to get him to the place where he's a whole, healthy human being. Add in yourself and Tom. And there's this house. All the energy and skill it took to build . . . the people who spent their lives standing at a saw or brick oven so you could have walls . . . and a brass handle on your dresser. Think about the friendships, the family ties. Think how long it's taken for us to get to know and trust each other. What kind of sum do you get? Multiply by 200, 400 million. Everything — not just dead — but wasted. And all it takes is one trigger-happy old man with four stars on his collar.

MEG. [After a pause] One general is not enough to create holocaust.

JENNY. You're right. Somebody will have to drop a wrench down the silo. Or a janitor, while dusting the computers one evening, leans his arm on the wrong button. No, not his arm. Hers. You know they'll blame it on a woman. May I have another cup?

MEG. [Pouring] It's more than waste. [Sits] The pain of holocaust is . . . it has to do with what God intends.

JENNY. Meg . . .

MEG. Listen, will you? Just sit and listen. [Slowly] God gave us life. This life includes both pleasure and pain, joy . . . and grief. Dying. God makes flowers and alligators. There's no way we can understand. We can suffer and die and still live. But disobedience, ingratitude — that's the pain that can't be endured. That is the pain that never goes away — not in this life or in any other. Being outside the will of God; choosing what is not God. Taking power. That's the real pain of holocaust . . . that we have chosen weapons and our own power for defense; that we have . . .

JENNY. It doesn't seem fair, you know, to blame this all on us.

MEG. It's a gift, Jenny. A wonderful gift. Love hurts and life hurts and there are alligators, but God gives us enough . . .

everything — if we'd just accept it and let go of our fear and trust
that . . .

JENNY. Trust?

MEG. I know it's hard. I can understand . . .

JENNY. You understand? You understand?

MEG. All right. I don't understand. I can't sit here and explain it.
I've shared your feelings.

JENNY. Feelings? You . . . . There are twenty . . . fifty submarines
skulking all over this planet with enough . . . . Just one of those
submarines could wipe out Chicago, New York . . . I mean
where do I go? Australia? Tahiti? Those fat, ignorant generals
with their war games. Have you ever seen them on TV? They
can't keep a straight face. It's the only way they can get it up
anymore. Play games with the fate of every human being on this
earth. They know they should look serious, but you can tell they
love every minute of it. "Look serious," the teleprompter says;
but underneath they are glad that millions of people live in
everlasting fear of what they might do or . . .

MEG. Power.

JENNY. . . . say. God, I feel helpless. I feel utterly helpless. The
Jews in Buchenwald had more dignity, more options, more
control. "Dear Mr. President. I wish to express my views on
nuclear warfare. Quite frankly, Mr. President, I'd eight hundred
times rather be red than dead. Sincerely yours, a person who is
quite close to hysteria."

MEG. Jenny. . .

JENNY. I hate them, Meg. I hate everyone and anyone who is
doing this to me. Do you know what we are? We're bugs. We are
little potato bugs that the boys throw into gasoline. And while
we are there swimming around in all this poison, waiting for
them to throw in the match, we . . . form committees. We . . . it's
insane. This whole civilization is out of its mind. Totally removed from reality. Whacko. Do you understand the kinds of
repression it takes? The layers and layers of deceit it takes to
keep this out of our minds?

MEG. I don't think it's that hard.

JENNY. Look at me. I'm standing here, shaking. [*Long silence.*]
It's no good, Meg. I know what you want to say. "Though I walk
through the valley of the shadow . . ."

MEG. It isn't a panacea. It . . . it may be harder even than despair.

JENNY. Yeah, well I can't do anything harder than I'm doing
already. I drank too much coffee. I'm sorry. I mean, "Thanks for
the coffee, Meg." [*Meg remains silent.*] When does Robby get
home?

MEG. For lunch.

JENNY. I'd better get going. [*Puts on her coat*] Thanks, Meg. [*Meg
nods. Jenny exits. Meg picks up the cups and leaves also.*]

SCENE 5

Setting as in scene one, with Robby's bed center stage.

TOM. [*From offstage*] Robby. What are you doing? Come on . . . get in bed.

ROBBY. [*Enters with Tom*] Mommy wanted me to put my books away.

TOM. OK. Hop in.

ROBBY. [*Checks under the bed himself. Climbs in*] Would you check the closet, Dad?

TOM. Any monsters in the closet? Nope, not a thing in there except toys and clothes. Tuck in these blankets. Here's a kiss for Robby and a kiss for Fozzly Blair. [*Meg enters and stands at the doorway, looking on.*] Good night, guys. Sleep tight.

ROBBY. Good night. Good night, Mommy . . . . Mommy, will you stay with me? Just for a few minutes? [*Two figures begin to emerge from opposite sides of the stage. They start from darkness and stop at a place where they are only faintly visible.*]

MEG. It's time to go to sleep.

TOM. What are you afraid of, Robby? I checked all the dark places. There are no monsters. [*Robby is silent.*]

MEG. You're afraid of monsters, Robby? [*He nods.*] Are you afraid that they will hurt you? [*He nods again.*] Are you afraid that they will eat you or kill you?

TOM. Meg . . .

ROBBY. The monsters will take me away.

MEG. [*Walks towards the bed*] Sometimes I'm afraid of monsters, too.

ROBBY. You are?

MEG. I am. And you know what helps me? [*Kneels at the head of the bed.*]

ROBBY. What?

MEG. I think about morning . . . about all the things that I will do if the monsters don't get me. I think about hugging you and Dad. I think about the clean clothes I will put on. I think about how it will look out the window. Maybe there will be a new snow tomorrow. I think about how the furnace comes on and warms up my toes. I think about the cupboard door swinging open and seeing the cereal boxes sitting there on the shelf — right where we left them . . . the bowls and the spoons clinking . . .

ROBBY. And sugar on my cereal and Fozzy Bear watching me eat. Can we go to the library tomorrow?

MEG. If it doesn't snow too hard tonight.

ROBBY. If it snows, will you take me sledding, Daddy?

TOM. As soon as I get home.

ROBBY. Oh boy!

MEG. We'll have another whole day to be with each other. [*Looks* to Tom] And we won't waste it, right? Is that a deal? [*Robby nods.*]

TOM. Do you feel better?

ROBBY. Yeah.

MEG. Would you still like someone to stay with you? [*Robby nods. Tom half grimaces, half grins. He lies down at the foot of the bed.*]

MEG. [*Gives them both a kiss*] See you in the morning.

ROBBY. If the monsters don't get us.

MEG. Right . . . if the monsters don't get us. Good night, guys.

ROBBY. Night, Mom. [*Meg exists. Lights to dim. Hold. Off.*]

Suggestions for Discussion

1. Get together with a group of people you trust. Let each person have a turn sharing his or her fears. What has it been like to live with the prospect of nuclear holocaust? Listen for at least ten minutes to each one without interrupting.

2. How do we block out the awareness of the nuclear threat? At times when we don't succeed in numbing ourselves, how do we cope? What is our source of strength, or basis for hope? How can we provide support for one another?

3. Talk about fears other than the nuclear issue. What helps you overcome them? How can we help children like Robby live with fear?

4. Meg and Jenny at the end of their conversation feel somewhat alienated from one another. How do their approaches to reality differ?

5. Meg feels that she has come to terms with her fear. How has she done it? Do you feel closer to Meg or to Jenny? What would you have added had you been part of their conversation?

A CANDLE IN THE DARK

by Gordon Houser

CHARACTERS

DOUG
STEPHANIE
JASON
SALLY

The scene is Doug and Stephanie's living room, in a midwestern town. It is winter; much snow has fallen. Jason and Sally have driven from a nearby town for an evening visit. Doug and Sally are brother and sister. Each couple has been married less than two years. Doug and Jason are conversing on one side of the room, Stephanie and Sally on the other.

DOUG. Yeah, we've been having to put in a lot of overtime the last couple of months. They keep pushing us to get this project completed.

JASON. That doesn't seem fair. They should hire extra workers instead of making you work such long hours.

DOUG. That would take too much extra time in training. We're working on a computer system for the cruise missile, and they want it done as soon as possible.

JASON. [*Pauses.*] How do you feel about that kind of work?

DOUG. I like working with computers. I'd rather not have to work at such a fast pace.

JASON. No, I mean how do you feel about work that helps produce missiles?

DOUG. [*Voice tightens, body stiffens*] How would you like to live under communist rule? Cause that's what would happen if we stopped producing weapons.

JASON. I wouldn't particularly, but that's not what I asked. Besides, we already have enough weapons to blow up the world twelve times. Why do we need more?

DOUG. Where did you get your information?

JASON. So what if it's only six times? What's the difference?

DOUG. Where did you get your information?

JASON. From *The Defense Monitor*.

DOUG. What's that? A lobbyist group?

JASON. Probably. I don't know.

273

DOUG. Well, I'm not going to accept that as accurate.

JASON. Of course, your sources of information are completely objective.

DOUG. Not necessarily, but you can't believe everything you read from those lobbyist groups.

JASON. Well, I wouldn't worry about them getting too influential. The Pentagon's getting more money than it's even asking for. [*By this time Stephanie and Sally have stopped talking, aware of the argument taking place. They sit quietly but uncomfortably, until Stephanie rises.*]

STEPHANIE. Anybody want more ice cream?

SALLY. No, I'm full.

JASON. No thanks. Sal, we should be going. It's getting late, and we need to work tomorrow.

SALLY. Yeah, we really should. [*Jason and Sally get up.*]

STEPHANIE. I'll get your coats.

DOUG. I'll tell you what. The air force base has their annual show sometime in the spring. I think you ought to come down and see it to get an idea of the other side. You should talk to some of the pilots and see what they have to go through in their conscience.

JASON. Oh I agree. I wish they didn't have to be in that position. I wish you didn't have to work in a military aircraft plant. I wish you could use your skills to do something that would help people.

DOUG. We're helping people remain free. Have you ever been in a communist country? I have, and I sure wouldn't want to live there.

JASON. Have you ever been in a Latin American country where the US supports regimes that torture and kill thousands of innocent people?

DOUG. I can't believe you'd just let Russia blow us up.

JASON. Why would they blow us up? They'd waste all our resources and the radiation would poison the planet.

DOUG. If we disarmed, they'd take us over in months.

JASON. How could they do that? They can barely handle the few countries they have influence over now, and their own people are starving because they spend so much on armaments.

DOUG. That's not a realistic scenario. I have access to information that I used to wonder why they told us not to tell anyone about. Now I know.

JASON. Even if the Russians took over, we shouldn't fight if we're followers of Jesus.

DOUG. Now what's that supposed to mean? You're mixing religion and politics.

SALLY. Jesus didn't fight back when he was arrested and killed. And he conquered death by rising from the dead.

JASON. And if Jesus didn't fight back, why should we?

DOUG. That's just your interpretation.

JASON. He said clearly, "Love your enemies." How can you love them by killing them?

DOUG. That was then.

JASON. Well, that's whàt we believe God is calling us to, to be like Jesus. And that means no killing.

DOUG. I can't believe you can be so naive. Do you realize if we were attacked, this area would be one of the primary targets? If we don't keep up with them in production, that's going to happen.

JASON. If we keep making bombs, it will become inevitable.

SALLY. Besides that, spending money on bombs takes money from the poor who need food and shelter. I'd rather my tax money went to the poor instead of to the military. [*Stephanie has brought out the coats and now sits down. Jason and Sally stand holding their coats. They are standing in the foyer between the living room and the front door. Stephanie sits staring ahead, no longer paying attention to the conversation.*]

DOUG. I feel a lot better about my taxes going to the military than to support those slobs on welfare who don't work.

SALLY. Doug, most of the money spent on welfare goes to the elderly and people whó are disabled, such as people in nursing homes.

DOUG. I've always made my own way ever since I was in high school. Nobody gave me any handouts, and I never asked for any. And that's how it's going to be. You have to work for it and plan for it.

SALLY. But Doug, what if you became disabled? It happens.

JASON. And the taxes that don't go to help them go to build weapons for killing people.

DOUG. If you believe that, then you should stop paying taxes and go to jail.

JASON. [*Pauses.*] I'm glad you said that.

SALLY. It's a bind.

DOUG. Man, this is the freest country in the world. Look, we can get up tomorrow and go to work and not have to live in fear like in communist countries.

JASON. Yeah, but we're white and middle class, and we don't live in fear in the slums or in Appalachia.

DOUG. It's still better than in East Germany.

JASON. Not if we're disobeying God.

DOUG. You don't realize how safe the air force keeps us. When I go to bed at night I feel safe because I know the air force is watching over us. You should be thankful.

JASON. Doug, don't you see what you're saying? When I go to bed at night I thank God for keeping me safe.

SALLY. Having all these bombs around doesn't make me feel safe.

[*Pause*] Look, we're not going to convince each other on this. And Doug, I don't want this to hurt our relationship.

JASON. Yeah, we don't mean to be attacking you.

DOUG. Oh no, I don't feel attacked. I just think it'd be good for you to come to that show and get a different perspective.

SALLY. Well, it might be good for us to go.

JASON. I wouldn't mind talking to those guys.

DOUG. I might give you a call when I find out when it is.

JASON. Well, we really need to go. [*He shakes hands with Doug.*]

DOUG. Sure, well, thanks for coming down. Take care.

JASON. Yeah, you too.

SALLY. Bye Stephanie.

STEPHANIE. [*Stands*] Bye.

[*Jason and Sally put on their coats and leave. Doug walks back in, shaking his head and muttering something.*]

STEPHANIE. Doug, you missed your show on TV.

DOUG. Oh, it'll be repeated sometime. [*He sits in a chair, staring. A moment of silence passes.*] I can't believe they actually think that way.

STEPHANIE. You knew they didn't believe the same way you did.

DOUG. Yeah, but I didn't know they were that extreme. Did you hear them say that if Russia attacked us we shouldn't fight back? They even said —

STEPHANIE. [*Interrupts.*] Doug, so what? Why can't they believe what they want? Why does it bug you so much?

DOUG. I don't like to see people living in this country where there is more freedom than anywhere else and then trying to tear it down. Especially when it's my own sister.

STEPHANIE. Why don't we have some ice cream and go to bed.

DOUG. [*Chuckles*] The kind of stuff they must read. [*They hear a knock on the door. Doug answers. It's Jason and Sally, shivering.*]

DOUG. Well, hello. Something wrong?

JASON. Yeah. Sorry to bother you. The car just died several blocks down the road. I don't know if the gas line froze up or what, but the battery's dead now.

DOUG. [*Acts busy, his mind racing*] Yeah. OK. I can give you a jump, and I think I may have some gas heat somewhere. Come on in and get warm.

STEPHANIE. [*Walks in from the kitchen.*] Oh, hi. What happened?

SALLY. Car trouble. Sorry to keep pestering you.

STEPHANIE. Oh, you're not pestering us. But this will make you even later getting home. I'm sorry we kept you so late.

JASON. Oh, you didn't keep us. That's all right.

DOUG. [*Comes out with a coat on and carrying jumper cables.*] You ready?

JASON. Oh, we've got jumper cables. I think it may be more than the battery though.

DOUG. Sure. Well, I'll go get our car started.

JASON. Sal, I'm not sure we'll get it going right away. You want to wait here with Stephanie until we do?

SALLY. [*Hesitates*] Yeah, I suppose I could if you don't need any help. .

JASON. I don't think we will.

STEPHANIE. Sure, why don't you stay.

SALLY. OK. We'll see you later. [*Jason leaves. Sally takes off her coat and sits down next to Stephanie.*]

STEPHANIE. You want something to drink?

SALLY. No thanks. [*Pause.*] Listen, Stephanie, I'm sorry for how we talked to Doug. We got carried away.

STEPHANIE. Oh, that's OK. He's the one who kept pursuing it.

SALLY. I feel bad for how emotional we got. I didn't want him to feel put down.

STEPHANIE. Oh, I don't think he did. [*A longer silence passes.*] I was thinking about one of the things Jason said about the effects of radiation. You see [*she hesitates, chokes up*], my dad was in New Mexico when they did the bomb testing there back in the fifties.

SALLY. You think that might be related to his cancer now?

STEPHANIE. [*Starts to cry.*] I don't know. [*Sobbing.*] He told me one time he was afraid he might get cancer because of being close to that. He'd read about other people getting it.

SALLY. How does that make you feel?

STEPHANIE. [*Still crying.*] I don't know. Angry, helpless. I just wish it wouldn't have happened.

SALLY. [*Puts her arm around Stephanie, hands her a Kleenex.*]I'll bet it really hurts.

STEPHANIE. Sometimes it feels like a nightmare. Doug talks about the Russians and how we need to keep safe, and he's probably right. But sometimes I don't care. I mean, I want to support him in his job, and he supports me in mine. He's good. But sometimes I wonder why they have to make more missiles. But that's what you said anyway.

SALLY. I think it's more real to you though, Stephanie. [*They hear cars pull up. Stephanie tries to dry her tears. Soon Doug and Jason walk through the door and stamp snow off their shoes.*]

JASON. Well, we got it going, but we had to let the gas heat work first.

DOUG. Man, I didn't think it was that cold out. You ought to look at your distributor.

JASON. [*Walking into the living room.*] You ready to go, Sal? [*Sally gives him a look, trying to communicate that something is wrong.*] Is something the matter, Stephanie?

DOUG. [*After putting up his coat.*] What's wrong, Steph?

STEPHANIE. Nothing. [*She looks down.*]

SALLY. [*Hesitates.*] We were talking about her father's cancer. She thinks it may have been caused by radiation from the A-bomb tests.

JASON. Was he living near Los Alamos then?

STEPHANIE. [*Fighting back the tears.*] Yes.

DOUG. Oh, that's crazy. There's no proof of that being the cause.

STEPHANIE. [*Cries out loudly*] So what, Doug. He's still dying. [*Everyone is stunned, silent.*]

SALLY. [*Hesitates, speaks quietly.*] It doesn't matter now what caused it.

JASON. [*Also quietly.*] That's true, except you'd hope we'd learn from it.

SALLY. [*Scolds.*] Jason! [*Doug goes to be beside Stephanie. She stands stiffly. He puts his hands on her shoulders, but doesn't know what to do.*]

JASON. Maybe we should go.

SALLY. Is there anything we can help you with?

STEPHANIE. No, that's all right.

JASON. Doug, thanks a lot for your help. And thanks, Stephanie, for your hospitality.

DOUG. [*Jumps up to see them off.*] Well, I'm sure glad you came down. It was sure good to get to see you again.

SALLY. I'm sorry we had to get into that hairy argument.

DOUG. Well, next time we'll have to steer clear of religion and politics.

JASON. [*Sarcastically.*] Yeah, we can talk about the weather and the wheat prices. [*Jason and Doug shake hands and laugh. Suddenly the lights go out. The electricity is off.*]

STEPHANIE. [*Screams.*] Oh my God!

DOUG. [*Trips over a coffee table to get to her.*] What's wrong, Steph? It's just the electricity.

STEPHANIE. [*Breathing heavily, leaning her head on her hand, looking down.*] I just had a terrible feeling. I was thinking about what you said earlier, Doug, about this area being one of the prime targets of an attack, and the thought flashed across my mind that — that this was the end, that everything would be gone. Dad's having to face death now, and he talks about having to give up so much that he loves. Not only his family, but his hobbies, his books, photography. Just now I suddenly thought of losing everything: you, Doug, our house, my silly stained-glass project, the new TV; everything would be obliterated.

DOUG. It didn't happen, Steph.

STEPHANIE. [*Loudly.*] But it could have. Don't you see? [*She puts her head in his arms and cries.*]

278

SALLY. [*After a period of silence.*] Do you have some candles?

DOUG. Yeah, in that top drawer, and there're matches on the refrigerator. [*Sally lights a candle, carries it in, sets it on the coffee table. A long silence ensues.*]

JASON. [*Staring at the candle, in a quiet, contemplative voice.*] That possibility is so terrible to think about that we have to retreat into the unreality that it can't happen, that it won't happen. And what's most terrifying is that we're not terrified by that possibility. We just talk around it. We don't face it like Stephanie's father has to. [*Another silence. Sally nods her head. Doug moves his eyes from the candle to Jason and back to the candle again. Stephanie stares at the candle, her eyes clinging to it as though it were her only hope.*] It's as though the darkness wants to swallow us in its terror and take away our hope, but Jesus can encompass even that.

SALLY. [*Holding up the candle.*] The light shines in the darkness, and the darkness will never overcome it.

Suggestions for Discussion

1. Imagine someone with whom you fundamentally disagree on an issue of importance. How do you handle the problem?
   - Avoid the subject completely.
   - Change the subject to "safe grounds" when the debate becomes heated.
   - Confront the matter and verbally fight it out.
   - Try to explain your viewpoint without getting the other one upset.
   - Disagree on the issue but affirm the other as a person.

2. Roleplay several of the above options with the topic addressed at the opening of the play. Start with confrontive argumentation. Then replay, exploring other options.

3. Which viewpoint do you hear expressed more often — that of Doug or that of Jason? Which one is yours?

4. Evaluate the behavior of the four characters. To whom do you feel most attracted? Did anyone change significantly over the course of the evening? Did they all change? Explain what they may have learned.

GENESIS

by Ingrid Rogers

CHARACTERS

3 SPEAKERS
3 OBSERVERS

The first speaker climbs on a podium, stage right, and starts speaking. The three observers draw near and listen. Over the course of the speech, they get more and more repulsed and end up withdrawing from him.

FIRST SPEAKER. [*The prophet of doom, in a slow, meditative voice*]
In the beginning
God created Heaven and Earth
And God saw that it was good.

So did we, since Heaven was a fit place to fly bombers,
and the Earth a fit place to drop them on.

God separated the land from the water.

We drew from both without returning,
depleting and polluting.
We fought over both land and sea,
craving to possess and rape which was not ours.

God created the animals and the plants.
People as caretakers began to slaughter and shoot,
extinguishing species, one after another.
Nature had to give way
to highways and slums and bomb craters.

God formed people
after God's own image, giving them the power to choose and
to create.

They used these powers to build weapon systems.

In the end,
people destroyed Heaven and Earth
and the spirit of destruction lay upon the waters.

SECOND SPEAKER. [*A liberal and status quo person gets on a podium, stage left, and begins to condemn the prophet.*]
Don't listen to him, the prophet of doom!
We live for today! Do not worry.
The human brain has always conceived of solutions.
Everything will work out all right.
We have the government and institutions to take care of things.
Let it be!
Why always emphasize the bad?
Hasn't there been enough weeping?
Let us enjoy life while we can! Let us laugh together!
[*The observers have surrounded this speaker, cheering, smiling. Their relief is obvious. Along comes the third speaker.*]

THIRD SPEAKER. See here, friends:
You don't have to make a choice between these two
approaches to life. Both will lead you astray.
Don't lose your laughter in despair, thinking that our global
situation is too far gone to be turned around.
Don't hang your heads in frustration
and let your minds linger on dust rather than the tall trees.

But neither must you deny that evil exists. Let your grief
and worry become the source for your visions!

Aware of the arms race, work for peace.
Aware of evil, strive for a better world.
Leave room for tears and laughter both.
Respond, create,
help hold the world together.
[*The others have been slowly turning toward the third speaker. She stretches out her hands and all five join her center stage.*]

Suggestions for Discussion

1. What effect does the first speaker have on you? Jot down words describing your emotional response. Then do the same for the second speaker. Share you responses in groups of four.

2. State in your own words which dangers are inherent in the approaches of speakers one and two.

3. Make a list of reasons to be pessimistic. Then make a list of reasons to be optimistic. Share with each other where you see your strengths as peacemakers. Affirm each others' talents.

POSTSCRIPT

The Church of the Brethren General Board is interested in compiling a second volume of plays that show global awareness and seek to integrate faith with social action. If you have written such material, please send the manuscripts to: "Anthology Project," attn. Ingrid Rogers, 707 North Sycamore Street, North Manchester, IN 46962.

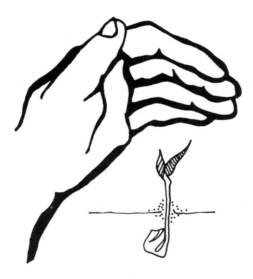